Travelling Light

Short stories and travel writing
to take you away from it all

by Kate Nivison

Acorn Independent Press

A catalogue record for this book is available from the British
Library

ISBN 978-1-908318-00-8

Published by
Acorn Independent Press
www.acornselfpublishing.com

Also by Kate Nivison:

How to Turn Your Holidays Into Popular Fiction

Tiger Country

The Wine Is Red

Praise for *How to Turn Your Holidays Into Popular Fiction*

'A stimulating, comprehensive guide, practical, yet highly imaginative.
An entertaining read in itself, as well as very helpful.'
Gaynor Davies, Fiction Editor, *Woman's Weekly*.

'The first thing I ask about this book is: why has no one ever thought
of it before?... all the advice you'll ever need... this book is a good read.'
Writer's News.

Acknowledgements

On the Road

To my travelling companions, Maggie Champkin, Elisabeth Drew, Cathy Smith who first suggested I should get into travel writing, Rosaleen Smyth, Lorna Wandless and my lovely daughter Catherine, many thanks for your wonderful company and support along the way.

Into Print

Many thanks to my husband John for listening patiently to most of what is in this book without nodding off, and so being my first and best critic. Thanks also to the London Writer Circle and the Society of Authors for their friendship and invaluable advice over many years. But what every writer needs most is a good editor, and I've been fortunate to have had some of the best. In particular I'd like to thank Sally Bowden (former fiction editor of Woman's Realm) who gave me my first fiction break, Gaynor Davies (fiction editor of Woman's Weekly) and Leila & Ali Dewji of Acorn Independent Press for their expertise, and above all for their faith in me.

About the Book

Do you love travelling but hate the packing?
Welcome to

Travelling Light

The holiday read with a difference

We've all done it – hauled out the backpack/wheelie suitcase and sworn, absolutely sworn, that this trip, we're travelling light. With all the extra security checks and CheapiJet's latest baggage restrictions in mind, it makes sense to pare it right down to the bare essentials – get back to the carefree days of 'just a toothbrush and comb'. It's just that the great heap of stuff on the bed is what the bare essentials look like these days.

Statistics show, at least they do in our house, that 99.9% of all packing is done by women, whether they are going on the trip or not, and they are also the ones who decide what reading material to take. No one's had time to load the right apps onto the latest reading device, so when push comes to shove, as it usually does when trying to cram everything back in, it's the thoughtfully chosen, weightier tomes that get dumped back on the shelf with a sigh.

Which is where this book could help. It's a 'holiday special' – a themed collection of the kind of thing you see travellers reading at airports, round the swimming pool, on beaches, cruises, long-haul flights or night journeys by train or coach, and that includes both fiction and non-fiction. So, like soccer, *Travelling Light* is a game of two halves. The first half is fiction, mostly in the form of short stories, but with some longer reads as well. The second part is non-fiction that can be loosely described as travel writing or, as I like to think of it, wandering about in someone else's mind meeting new people and places. Almost every piece has appeared before, in magazines and anthologies both here and abroad – a reassurance, if nothing more, to the reader, that someone, somewhere, must have liked it enough to publish it. (List at the end.)

The unifying theme of *Travelling Light* is travel in its broadest sense. That can include the actual travelling (there's a group of short stories with a *Come Fly With Me* theme), or arriving somewhere exotic or challenging (try the non-fiction in the all-too-true *Expect the Unexpected* section). Often it's about simply being there, experiencing the difference and wanting to go deeper into the spirit of a place.

Of course in both the fiction and non-fiction sections there's bound to be a strong personal element, but in no way is this any kind of spiritual odyssey, and it is definitely not a guide book that tells you where to go, what to see and even what to think. Some of the short stories may make you smile in that 'know the feeling' way, or even chuckle. One or two of the non-fiction pieces should perhaps be in a separate 'let's not go there' category, but at least they might make you glad you didn't. Above all, the pieces were picked to provide a variety (within my own rather limited scope) of 'voices', moods, themes and subject matter.

So this is a Jack Sprat kind of book, in that your travelling companion may prefer fiction to non-fiction, or vice versa, so between you you'll eat it all up and swap notes over breakfast. Whether in company or going solo, maybe you won't mind either way and will enjoy the feeling of liberation, pure escapism and seeing the world from a different perspective that runs through the whole collection like a streaker at a parish garden fête.

Hopefully it's the kind of book to take your mind off flight delays, endless queues and unexplained noises outside your room/cabin/tent at night. It could be good for curling up with in a strange bed as a cure for jet lag (staying awake if you can, or nodding off with something soothing if you can't). A small dose of Mary Kingsley from the *Travelling Women* section can be a great tonic, especially for those who hate packing. It didn't matter whether she was hacking her way through evil mangrove swamps or sleeping in a rain forest village, she always took the same clothes she wore back home in England. That included whalebone stays, her beloved 'good thick skirt', and one pair of boots which she kept on day and night in mosquito areas, sometimes for weeks at a time. A pair of cotton slippers is mentioned as a frivolous indulgence. It must have made the packing enviably simple, but they just don't breed them like that any more.

This book won't stop you from getting ripped off in Rio, mugged in Monrovia or feeling broken-hearted in Bangkok, but at least it might help you to 'travel light' in all sorts of ways, even if you prefer to make the trip from your favourite armchair.

Bon voyage and happy landings, wherever you may find yourself.

About the Author

Kate Nivison

I'd love to be able to claim that my liking for 'those faraway places with the strange sounding names' dates from being born on the back of a camel while my mother was escaping from a white slave caravan bound for Outer Mongolia, but things like that didn't happen in the London suburbs where I grew up. But we had books, lots of them, and I particularly liked the ones about explorers and mad missionaries. There were serials on the radio with archaeology professors or secret agents being chased around places with impossibly exotic names like Istanbul, Zanzibar and Jamaica, with sound effects so realistic that we would sprint home from school by way of forbidden short cuts across untamed areas of the local golf course just to be in time for the next episode.

My first unaccompanied journey by train, aged eleven, went a little off the rails when the train I'd been told to catch was rammed by a runaway engine right beside me on the platform, and I found myself wondering if having to dodge showers of hot coals while some people were screaming was quite normal. It's probably just bad luck, but I only have to get on a proper train for something weird to happen; windows blow in, the lights go out, it stops in a tunnel or it's going the wrong way – or I am.

Undeterred and looking for something different, I left home on my wedding day for Nigeria – as foolhardy a proposition today as it was then – for a spell of teaching abroad. It certainly wasn't boring. Nigerian trains turned out to be even worse than British ones, and so did most other things. There, I had a baby (who was very good about it), malaria (twice) and other character-forming experiences including riots and a hasty evacuation because of the civil war. But by then it was too late – we'd caught the Africa bug, and spent the next six years in Zambia.

Back in London with two more children, I took to writing down what I could before I forgot, although it was clear that the eyes of relatives, friends and publishers would quickly glaze over at yet another TIA (This is Africa) reminiscence. In the end it seemed that the only thing to do was fictionalise some of them in the form of short stories, and these began to sell. Magazine readers rather liked stories and serials with exotic backgrounds, so every trip abroad, whether it was a family camping holiday, an all-inclusive package, cruising on ships large and small, looking up old friends or just wandering about anywhere in the world, went down in the notebook for background and possible plots. Some of my own favourites have gone into the fiction section of this book and there's a strong element of pure escapism and longing in many of them. Often they grew from watching and wondering about other people's lives and running with the idea of how simply being 'somewhere other' can be such a transforming experience. It certainly has been for me.

Writing-wise, the wheel turned full circle when a colleague suggested I tried travel writing, on the grounds that if you could make up stories about places, you could probably tell some kind of truth about them, even if that truth had to be tailored to specific markets. I've done my fair share of 'fact box' travel features, but you won't find those in the non-fiction section. Here, the selection fell on the kind of factual reading that I'm instinctively drawn to myself for wiling away a long-haul flight, or maybe relaxing beside a pool or under a palm tree. Sometimes it's good to take a break from people-watching – say in an Indian bus station or an interminable queue for visas. That's where the sort of read that isn't exactly *War and Peace* or *The Universe in a Nutshell* can create an oasis of personal calm and make me appreciate yet again, just how lucky I am to be there.

It's inevitable that what seems like a lifetime of Africa-watching comes through strongly in both the fiction and non-fiction sections, but continents are not like children – we are allowed to love just one the best. But sometimes you have to leave the places and people you love and look back on them over time to see them more clearly. They say 'never go back', but I do, whenever and wherever I can – to add yet more perspective. Of course, there are many parts of the world, conspicuous by their absence from this very limited selection, which I would really like to know much better, or see for the first time. Perhaps right now, like me, that's a project you are already working on yourself.

Contents

Short Stories To Take You Away From it All

Travel Writing: People & Places

Short Stories to Take You Away From it All

To travel happily, one should travel light.

(Antoine de Saint-Exupéry, French aviation
pioneer and author, 1900-1944)

*All journeys have secret destinations of which
the traveller is unaware.*

(Martin Buber, Austrian-born Jewish
philosopher, 1878-1965)

Come Fly With Me

Let's fly, let's fly,
Pack up, let's fly away!

(Popular song, 1957, Van Heusen and Cahn)

I think it is a pity to lose the romantic side of flying and
simply to accept it as a common means of transport.

(Amy Johnson, aviation pioneer, 1903-1941)

South for the Winter

Sometimes you just want to leave it all behind and soar off into the blue.

They said you shouldn't put out white bread for the birds, so she didn't. Well, only the crusts and crumbs. Crumbs from the rich man's table – ha – she knew all about crumbs.

There you are, she said to the empty sky. Some bacon rinds too. He loved his bacon. They said you shouldn't give husbands bacon, but she did. And to follow, my dears, the last of the cake with all the fruit sunk to the bottom.

Soon they'd come. Starlings, of course, and the resident robin; spotted flycatchers too, but they should have left by now. They had nests in the ivy up the side wall and came back every year to the same one. There was plenty of energy there with all that fat and fruit for those going south.

She rubbed her cold hands down her apron, with *Save the Rainforest* and a bright macaw where her stomach, no longer flat, rubbed against the sink. Save some of it for me, she thought, her nose nipped and the wet grass biting her feet.

Inside, still shivering, she turned up the thermostat. There was the usual breakfast mess in the kitchen. She ignored it and sat down where she could see the phone wires outside; four strands. The swallows were there, line by line, like a song waiting to be sung.

Come fly with me, let's fly away./ If you could use/ Some exotic booze,/ There's a bar in old Bombay./ It's perfect for a flying honeymoon, they say...

So why hadn't she gone on that flying honeymoon, with her bird man fifteen years ago when she still had the chance? He was the lean sort who tanned well. Long-legged like a wader. 'Botswana's lovely in the dry season. They'll need some serious studies now they're opening up for tourism.' He'd never have wanted fry-ups and white bread or needed a pub round every corner, or taken more notice of the telly than he did of her. He could spend all day in a hide with his field glasses, but his silences had warmth, and when they'd made love the nights had never been cold.

'Come on, you'll love it. What are you afraid of?'

It wasn't fear of flying, that's for sure. She looked out at the swallows as they fidgeted and changed their tune. More like fear of the new – new places and people. Fear of being uprooted, of becoming *un*-rooted. So her bird man had flown. Every few years another field posting. Postcards from Kenya, Morocco, Rajasthan, always of birds - spoonbills and storks, lily-trotters, ox-peckers and carmine bee-eaters, of fish eagles, crowned eagles, crested cranes. She'd kept all the cards, but Married Another. And each year the winters got colder.

'It's all right for you in your fur coat,' she said as the striped mound in the cat basket rolled over and stuck out a languid paw. 'No, please, don't get up.' Half-closed, calibrating, amber eyes watched her upside down. 'And stop trying to look cute, Sultan, you old ratbag. It doesn't suit you.'

Maybe she could hibernate. Curl up on the top shelf of the airing cupboard with a bottle of Drambuie and a straw and refuse to come out until Easter. Would they even notice? They might eventually, when the food ran out. But husbands and sons were highly adaptable creatures. You bet.

She shivered again and found another sweater. On the mantelpiece was the latest postcard - from Lake Manyara, with flamingoes. She lit the gas fire that looked almost real and settled back to watch the blue flames lick at the fake coal. How could they not be consumed by such passion?

The bright gaseous blue hurt her eyes; like the sky above the flame birds' lake – gas-flame blue. The birds and flames rose together, wheeling, swerving, unstable as woodsmoke, and she began to relax as the warmth of it crept into her at last. Was that all it took? A surge of warm air to lift the spirit, to stretch a-tiptoe on those slender legs, to dance along the surface of the lake and up into the blue...

Outside, against a pile of unwashed grey clouds, a swallow detached itself from the rest and looped after some fly that had survived the autumn chill. It looked easy – so easy when you knew how – how far it was to Manyara, as the swallow flies...

Must get up – up, up and... It was really quite simple. You only needed lots of lovely warm air. Up on the toes, stretch the wings. They were waiting for her up on the wires, twittering and calling. She was part of their song. They would lead her to him, high above the Channel, over wet hedges and wide fallow fields, along gleaming river valleys, to skim the bones of dead mountains, across the blue water and into the swirling red dust – over the tall grasses where the cicadas sang and sunsets flared like the end of time.

A hop and a flutter, almost there. South for the winter. Just for the winter. Yet something still held her back, was pinning her down – and it hurt, hurt so much, like biting cold or claws of steel. 'Sultan!' she screamed as the amber eyes narrowed pitilessly. 'It's me. Put me down, you fool,' but the only sound that would come was a frightened twittering.

They were back soon, but not soon enough. Their voices were so close . .

'It's like a tip in here, and what are all those feathers?'

'Hey Dad, Sultan's got a bird.'

'*Help me...*'

'Is it dead? Dad, why's the back door open? Mum?'

'*South for the...*'

'Ooh look – it just gave a little squeak and went all floppy. Anyway, where's Mum? Hey, Dad, where is she?'

Flight Path

'It is too rash, too unadvised, too sudden;
Too like the lightning....'
Romeo and Juliet

Their flights had taken off on time from Bangkok, one going west, one east, within minutes of each other, so the parting had been short. For once, they'd both been hoping for delays – for just a little more time.

Each is staring out of the plane window now, trying to remember every last detail. Down there, every grain of rice had seemed important, but now the paddi lands are already a blur of monsoon greens and browns. Soon even that would only be a memory.

I won't let it be like that, Laura tells herself as she unfastens her seat belt. *I won't.*

'Don't let it get to you,' says Marcie, her agent, patting her arm. Marcie has been cursing the Bangkok stopover and wondering if Laura was going to turn mystical on her all through the Australian tour. Young actresses could be so emotional. 'Remember, sweetie, the best things in life are *short.*'

But Laura has closed her eyes and is conjuring up the sound of Gerry's voice – which even now, on the other departing jet, is asking the stewardess for a Coke as the brain behind it listlessly combines the speeds of the two planes. We're being pulled apart at 900 miles an hour, he muses. No wonder it hurts. Then he too, closes his eyes, remembering.

Trained at New York State University to go for the essentials, he starts with her smile. Since his doctoral thesis is on Australian Aboriginal sacred sites, he thinks it's really neat that the fatal glance should have occurred in a culturally significant place. And they don't come much more significant than the Temple of the Emerald Buddha. The guide had just said that the golden statue is given a change of clothes according to season, and it was this that had made Laura look up – and smile.

Alone and homeward bound, well used to stopovers pungent with spices, jasmine and drains, Gerry had been watching Laura's group without quite knowing why. Marcie could have told him that it was Laura's star quality, of course – that indefinable something that makes one person eclipse the rest – but Marcie, for once, hadn't been there that day.

'The Buddha's robes are changed ceremonially three times a year,' the guide was explaining. 'This is his monsoon outfit.'

A matronly type said, 'Isn't that cute? And I just love that inscrutable smile,' and the tall girl with the long cork-screw curls of dark blond hair half turned and smiled too. And, in that moment, an entire lexicon scrolled through Gerry's considerable brain and stuck at *'fair'*. This girl was fair – as in *'fair as the sun and moon'*, earth not having anything to show more, and what only the brave deserved.

When she glanced up and saw him watching her, there were only two thoughts in his mind. Yes! And – How?

But, for Laura, it was always voices before smiles. At drama school they were blindfolded and made to listen. So for her the lightning struck when she first heard him speak. Inside the temple when their eyes had met – do eyes ever meet accidentally? – her only impression of him had been of height, of wholesome American-ness, educated, and not at all gung-ho.

Behind their closed eyes, both of them had moved on and were outside the temple now.

'Pardon me, could I trouble you to take my picture in front of the Golden Chedi?' says the voice behind her, and she remembers thinking lightly, Oh it's him – please let him be going to Sydney tomorrow, too. No, don't be silly. Then aloud, 'Maybe you would take one of me? I only joined this tour at the gate. My friend's back at the hotel with the, you know, Thai Tummy.'

Gerry remembers the exact words too – remembers wondering how this girl could make even something like that sound like Shakespeare.

'Would they mind if I tagged along too?'

'I shouldn't think so – it's almost over, anyway.' She smiles again.

So far, so good. Another year, and Laura will realize just how beautiful she is, but for now her sole ambition is to be an actress – a very good one – so that people will say, 'Of course, Laura Underwood's interpretation was definitive.' She wears her looks easily and will not be destroyed by them. Even her parents seldom think of her as 'beautiful', although her mother did cry unexpectedly at the airport. A year was too long to be without Laura.

Perhaps Gerry saw all this in the face lit by the golden beeswax candles, and that's why he followed Laura's group into the Palace courtyard. All he knew for sure was that he was hooked. That smile – it's wonderful. Idiot! *She's* wonderful. Say something quickly, or she'll vanish.

'Can you believe this place?' he says, falling into step with her. 'I've seen a few temples, but this one is incredible. Your friend will be madder than hell to have missed it. If you want, I've got some medication.'

'That's kind, but she's brought some stuff from home. She wouldn't let me stay in with her, and you're right – she's furious!'

Her. It's a *her*. Thank you, gods, Buddha, the Great Sky Dragon, the whole bunch of you, thinks Gerry.

He asks if she'd like a fruit juice at the little café by the Palace Treasury, and as she says, yes, let's – it really is hot for ten in the morning, they will both relive the feeling of elation that the whole day is still in front of them, and how they tried to avoid the inevitable question: 'And how long are you in Bangkok?'

These days, even the young know full well that the odds are stacked high against them that this could be a once-and-forever kind of love.

By the time they have finished their juice, followed by a coffee, he is well into explaining Aboriginal beliefs about how the ancestors would sing their tribal lands and sacred sites into existence in the Dreamtime. He draws a songline for her on a paper napkin, and, fascinated, she asks to keep it. He wants to know all about Equity cards, agents, Shakespeare, Stoppard, Pinter... Each is entranced by the way the other speaks, and neither wants to suggest a move in case it breaks the spell.

'I'd better see if Marcie is okay,' she murmurs at last, looking round for a pay phone booth. 'My mobile's no good here.'

'Try mine,' he says and pushes it along the table towards her fingers, wanting so much to stroke them, to have them touch him.

Suddenly Laura feels wonderfully safe with this man. Not safe as in he-won't-try-anything, but safe as in I could trust myself to him. She's never felt that about a man before, and doesn't know what to do.

Marcie, hotel-bound, catches something in Laura's voice, says she's feeling a bit better, but makes her promise to call again later.

There was no question then that they would spend the day together. They take a river bus as far as it goes one way, and then back the other. When Gerry takes her hand to help her onto the boat, he doesn't let it go. He's never been so scared of making a wrong move. They talk and talk, about so many things, and once he thinks he's blown it when he says that the Bollywood film industry is onto a good thing by not allowing kissing – it leaves so much to the imagination.

She looks away for a moment and he holds his breath. Then she pushes her hair back in a gesture so artlessly sensuous that he can't bear it any longer.

'*You fill up my senses...* Um, *Annie's Song*', he says, almost to himself. 'I feel as if I'm drowning...'

She says it must be the river, and anyway, it's a beautiful song.

The boat is passing his hotel among a line of big international names almost on the river front, and he points it out. 'After six months in tribal territory, I needed one with a bath,' he jokes, desperate to keep it light. 'Not quite true – I got a good deal. They even put an orchid on your pillow.'

'Ours is in the old French quarter'. She knows a graceful invitation when she hears one, but isn't yet quite ready to accept.

'I've got another year back home to write all this up before I can be sure of a university post,' he tells her over chicken fragrant with lemon grass and ginger at a floating restaurant. 'Have you ever thought about the States?'

She sighs. 'It's this Australia thing. The rest of the company's already there, and I've been waiting so long for a chance like this.'

Why can't it be easy, he thinks, the way they said it used to be? Then this luminous girl would change her ticket, her plans, her life, and come with him. Six years of studying and fieldwork, his parents' support –

he can no more abandon it, any more than she can *not* want to be an actress, and *not* take this chance in Australia, ironically, just as he's left the place.

'What colour orchids do they put on your pillow?' she murmurs as they stroll along the river bank. As in a dream, he buys a bunch of every colour he can find, and she says, 'Don't kiss me – not yet.' They take a tuk-tuk to his hotel, and the driver grins, and says, 'Honeymoon – good.'

They make inspirational love in the shower and fall asleep on the silk bedcover. When they wake up he says that didn't count because it was over far too soon. She throws a pillow at him and he tickles her bare shoulder with an orchid, but afterwards when they are telling each other softly that was the most wonderful ever, neither doubts it.

Fingers and arms entwined, they go out to the Night Market for a snack and buy each other carved jade horoscope signs. Laura suddenly remembers Marcie, and calls to say she'll be back tomorrow in good time to pack.

There seems to be a pact between them that sleep is a waste of precious time, so they are up to see sunrise at the Temple of Dawn. They make no promises, except to email when they can. When Marcie looks at Laura's rapt face, she wants to tell her that a career, ten thousand miles, a whole year, are nothing – such feelings truly can last for ever. Instead she says nothing and just sighs for them, and a little for herself.

High above them, two vapour trails cross. Far away, over the land, a streak of lightning splits the impassive sky. Between them, below them, before them, lies an ocean. Yet the signs could be wrong. True lovers do not *always* have to part, and next year the Emerald Buddha will be dressed in his monsoon-season robes again. And he will still be smiling.

Nowhere Man

It's all very well to travel hopefully, but what if you never arrive?

At first I didn't think much about him. He looked just like any other business type who'd nearly missed the plane. It takes one to know one. At the time, which was German time, and therefore an hour ahead of everyone else, I was actually more interested in whether the stewardess, a Scarlett Johansson look-alike who'd herded him up the steps at the very last minute would come up to expectations out of her Lufthansa gear beside the Bahrain Hilton pool.

A large female who'd come dressed as a polar bear had bagged my window seat, but there's nothing to see on a night flight from Frankfurt to the Gulf, so I'd left her to it and taken the aisle seat in our row of three. Sure enough, she had just begun to offload her cabin bag into a mound on the seat between us when Scarlett turned up with *him* in tow.

'In here, Mr Vandenberg,' she said briskly, while fixing me with a wicked-queen smile. 'Please, the aisle seat should be free, I think.'

There was a bit of a *manifestation folklorique* as the Frankfurter moved her defences and I edged over. Then this Vandenberg character took the aisle seat without so much as a murmur. He wasn't even flustered – as if he always walked into a spare seat at the last minute. But so far, that was all.

'That's what I call good timing,' I said, just to break the ice as the engines started.

'Timing?' he said in slightly accented but excellent English. 'I've lost all sense of time.' Just like that.

Vandenberg, I thought. Anglo-Dutch, maybe?

'Know the feeling,' I replied cheerily. 'I'm already bushwhacked. Bags went missing at Aberdeen and this was the only way I could make it to Bahrain on schedule.' I sighed. 'You in the oil game too?'

I remembered where I'd last tried that line at one of those parties somewhere hot and sandy where the hard stuff comes in Lucosade bottles and the stewardesses really take good care of you. I can't remember her name, but I think she was with Qantas. 'Oil?' she'd cooed. 'Would that be baby, cooking, or just plain crude?' It was the start of a beautiful, if all-too-brief, relationship.

Vandenberg blinked wearily. 'Oil? I used to be. I sometimes wonder if they missed me.'

The drinks trolley was already rolling and the captain was crackling away in German about how welcome aboard we were, and how high we were going to get before hitting Bahrain. You can keep all that stuff about travelling hopefully. These days, all I want to do is arrive, even if it's 2a.m. Gulf Time.

Seeing that Vandenberg was still looking vacant, I asked if he was staying there long.

'No,' he replied. 'I'm just passing through.'

He was mid-thirties, I suppose; not bad looking, but pale. Blue-green eyes, mid-brown hair, well cut; medium build; good casual gear you could pick up anywhere. Nothing to make him stand out from the herd except an air of - what? I don't know – misplacement was the nearest I could get to it. I felt as though he'd lost something. Maybe himself.

It got worse. When Scarlett and her trolley partner rolled up, Vandenberg seemed to shrink in his seat and go even paler, like they were the Angel of Death in duplicate.

'You look as if you could do with a brandy or something,' I said as I ordered my usual.

He shook his head.

'You're not allergic to them, are you?' I asked jokily as they trundled on. 'Stewardess, I mean. Personally, I love them all.'

'So did I, once,' he relied. 'That was the trouble.'

Cracked it, I thought. *Cherchez la femme.* He'd probably had an unhappy fling with one of them – maybe several of them. Maybe the whole damn' fleet. It was as simple as that.

Then the flat voice began again. 'And then it started, you see. Once you're in their power, you lose the will to resist.'

'Sounds great – when do I start?' I said, trying to see him as the world's greatest dead-pan artist. 'How about an intro to Scarlett over there?'

'Her name's Trudi, and the dark one's Barbara.'

'Well', I said, 'you certainly know your way around.'

'Yes,' he murmured distantly. 'Around and around and around. If you travel east at the speed of eight hundred kilometres an hour in these latitudes, the days are only sixteen hours long. With good connecting flights, it's even less. And now it's too late. They've got it fixed, and I can't break out. Once you upset them, you see, they wait until you're jet lagged out of your head, log you into the system, and that's that.'

Okay, if travel broadens the mind, air travel can really freak you out, and here I was strapped in beside the worst case of jet lag on record.

'Look, we all get a bit frayed round the edges on the long-hauls,' I said. 'How long have you been on the go on this trip?'

Even downing the rest of my Scotch in one didn't help with the next bit.

'Since 2008,' he replied, without changing his tone. 'April, I think it was. I suppose they told the company I'd gone missing or something.'

You know what it's like when you wish someone would just crack his face or let out a guffaw and everything would be all right? Well, he didn't. Now I've sat next to some hard cases who didn't know whether it was Tuesday night or Thursday morning. But 2008? What was this guy on?

I must admit that at this point I thought I was beginning to lose it myself. Maybe I should have just hung in there and tried to get some sense out of him. It was time for a trip to the lavatory to mull things over, and perhaps have word with Trudi, as she now was. There was a queue, but it gave me time to think.

Of course I knew it was crazy. After two days of airline food and very little sleep, my mouth made the bottom of a parrot cage look neat. I was a bit out of it, that's all, and probably so was he.

I looked round. Weren't we all? Most of the other inmates had their eyes closed, but they didn't fool me. No one could sleep in a sardine can belting along faster than the earth was turning, high above the Med with no visible means of support. Even at school that used to fascinate me. Then there was watching stuff like *Dallas* and *The Troubleshooters* at an impressionable age. So when I started at Hague International, it wasn't to join the nine-to-five brigade. I wanted travel and adventure. That was before I found out what long-hauls did to your biorhythms.

I had to find Trudi, just to talk to someone who wasn't going to spook me. It was nearly feeding time and she was doing her juggling act with food trays in the back galley so I didn't want to upset her.

'It's about Mr Vandenberg in 17C, Fraulein,' I burbled. 'Do you think he's alright?'

She looked at me as if I'd asked for a bacon sandwich in Mecca during Ramadan.

'Mr Vandenberg doesn't wish to be disturbed, sir. He's one of our most regular passengers and we take good care of him. Please return to your seat – we are about to serve a light supper.' She almost smiled then. 'We call him our Flying Dutchman.'

Then it clicked. This was really him, just like that story about the ship doomed to sail the seas forever because of some horrible crime on board. Vandenberg had broken one heart too many, and the girls had fixed it so that he'd never make port again. What a fate! Permanent jet lag, canned air, endless queues and baggage searches, airline food and filling out landing cards – but for where? They plugged you into the system and left you there – for good.

Vandenberg seemed to be asleep when I got back. As I squeezed past him, I swear the cold draught was coming from him and not the air blower. The food came and went. Only the Frankfurter munched her way happily through the lot. I didn't sleep a wink.

Vandenberg didn't wake up until we were due to land. I couldn't face another blurred conversation, but I watched as Trudi and Barbara escorted him to the transit lounge. Then I hung around where I could see the tarmac.

Dawn was doing all the things it is supposed to do in the mystic East when I spotted him again, through rose-tinted eyeballs, I have to admit. Sure enough, two lotus-blossom types in sarongs had him gently by the arms and were leading him towards a Cathay Pacific ('Enjoy your fright') to Singapore.

He was the last to board. They were taking good care of him all right – they were going to fly him all the way and never let him go. They'd club-class him, shuttle him and stand-by him; stop-over him, have-a nice-day him, Ryanair, EasyJet, Aeroflot, Qantas, BA and Virgin Hot Air him – from here to there. Anywhere and nowhere. And me? That was the day I decided to find a nice girl with her feet on the ground, get a desk job and settle down.

Wish You Were Here

When a girl like Keeley signs up for the school trip to Amsterdam, what do you do? You just have to take her, knowing there's bound to be trouble.

There comes a time in every teacher's life when you wish, oh how you wish, you'd become a dentist, a shepherd, an astronaut – in fact anything where no one can answer you back. For me, that day came in July two years ago on the school trip to Amsterdam.

Now I must say that Collier Lane Comprehensive hadn't been my first choice when straight out of college and looking for somewhere to cultivate a love of art. From the comments in the staff-room, it hadn't been anyone else's either. The general feeling was that we were there because we were there, and so, like Mount Everest, or possibly the Battle of the Somme, was Collier Lane – in which case we might just as well get on with it.

Unfortunately for the teachers, not all the pupils shared these noble sentiments – least among them Keeley Pendle. Of course, every school had its Keeley Pendles and Gary O'Houlahans, the kind that bring tormented dreams of early retirement even to hearty full-backs like Bill Hawkins (not for nothing known as Hawkeye) whose idea it was to set up the Amsterdam trip.

Bill's method of getting staff volunteers for such ventures was to sneak up behind the young and inexperienced and murmur things like, 'Joanne, you warm and wonderful human being, think of the Rembrandts, the Vermeers, the Van Goghs.' I could always resist a Hawkeye, but never a Van Gogh.

To the relief of the five staff who'd been likewise sweet-talked into signing up, the O'Houlahan clan decided that their Gary couldn't take any more culture, but Keeley Pendle's name on the list was greeted with raised eyebrows and a deep sense of foreboding.

It wasn't that we were unsympathetic to Keeley's problems, the greatest of which was her father, if such he was. If he bullied Keeley the way he bullied the teachers at parents' evenings, it was no wonder the girl was trouble. In her first two years at Collier Lane, there'd been that tell-tale mixture of withdrawal, cunning and neglect which sapped the stamina of anyone who'd tried to help. It was my lot to catch her in the third year, and that's when Keeley really began to make her mark – on the walls, the desks, the other girls, and even once on a dinner lady's shins.

For a while, I'd been hopeful that Keeley and I might somehow rub along. What little work she produced between frequent bouts of truanting showed real flair – in particular, one lovely watercolour on the theme of 'Wish you were here'. Her interpretation of this had been highly original – a startlingly revealing self-portrait of the girl as we knew her, hunched, dishevelled, staring angrily at a mirror, where her image was reflected as a completely transformed Keeley – smiling, confident, even pretty. Not only was the meaning touchingly clear, but the technique was bold and original. Even Hawkeye was impressed. But whatever the girl had been trying to show us in that brief flash of inspiration stayed well hidden in reality.

Naturally I praised 'Wish you were here', pinned it on the art-room wall and offered extra help. The results were not encouraging. After a few days, someone daubed the picture with red paint. No one owned up, and I was left with an uneasy feeling that Keeley had done it herself.

'It was crap anyway,' was all she said, with her usual shrug.

'It was good,' I'd replied, 'and you know it as well as I do, Keeley.'

'If you're so hot,' she flung over her shoulder, 'whatcha doing in a dump like this? Why aren't you a *proper* artist.'

Of course it hurt. It was more upsetting than any amount of noise and cheek from the others. But when someone like Keeley signs up against all the odds for a school trip, what do you do? Refuse to take them, so that they behave even worse for being left out? Say they can come if they turn over a new leaf, and risk the numbers being short if they don't – or let them come, hoping they'll see their friends and teachers in a different light in new surroundings, and maybe even benefit from the experience? With Keeley, I favoured the latter, and said so to Bill Hawkins.

Most teachers are born optimists. They are also quite cute at sharing the responsibility (and therefore the blame) if anything goes wrong.

'Well, if you really think you can handle it...' Hawkeye was at his manipulative best, 'so I can count on you to have her in your group, then, Jo?'

Suddenly, a whole week of being accountable for six of Collier Lane's finest, among them K. Pendle, was enough to cast a long dark shadow over the brightest Vermeer in the Rijksmuseum.

When it actually came to it, I had to admit that things went much better than expected, at least for the first part of the trip. Hawkeye had decided on flying to Amsterdam from Birmingham rather than a gruelling trip by coach and ferry, with accommodation in hostels to keep the price down. Collier Row wasn't exactly in the gin-and-jag belt so most of the kids hadn't flown before. Consequently, their behaviour on the outward flight was positively reverential although, as Jennie Flaxman (PE and more of realist that I) remarked, it could have had something to do with them being strapped in, and why couldn't we introduce seat belts in schools.

Hawkeye's itinerary kept up a stiff pace – one day for the Delta Scheme, another for Amsterdam by canal, Anne Frank's House, the Cheese Market and so on. The clanking, grinding works of a windmill went down well, and so did the gin factory (minus samples). He'd decided that half a day was the limit of their tolerance for Art, and it hurt me to rush past those gorgeous rooms full of Dutch and Flemish masters – but duty was duty, and I promised myself a return visit very soon.

That was the morning I found Keeley in front of a Van Gogh self-portrait when the others were already on the coach. It was the one of him painting at his easel. She didn't say anything when, short of breath and running out of temper, I finally found her, except, 'Oh, it's you.' She never called me Miss Hundleby like the others, or even 'Miss'. It so happened that the postcards I'd bought included one of that particular painting, and I showed it to her as we hurried outside to join the others. I'd have given it to her willingly, but I think she sensed it, and both of us knew she'd refuse.

It was sad, I thought as we boarded the coach, that it was the only thing I did know for certain about Keeley's state of mind just then.

That night came the moment I'd been dreading. They'd been allowed to go shopping in the afternoon, with strict instructions about alcohol and anything smoke-able, legal or otherwise, but that hadn't stopped Keeley. By the time one of the girls called me, it was too late. Keeley stank of marijuana and was already drunk – quietly and desperately drunk – and then very sick indeed, mostly, but not entirely, into the washbasin in the room I was sharing with Jennie Flaxman.

We sat her on the bed, cleaned her up and gave her some Alka Seltzer, then walked her up and down the quiet street outside.

'Why?' I asked. I'd learned not to waste words with Keeley.

'Why d'ya think?' was her mumbled reply. I could do little but exchange despairing looks with Jennie Flaxman over the spiky, fake-red hair. We got her back to bed, discretely checked for remaining bottles and stashes, and hushed her room mates.

'You know those Westerns when someone says they don't like it, it's too quiet?' I said as Jennie and I tried to get some sleep.

'Just what I was thinking,' she replied. 'She's always quiet, but this is different. Anyway, only one more day.'

'Do you know, she hasn't bought any presents, nothing at all, in fact, that I can see.'

'I wish you hadn't told me that,' said Jennie.

Our last day was at a dairy farm, with lots of smaller animals for the kids to pet, and the flight was at 6:30 pm. Beside those contented animals and the rest of our cheerful herd, I could only think of Keeley as a hunted vixen.

We got to the airport with not much time to spare before check in. It was pretty crowded, and my group was at the back, as usual. I moved forward to check in my case and show them what to do, but there was a moment or two's delay at the desk to get more baggage tags. I don't know what made me look round before I put my case on the scales, but when I did, Keeley had disappeared.

'She said she was going to the loo, Miss Hundleby,' said Tracey Earnshawe. 'She's left her case, see?'

'I bet she's done a runner,' said one of the boys cheerfully.

Not without her case, I prayed fervently as I shot off, but the feeling was growing as I called her name along lines of cubicles in the nearest toilet and emerged without her, that he could be right.

Hawkeye came over. 'Trouble?' he said. The rest had already checked in. He looked at his watch and then at me. 'Right, I reckon we've got about twenty minutes. I'll get an announcement over the PA. Jo, you do all the loos. Mike, stay with the kids and get them through passport control. Jennie and Ian spread out, and I'll take the main stairway after I've raised the alarm. When you hear the last call, get back to the departure point regardless, and I'll have made sure you get priority. Then we'll take it from there.'

It's amazing how much ground you can cover when you have to, and how many loos and other likely hiding places there were in that airport. I was certain now that Keeley wasn't just being difficult – she wanted out, and the school trip had been quite literally what she saw as her passport to freedom. But what kind of freedom was she planning, in Amsterdam, for goodness sake? I wasn't angry, I was sick with fear and failure as I threw myself round every last corner of the place.

Quite exhausted, I was last back at the departure point where, as I feared, the only sign of Keeley was her tattered wheelie case guarded by an official, and my three harassed colleagues. 'But she *can't* have!' had quickly become '*She has!*' It didn't matter how. Every teacher knows that any child determined or desperate enough can do almost anything, and that short of leg-irons or electronic tagging, there's nothing much anyone can do.

We went into a disconsolate huddle. 'Take off's in ten minutes,' said Hawkeye. 'But they can hold the door for another five without losing their slot. The rest are on board and so are our cases, except for yours, Jo. Seriously, what do you reckon? Is she just trying to put the fear of God into us?'

'No,' I said glumly, and the others agreed.

'I'll stay, of course,' I said, trying not to feel like Sydney Carton bravely going to the guillotine. 'I'll sort it out somehow and phone the school, or your place when I know what's going on. Tell those parents of hers she's not well or something.'

Hawkeye nodded at the Dutch officials as he passed me the emergency money and crisis packet. 'They'll get you on tomorrow's flight. Thanks, Jo.'

'And if I don't find her by then, it will have to be Interpol, but I'm going to stay until I find her.'

There were hugs and comforting pats. 'That picture she did – Keeley-flaming-'Wish you were here'-Pendle – God, that's ironic,' said Jennie. 'Keep ringing in.'

As they moved off quickly to the departure gate and out of sight, the enormity of it began to sink in. The unthinkable had happened. I'd lost a child – someone else's child – in a city whose red-light district made Soho look like Tunbridge Wells, and I was on my own with a fistful of euros, two wheelie cases and my flight bag. Headlines swam before my eyes. Soon I'd have to give a full description to the police. Even if Keeley managed to change her appearance with another dye job, she knew nothing about papers and regulations. How long could she lie low, and what might happen to her in the meantime? Right now, she could be heading for... I shuddered. Van Gogh had gone to the South of France to find himself. Paul Gaugin had gone to Tahiti...

I braced myself and went to talk to the officials, managing to convince them that if they left the suitcase where it was and put out an announcement that the flight had left, she might just come back to get it. Reluctantly they agreed to stay out of sight and let me approach her alone if she showed up. It was a long shot and we set a thirty-minute deadline. Meanwhile Security was checking the exits for a smallish figure with spiky red hair, in a short black leather skirt, a tight purple top, black tights and black ankle boots.

The flight left, and the time had nearly run out when I spotted her. I was in such a trance of worry that I almost didn't recognize her first. She'd jammed a black beret down over her hair, ditched the tights and boots for sandals and replaced the purple top with a baggy white one – just enough to fool anyone who didn't know her.

'Keeley,' I said quietly, behind her.

She didn't jump, but her shoulders seemed to drop, and she ripped off the beret in what could have been an admission of defeat.

'Oh, it's you,' she said tonelessly.

'Just me,' I replied. 'They've gone. Fancy a coffee?'

In the split second of hesitation before she agreed, I knew there was an even chance we'd be on that plane tomorrow – if I didn't blow it. But as I gave the thumbs-up to the watching officials, I knew it was going to be a very full-on twenty-four hours.

She began to talk, slowly at first – how she'd planned it as soon as she'd heard about the trip, got money by working in the evenings, even got drunk to make us glad to be rid of her. Kids – honestly! It had been a doddle, she said, to hide in the loos and change her clothes for the ones in her flight bag. She'd got around £50 in euros, and was going to get work as an artist's model, and then support herself by painting. She didn't make excuses, look for sympathy or ask for advice, and I didn't give any, but when she started talked about her home, I could have wept at the sheer unfairness of it all, even if only half of it was true.

The hostel still had rooms, and we spent all next day in the museums. For each of the artists I told her a little of their often tormented lives, hoping perhaps she would see how often great art could be born from life's difficulties. It was the nearest I felt I could get without breaking her down completely.

'Van Gogh used to be a teacher,' she ventured. 'You left that bit out.'

I hope she meant it well, but with Keeley, you could never be sure.

When we got home, the incident was more or less patched up as best we could, and although she carried on in my classes, and was much more co-operative, she never mentioned it again. For two years, I wondered if I should have said more, or less, on that strange day in Amsterdam.

Last year, she took her exams and went to the local art college. Last week I got a postcard. It was the Van Gogh again, postmarked Amsterdam. It said,

Dear Miss Hundleby – guess who! Got a job in a studio mixing paints
and things for the summer through someone at coll.
Thanks for everything, Keeley.
PS Wish you were here.

On days like that, I think maybe I don't need to escape to Tahiti for inspiration after all, and that on the whole, I'd rather be a teacher than an astronaut.

I Dream of Africa

A foutra for the world and worldlings base!
I speak of Africa and golden joys.

(Falstaff, from Shakespeare's Henry IV Part 2)

Please leave Africa as you would wish to find it.

(Graffiti on a loo wall in a West African teachers' college)

The Road to Kachinga

Tomorrow, to ease their father's spirit, there would be a ceremony, led by
Chief Kapemba if he was willing, to break the gun and bury it like a snake.
But the leopard must not be killed – their father had said it.

They were almost there now. Sandwiched between Andrew at the window
of the Land Rover and Foto the driver, Vicky Carstairs made both men
jump as she pointed excitedly ahead.

'Okay, this is the place. Can you pull over, Foto, just before the bridge?'
They braced themselves as the Land Rover almost stood on its nose in
the mud. Andrew reached automatically for his camera, but she grabbed
his arm. 'Maybe later, I think. Don't worry, I'll see you get so many prize-
winning shots, the editor will promote you. I just want you to get your first
view of Kachinga with nothing in between.'

Laughing with sheer exhilaration, she pulled him towards the wooden
bridge. After the four-hour drive from the airport, it was so good to feel
the muggy warmth that soothed away the travel stiffness. And the mud –
the red, gritty, wet-season African mud she always loved to see on the way
back home, because it meant Christmas holidays.

'Sorry, darling,' she laughed, as Andrew almost slipped and made a
grab for the splintery handrail. 'You forget how wet it can really be.'

He was looking down with disbelief at his designer trainers.

'There,' she said, and gave him a dab of mud on the nose. 'Dad always
says instead of christening us, they just said a prayer and rolled us in
Kachinga mud.'

'I don't believe this father of yours,' muttered Andrew. 'My God, is that
meant to be *water* down there? What a colour! Has it got a name?'

She chuckled at the look on his face. 'We've got maps round here, you
know. None of this "Here be crocodiles" stuff. That's the Langwa. Not bad
for a tributary, of a tributary, of the mighty Zambezi, is it?'

'It's like bloody Campbell's soup.'

'And very good for you too, if you're a hippo – full of Nile cabbage weed and bits of trees. I was hoping we'd see the hippos, but I suppose they'll be in the reed beds at this time of year.'

'Hippos? So near the road?'

'They're not a bit shy. Listen.'

At first they could hear nothing above the rushing water. Andrew put his hands round her waist and squeezed. 'It's all this nature in the raw,' he breathed into her hair. 'I think I'll carry you off right now and...'

'Ssh!' Gently she disentangled herself. 'Not now – Foto's over there.'

Andrew drew away. 'Don't give me that not-in-front-of-the-servants stuff,' he grinned. 'Surely that went out years ago – even with Daddy.'

Vicky made a face at him. Nothing was going to spoil this moment. After all, she was bringing the man she loved – and it had to be love if you felt like this – to the place where she was born. Back in London, it was Andrew who'd made the running – led her into the strange customs of the tribe – where to eat, what to wear, street markets, galleries, and into grown-up love-making. At times it had left her gasping. But this was *her* home ground, and Andrew could try a bit of the wide-eyed wonder for a change.

Yet there was so much it took some time to understand. 'Look, Foto may be Dad's driver, but I was brought up with him, and here, you don't grope in public – much as I might fancy the idea, you understand.' She gave him a sexy smoulder.

'Boarding school girls. I've met your sort before. Just wait until lights out...'

Her response to his touch was so predictable that it almost worried her at times. It blurred things, like the way he seemed to have got it wrong about her father. By the standards of the other settlers in the area, Douglas Carstairs was a flaming liberal, if not a Commie pinko, even before Independence. He'd never bothered talking politics. He simply liked Africans and had always said they would be running the country themselves one day. You had to get outside it all to see how much that said about Doug Carstairs.

She touched Andrew's arm. 'Hear that?'

This time Andrew heard it – a blowing snort, a distant bellow and some splashing. 'You know, whenever I come back I have this nightmare that the hippos won't be there – that Kachinga will have changed. Every school holidays I always used to stop here first. Then I'd walk over the bridge for the first view of the house. Come on!'

He followed her across the splintery planks and... Perfect timing. Less than a mile away now, across the high grass and a flood-mark of fever trees, a shaft of golden afternoon sun lit up her old home. Kachinga – a long low bungalow with a high roof of darkened thatch overhanging the veranda. A lawn of carefully tended Bahama grass blending with a blue-green eucalyptus windbreak framing the back. Clumps of hibiscus, huge star aloes and shoulder-high canna lilies, and over the porch the vivid purple flash of bougainvillea.

'M'mm, I'm impressed. And look at that light! So okay, let's have the guided tour.'

Excitedly she pointed out the cluster of guests' chalets, empty at this time of year with the rains churning the park tracks to quagmires and the animals dispersed. The workers' compound – beehive huts and conical wicker grain stores topped with pan roofing; the workshop area with the generator and fuel dump hidden by a flowering hedge from the barbeque area. Her arm in his, she told him how her mother used to hang a bright *chitenge* welcome cloth over the veranda for her to see from this very spot. Since her mother's death twelve years ago, it always left an ache when the cloth wasn't there to greet her.

'There's a lot of cars,' said Andrew. 'I thought the place was closed for the season.'

'They're mostly ours. That looks like a new lorry round the back. There's the Land Rover, Dad's pick-up, Josh's old station wagon, Maureen's run-about.' She shaded her eyes. 'But I don't recognize that Peugeot.'

Andrew was frowning and saying something about quite a reception committee. He could be so transparent at times.

'Don't worry, my love,' she said. 'Dad's not going to come after you with an elephant gun for comprehensively seducing his darling daughter. I told you, it's just going to be the family. No pressure, and no guests because the place is being done up. It'll be a Christmas you'll never forget, and you'll get so much footage you'll run out of film.'

Foto had started the engine and was coming across the bridge after them.

'Home, my friend,' she said to him in Chewa. It wasn't an order, just a statement of fact. Foto laughed and said the time had been too long. The soft African phrases hung between them like a conspiracy, but she didn't want Andrew to feel excluded. 'Whose is that Peugeot, Foto?' she asked. For one crazy moment, she thought it might be Greg's. Greg Hamilton, one of her reasons for leaving Kachinga. But they'd lost touch now, and there was no earthly reason why Greg should be here today.

Foto did a double take, and his answer took her mind off Greg. 'It's the doctor's, from Katondwe.' He was speeding up even as he spoke.

She asked if everyone had been all right when he left, and Foto said all had been well enough, but he'd been three days in the capital getting stores.

'How about Maureen?' If anyone was poorly, it was likely to be her sister-in-law. Josh had married Maureen six years ago, but things hadn't gone too smoothly for the rather spoilt girl from town. She'd met Maureen only once during a brief holiday, and heard her father wonder aloud if she had the makings of someone who would one day be running Kachinga. But to get the doctor out here? Well, you didn't – unless... And why were the shutters closed?

As they crossed the narrow culvert to the home compound, Foto gave his usual three blasts on the horn. Normally it brought the local kiddies running out and shouting. Then the door would open and her father would appear...

They swung to a stop but the door stayed shut. Really anxious now, she bounded up the veranda steps. The door opened almost reluctantly, but it was Josh who stood there, with Maureen hovering behind him. Vicky flung herself laughing into his arms. His hug was hesitant, as if he was treating her gently, and he seemed older, tired – as if he'd shrunk.

'Vicky love, thank God you've made it.' He held her at arms' length for a moment. Maureen had been crying. 'It's Dad,' he said shakily. 'He's – there's been a ghastly accident. His gun went off. There was this leopard, you see...'

Her father's bedroom was dark as she tiptoed in. The bulky figure in the big double bed did not stir and the shock that had almost frozen her in the doorway, suddenly melted in an overwhelming relief that she was here for him now. They'd placed him to one side of the big double bed to allow for the tangle of drips that seemed to be pinning him down, and he looked so lonely there.

'Dad – it's Vicky. It's okay, I'm here.'

But it wasn't okay – although mercifully his face and chest weren't marked above the great swathes of stained bandages where his own gun had blown a hole in his side. Someone from the dispensary had given him morphine, and they'd got the doctor on the radio, but he said it was too late for the hospital. They'd said it would be some time tonight.

'You made it, sweetheart,' was all the still figure could say at first.

Vicky sat there unable to speak, stroking the roughened hand that was now cold and clammy to her touch. She wanted so much to know that he wasn't in pain.

He might have read her mind. 'It's good stuff that,' he murmured with the faintest movement of the arm attached to the drip. 'Better than Scotch any day.'

The room smelled strongly of disinfectant. When you were a child in a boarding school sick-room and your parents were six thousand miles away, it was the loneliest smell in the world. How ironic. Today, she was the parent, and he was the child.

He seemed to drift for a while, and then squeezed her fingers. 'You should have seen it, lass. After all this time, a leopard at Kachinga. She was a beauty... a female in milk. Don't let them kill her, or I'll come back and haunt the lot of you. She'll be the star attraction next season... wasn't the beast's fault... always was a clumsy bastard...'

It had all happened so quickly. Josh had said they'd been sceptical when the tracks were reported. But then chickens and goats started disappearing with the usual trademarks. They hadn't been out to kill it, of course. Leopards were a protected species, but then last night, after a third raid on the poultry run, they'd waited in the Land Rover, flashlights ready, safety catches off, to spot where it was getting over the ten-foot wire and fire shots to scare it off. The creature hadn't meant to attack them. The smell of engine oil hid human scent, and she'd simply tried to use the vehicle as a springboard to clear the wire. In the awful, bloody confusion that followed her jump almost on top of them, and the gun going off, the leopardess had escaped unscathed.

It seemed to get dark early that night as they took turns to sit with him. Vicky was so shaken and distressed that she barely had time to think of Andrew, dumped into a family crisis of first magnitude in a strange country, with people he'd never met.

Douglas Carstairs lingered until just before sunrise. Leaving Josh to complete the formalities, Vicky wandered blindly out of the house just as a damp dawn was breaking over the distant escarpment. In Josh's Holden, she drove down to the fever trees beside the river and waited for the tears to come.

It began to rain, great heavy sad drops, then streaming down the windows and blotting out the landscape. She wept for maybe half an hour, then wondered what her pathetic tears could count for in such a torrent.

At last she drove wearily back to the house to find Andrew in bed waiting for her, concerned, attentive. With an instinct that some men have, he seemed to know that what she needed then was wordless, exhausting passion. That was something Andrew did very well.

The next day was a grey blur. The village women came, keening as they prepared the man they'd known all their lives for burial, in their own time and in their own way. The family left them to it, saved from not knowing what to do by the African nearness to the core of things. On the small knoll about a mile from the house, the men were already digging beside the other grave out there under the flame tree. The funeral would be tomorrow.

They buried Douglas Carstairs as deep as they could beside his wife in the red rubble that passed for soil at Kachinga.

As Vicky watched the men pile river-smoothed cobbles over her father's grave, she held Andrew's arm and wondered yet again how her mother had lived through those first difficult years. She'd never once heard her complain – it was Dad who did that, loudly, comically, honestly. Now they were both at rest before their time under the flame tree. Sleep well, you two, said Vicky's heart. You've earned it, but oh God, how we'll miss you – Josh and Foto, all of us. Even Maureen. I suppose. But I'll miss you most.

Father Conway from the mission said some prayers, the local children sang, and they all somehow managed *The Lord is My Shepherd* before distant cloud veiled the line of the Zambezi trench. Normally they would have walked back to the house, but with a leopard about, they'd brought the cars and the lorry to get everyone back safely.

The little convoy was bumping its way back in the mud when Vicky spotted a large estate car heading towards them.

She blinked. 'Who's this, Josh – someone hoping to make the funeral?'

Josh grunted that he didn't recognize the wagon, but they'd be in time for a drink, and by God, he could do with one.

Yes, thought Vicky, I'd noticed. Josh hadn't been what you might call completely sober since she'd arrived. Perhaps understandable in the circumstances, only now he was master of Kachinga, and that was something none of them had yet been able to absorb.

The oncoming car stopped. All Vicky could see was the arm of a light formal suit propped at the window, but something about the blurred figure behind the windscreen made her stiffen.

'Good Lord!' Josh leaned out for a better look. 'It's Greg Hamilton. Bad news travels fast. Last I heard, he was in Western Province. He must have travelled half the night. And who's that with him?'

Confused, Vicky muttered something to Andrew about how fond he'd been of Dad, but Josh was waving and pulling over to let the rest of the convoy through.

In the passenger seat was a well-dressed, attractive African girl who seemed to distance herself from the proceedings as the two men got out and shook hands warmly.

'Couldn't believe it... just had to come... wonderful man...'

She watched numbly as her brother told Greg that she was home and saw him start visibly. He looked towards her and waved, then gestured to the house. She raised her hand in reply.

'So that's the one,' said Andrew's voice beside her.

Vicky bit her lip. Of course she'd told Andrew about Greg, the boy she'd once thought she was in love with. Telling him everything about herself had seemed the right thing at the time. Those whispered confidences in Andrew's arms, when nothing had seemed more unlikely than that the two men would actually meet, here, at Kachinga – and today of all days.

Now she felt a faint brush of distaste with herself for giving so much away. That teenage time with Greg had been so sweet in its way – very young love, inexperienced, untested, just there for the asking. Well, now it looked as if Greg had tales of his own to tell, judging by the elegant young woman he'd brought with him.

'Looks like we've got two more for the party.' Josh tended towards heavy irony even at the worst of times.

'Who's the woman?' asked Maureen in the thin voice that grated slightly on Vicky's nerves.

'Friend?' Josh never wasted words, especially when thirsty.

'Local tart, more likely.'

Suddenly Vicky felt irritated, and then ashamed of them. Why on earth had Josh married someone like Maureen? Okay, she was pretty in a fairish, dolly sort of way, but the type who didn't wear well in strong sunlight. She'd really tried to like her sister-in-law, but had found her colourless and inclined to be petty. Life at Kachinga demanded something more than that.

Josh said nothing and Maureen sniffed. 'Well if they've got to stay over, they can have a chalet. I'm not having her in the house.'

Vicky put a hand wearily to her forehead. Catching Andrew's eye, she saw stunned disbelief, and a rush of all kinds of dark emotions swooped on her from nowhere. It was like the time she and Greg, as children, had gone into a hillside cave and been mobbed by a horde of disturbed bats.

Burying your father was bad enough, but what was Maureen trying to do, for heaven's sake? In a couple of sentences, she'd assumed that Greg was sexually involved with this girl, taken control of domestic arrangements at Kachinga, and managed to show herself up as a complete bigot.

'Can't we leave this until we get a few facts?' she shot back.

'Or a few drinks,' said Josh, while Maureen retreated behind a sulk.

'Anyway, Greg will surely be staying at his folks', won't he?' she asked. 'It's only half an hour away. Not that they wouldn't be welcome here,' she added pointedly.

Josh looked round at her. 'I suppose you wouldn't know,' he said. 'The Hamiltons have packed up and retired to England. Mrs Hamilton was never all that strong. They sold out to the government agents a few months ago, and not for a good price, so I heard.'

'Oh no! Poor Greg.' Already almost drained of emotion, Vicky still felt a pang for him. How dreadful – to lose your home. It was unthinkable. But then, so was everything today.

Back at the house there was chaos. When a man like Doug Carstairs died, everyone for miles around had to come. They'd drive, ride, walk, even run for hours just to be there. No one would have dreamt of staying in the house to prepare the reception, but huge quantities of beer and roast meat for an African funeral were as necessary as champagne and cake at an English wedding. For such an occasion her father would have done everything in advance, so before leaving she'd reminded Josh to get the barbeque pit alight. A couple of pigs had been slaughtered, and crates of beer were cold-soaking in bowls, buckets, baths, anything. On the outside stoves, huge pots for mealie porridge stood bubbling. Now it just needed organizing.

'My God!' muttered Andrew as the car drew up. 'Who are all these people? It's like a crowd scene from *Cry Freedom*.'

Vicky smiled wanly. 'Dad would have loved this, but what we need is Richard Attenborough with a megaphone.'

It seemed so strange not to see her father's solid presence in the middle of it all – as if nothing at Kachinga could ever be quite right without him. She didn't dare to voice the thought aloud. Who would understand? Except possibly Greg, and he was nowhere in sight.

The little family group stood rather stiffly at the foot of the veranda. Josh, glass in hand, seemed ill-at-ease, unsure of his new role. Rather too quickly after talking to the leading villagers, he made his excuses that the barbeque needed attention. Maureen stayed to exchange a few words with the whites among their neighbours and then disappeared with some of her cronies into the house. Which was how Vicky found herself left with Andrew at her side and a seemingly endless queue of people wanting to offer elaborate, heartfelt speeches appropriate for such an occasion. Some of the older men wept or held her hand, while the women gave her the traditional hand-clapping bob of greeting which she returned. Andrew seemed bemused by the whole performance, and it occurred to Vicky that the entire district would now assume that they were married or soon would be, simply because he was standing beside her today.

They were talking to Father Conway, but she felt her eyes wandering away from the priest's open freckled face as she saw Greg and his companion threading their way towards them. Greg – the boy-next-door in her life for so long, when next door had been a lonely farm twelve miles away.

Of course he'd changed. He'd filled out from the lanky youth of their teen years. His hair, so blond it was almost cherubic when he was a boy, had darkened a little. With an inward smile, she remembered when he'd turned up one day with it cropped short, saying things kept getting caught in it, but she knew he really hated the way it crinkled. Cropped still closer now, it made him look harder, older than his years.

It was only when he was nearer, that she realized how hard she'd been trying to see him as someone foreign to her, a throwback to the sort of life she'd left behind her for good. But now she saw those same blue eyes that always looked so good in bright African light, unusually striking eyes for a man, and that's what Greg was now. The kind of man who had the confidence to come towards her after so long, arms outstretched, as if she was the only person in the whole confused scene.

'Vicky! I'm so terribly sorry about your Dad. Everyone loved him – we all did. I thought I wasn't going to make it. But it's just so good to see you...'

'I'm so glad you're here,' she managed to say.

What else could she say? He didn't kiss her, just wrapped her in a bear hug and then released her gently, but the sheer warmth of his greeting took away some of the pain. Somewhere between laughter and tears the jumbled phrases poured out – her father, the shock, how he'd picked up the news by chance at the local government offices. And then came the inevitable introductions.

'Angie, come and meet Vicky Carstairs. I only wish you could have met her father too. Vicky, Miss Angela Kazilimani, my fiancée.'

It came as a prickling sensation – like the feeling of touching something squirmy in a bank of leaves and wondering if it would bite or sting. Accustomed from childhood not to flinch at the unexpected, she prayed it didn't show.

The girl offered Vicky her hand as if it was an expensive present, but it was the impact of her surname on the bystanders which was even more dramatic. Those within earshot stopped talking and eating and simply stared at Angela Kazilimani. While Vicky was still coping with the thought that Greg was actually going to marry this girl, she could also read the signs. This was the relative of someone important, a local big man, a politician maybe – a man of power.

Angela politely murmured her condolences and Vicky offered her congratulations on the engagement, but it was all rather strained. As Vicky introduced Angela to Andrew, she thought she sensed him relax. So the famous Greg was no longer a threat after all.

She explained that Andrew was a good friend from the agency who'd come out for a working holiday, only to arrive in the middle of the tragedy. Yes, they'd be returning to London in four weeks as arranged. But as she said that, she realized that all she really wanted to do was drive away there and then somewhere quiet and talk, just talk, to Greg – about her father, the old times, and Kachinga.

Almost overcome by the sheer press of people, Vicky survived the next half hour on a warm wave of goodwill and sympathy. Uneasily, she wondered how Josh and Maureen were coping with the barbeque.

On the steps the pile of funeral gifts – fruit, eggs, maize meal and beer – was growing ever larger. A live duck, trussed and quacking disconsolately, was placed in her arms by Kapemba, the chief elder of the workers' village. With tears in his eyes he suddenly began to address the crowd in Chewa. Bwana Carstairs was a good man who had respect for the people. When would another come like him? All the animals feared him. Why should the leopard live who had taken this good man's life? If he were young again he would go out this very day with his spear and bring her the head of this wicked animal who would surely kill again. It was right that everyone should be eating and drinking today to make them brave like himself and Bwana Carstairs.

The bystanders clapped and murmured in deep approval. Vicky caught Father Conway's eye, and knew what he was thinking. Josh was nowhere in sight, down by the barbeque pit, and unless someone said something quickly, there would be a leopard hunt at first light tomorrow.

'What was all that about?' asked Andrew as the crowd gathered round Kapemba. She gave him a rough translation, thinking how quaint it must sound. Angela said rather stiffly that the people in this area were not educated. But Vicky knew Kapemba meant it. The tragedy demanded some kind of action. Also, it was plain that they were frightened.

She stepped forward, thinking rapidly. Not trusting her Chewa, she beckoned Foto to come and translate, and the villagers pulled themselves into some kind of order. Speaking slowly and carefully, she thanked everyone for coming and said that her father would surely know all their names. As he was dying he said that the leopard was not a bad animal. Truly, it was his own gun that had killed him. This gun was like a snake that had caused sickness and death. And with snakes you buried the head at one end of the garden and the tail at the other. So it would be with the gun. Tomorrow, to ease their father's spirit, there would be a ceremony, led by Chief Kapemba if he was willing, to break the gun and bury it like a snake. But the leopard must not be killed – her father had said it.

Even as she was speaking, she could feel Andrew's eyes on her and wished she'd risked it in Chewa instead. How strange all this must sound to him. She was also conscious in the sudden silence, that she was speaking for her brother, the new owner of Kachinga, and that she was a woman, and his younger sister, and that, as such, saying all this was not the local custom. 'As you know, my brother is preparing the meat for us,' she added, 'but our father told us both it was his last wish that the leopard should not die because of this horrible accident. And now, as Chief Kapemba has said, it is time to eat and drink. Come, my friends' – she extended her arms to where the smoke was rising from the barbeque – 'and let us be together today as we give thanks for his wise and brave spirit.'

Amid deepening murmurs of approval, she turned to Andrew, quite weak with the effort, and whispered as she took his arm, 'I've got to find Josh, quick.'

They set off, trying not to seem hurried as the bystanders gave way to let them pass. At the barbeque pit, as she feared, Josh was looking tired, fraught, and not entirely sober. Without a word, he pushed a basting ladle into her hands and went off to shout at some children to get down from the jacaranda tree shading the picnic area. Testing the huge sausages bursting on the grid, she wondered how much of his flush was the cooking and how much was whisky.

Grumbling, he came back to join her and she tried to smile. 'Dad's special recipe?'

Josh nodded grimly. 'He made a whole batch a couple of days before it happened – for your homecoming cook-out. Just as well too. I could never get the hang of that sausage machine.'

Maureen apparently was inside the house 'whingeing to the neighbours', as Josh put it, and for the next hour Vicky was in a whirl of spitting sausages, pork crackling, and red pepper sauce, as she sliced and hacked, slinging slices of meat and dollops of sticky white maize porridge onto any utensil thrust in front of her. Many of the guests had brought their own bowls just in case.

'Talk about the feeding of the five thousand,' muttered Josh. 'Who the blazes are half this lot anyway? We'll never get rid of them.'

There was a distant rumble of thunder. 'I wouldn't worry about that,' said Vicky quite exhausted. Within half an hour it would be pouring and there'd be a wild dash for home. For everyone, that is, except Greg and Angela Kazilimani.

The rain did its work, and at the end of a shattering afternoon, Vicky and Andrew were left with their guests while Josh and Maureen, having finally realized who Angela was, made their excuses and went for a siesta. They sat around drinking tea politely, until the rain stopped and dusk was falling. Eventually Vicky found the courage to ask Greg who had bought his parents' farm. There was a pause. Greg looked at Angela, who then opened her classically shaped mouth and blew the conversation to pieces.

'The farm was bought by the government land agents,' she said smoothly, 'and my father bought it from them.'

'Ah!' There must have been something in Vicky's voice, because she was suddenly aware that Andrew's attention was back on the conversation again. Something didn't smell right. Things often didn't, out here.

Unperturbed, Angela explained in her soft, measured voice that the place wasn't ready because her father was having it done up for Christmas. Meanwhile she and her mother were still at their house in town.

Andrew opened his mouth, but Vicky managed to give him a gentle nudge under the table and quickly changed the subject to Greg's conservation work in Western Province.

Outside on the lawn, a few bedraggled vultures were flapping around the soggy remains of the feast. It seemed a fitting end to an awful, wrenchingly dismal day.

Eventually Josh and Maureen roused themselves and came in to join them and Maureen went off sullenly to get a chalet sorted out for Greg and Angela. No one mentioned the Hamilton farm again, and for supper they picked at some leftovers from the funeral feast.

'I'm sorry, I've been driving half the day,' said Greg, yawning. 'What time is lights out, Josh?'

'Ten thirty, out of season,' was the curt reply. 'I'm sure we're all pretty shattered.'

Vicky tried not to show her surprise. On special days the generator wasn't shut down until midnight or later. Surely today was special enough for that. She'd already asked them to stay for the weekend, but

Greg, picking up that Maureen was less that enthusiastic about the prospect, said they had to get back tomorrow as he had a lot to do before the Christmas break. After that, there were hurried goodnights.

'I'm sorry,' she whispered to Andrew tiredly in the last minutes before the generator shut down. 'It's been a dreadful day. You go ahead – I just need some time to myself.'

He seemed glad to get away. Vicky got up restlessly and stared into the immense darkness beyond the veranda, her grief sharpened by a sudden dreadful fear. Nothing could bring her father back. But suppose now she had to face another loss. Suppose Josh and Maureen couldn't cope and one day it came to selling Kachinga. It had happened to the Hamiltons after all, and Vicky wasn't convinced that she'd heard the whole of that particular story.

The horror of it almost engulfed her and she sank back into her chair, gripping its worn chintz arms. The electricity gave its warning blip, but she didn't light the kerosene lamp. As a child, she used to wait for this moment with her eyes closed. This was when the night really began, when the comforting chug-chug of the generator was stilled, and every switch in the house was useless. There was no moon tonight, not even a star. You had to close your eyes. Yes, that was the trick – so when everything was quiet and you opened them again, it would never, *could* never, be quite as dark as you'd feared.

Next morning, Vicky and Andrew were already having breakfast when Josh appeared in the doorway, unshaven and in his sleeping shorts. 'Sleep well?' he growled. 'Stupid question.'

Vicky could only smile wanly at her brother. 'You mean apart from the hyenas down by the barbeque? I made it three.'

Andrew stopped eating his papaw. 'Why didn't you wake me up? I might have been able to get a few arty shots in with the infra-red gear.'

They both looked at him blankly. With a leopard about, roaming around in the dark simply wasn't safe any more.

'Don't worry, we'll get you some really good pictures when things have quietened down,' said Vicky.

In the bright morning light she couldn't help noticing the difference between the two men, and it was just the opposite of what anyone might have thought. Josh, supposedly the great outdoor, safari–boss type, wasn't much older than Andrew, the city smoothie, but it was Josh who looked unfit – a slob in fact. God, she thought miserably, Dad had been in better shape at nearly sixty.

'The bush is too thick at the moment,' said Josh. 'Game's pretty well dispersed – but we'll see what we can do.'

Suddenly Vicky remembered old Kapemba's speech at the funeral.

'Er, Josh?' She was going to have to put this carefully. 'You remember I told you what Kapemba said about a leopard hunt? Well, actually I suggested we have a gun-breaking ceremony, then bury the pieces. You know – like with snakes?'

Josh stared at her. 'What, are you crazy? Do you know what that gun cost?' His voice rose just as Maureen came in, her face puffy from sleep.

'If you want to know what the blacks really think, why don't you ask one?' she said without so much as a good morning, and nodded towards the chalets where Greg and Angela had just emerged.

'Okay, let's drop it,' said Josh uncomfortably. 'But the next time you get a hare-brained scheme like that, for God's sake ask me first.'

Vicky bit her lip and said nothing. If no one turned up, she'd soon know if her calculated risk to defuse the situation had worked.

Greg and Angela were already packed. They had some coffee, then thanked Josh and Maureen for their hospitality in the same cool way it had been given. In that atmosphere, Greg didn't even give Vicky a hug, just shook her hand, and she tried not to let it hurt.

'Maybe we'll be over this way for Christmas,' said Greg. 'What do you think, Angie?'

The tall, elegant girl seemed to give the matter some thought. 'My father has important entertaining to do and I may be needed at the farm. Yes, it might be possible.'

'Mind if I take a few pictures before you go?' asked Andrew, reappearing with what looked like most of his camera equipment. 'The light's wonderful today. I'd really love some shots of Miss Kazilimani against the bougainvillea.'

Andrew's interest in the girl as a model didn't surprise Vicky. In fact she'd got used to this sort of thing. If Andrew saw anyone in the street that might give him a good shot, he'd just go right up and ask, or take it anyway. And of course Greg had found her attractive too. Angela Kazilimani was beautiful, unusually so, with her long face, like a classical African mask. Her eyes were slightly tilted towards her high temples, the short lashes curling charmingly like a child's. But there was nothing childlike about her sensual mouth and the way she held her head with its tiny plaits twisted into a kind of tiara that accentuated her fine profile. When she saw the camera, she responded to it immediately.

Andrew suddenly went all professional. He'd found a 'natural'. Angela picked a spray of the violent purple bougainvillea, and used it to startling effect. She peeped over it coyly, wrapped it round her face, swung her hips, and even pretended to eat it like a bunch of grapes. Well well, thought Vicky.

'Terrific,' said Andrew. 'I'd love to do some more – maybe in your national costume too...'

The words dried as Angela stiffened. 'That wouldn't interest me,' she said coolly. 'I have plenty of fashionable clothes in town. Maybe over Christmas?'

'That's settled then,' said Greg firmly. 'We'll ring later about times – if I can get through.'

They all smiled. Phones were not a strong point at Kachinga. But Andrew was kicking himself as they waved them off. 'Oops – almost an own goal there. Honestly, I thought she might like the idea.'

'She'll be back,' said Vicky with a wry smile, comforted by the thought that seeing Greg again would make the first Christmas without her father a little more bearable.

'I could get that girl a modelling contract, no trouble,' said Andrew staring after them. 'Did you see the way she moved? With the right handling, she could go right to the top.'

'Bit of an eye-opener, eh?' Josh, still in his undershorts, made to go back inside. 'Didn't know Kazilimani had a daughter like that. But thinking of that old crook in the Hamiltons' place really sticks in my gut. Bloody politicians.'

'Typical,' sniffed Maureen. 'And I suppose Greg just happens to be in love with the old boy's daughter? That's one way to cover your back in this goddamn country – not to mention keeping one foot in the old homestead.'

'Oh Maureen!' cried Vicky in exasperation. 'She's a beautiful girl. I'm sure he's doing the right thing.' The truth was that, for all Maureen's prejudice, she'd thought the same herself. It did seem rather convenient. And yet – how far would she herself have gone not to lose Kachinga? In traditional African society no one would think the worse of Greg for it, so neither should they. But did he *love* Angela? Did he?

'If you'll excuse me, I'm going to put some flowers on the grave,' she said abruptly.

'Take my wagon and load up the second gun,' said Josh and slung her the keys.

It was only common sense. Vicky went through to the huge carved mahogany cupboard where the guns were kept. She'd always hated them, and only learned to shoot because one day they'd come across a dying hippo that it was a kindness to put out of its misery. 'Look, love,' her father had said. 'Being a good shot is the least you can do for the animals if you have to – and I won't always be around.' She'd never let Andrew know she could shoot. No one back there really understood how it could be, out here. Well, he knew now.

There were six guns, and an old service revolver on a shelf. Her father's heavy game rifle was on the left, and she shuddered. Yes officer, that's the gun that killed my father. Take it away. But Chief Kapemba hadn't showed up. There had been drumming half the night as well as the hyenas, and there'd be a few thick heads down in the village this morning.

She took Josh's light gun from the rack, opened the ammunition drawer, and then froze. On top was a sealed polythene envelope, and inside it was a large damaged bullet. There was no need to read the doctor's note. It was the bullet that had ripped through her father's side. There had been no need for an inquest, and without quite knowing why, she slipped the little envelope into her trouser pocket.

It was a glorious morning, the sort that came sometimes in the rains when the clouds lifted unexpectedly. It was humid, but not unpleasantly so, and the air smelt of growth and life. The waving elephant grass was not yet at full height, and she could see a rippling ocean in shades of green, shading to purple against the distant escarpment. She picked an armful of red canna lilies and fragrant frangipani blossom for the graves and threw them over the gun on the back seat.

A bateleur eagle, a male in full breeding plumage, soared overhead in the blue and a flight of snowy white cattle egrets swooped across her path on their way to the river. Once, she had taken all this for granted – thought everywhere was as beautiful and free as this. But if she'd never left it, would she be able to see it now, the way it looked to her this morning?

Leaving the car at the foot of the little knoll where the flamboyant tree stood guard over her parents' graves, she walked on, arranging the flowers in two sprays as she went. 'Hello, you two,' she said aloud. 'It's such a lovely morning.' She stooped to place the sprays – and then almost collapsed with fright. The spreading branches rustled, and there was a strange noise like a cough. They said leopards coughed. The gun was in the car. Petrified, she knew she should run.

Then down came a long, very human, skinny leg, followed by another, and then the whole body dropped stiffly from the tree and stood before her. It was Kapemba.

Instinctively she let out a frightened gabble of Chewa – 'Great God, grandfather. I thought you were the leopard.'

'Good morning, Miss Vicky,' replied the old man. He always used English when he was standing on his dignity. 'As you see, I was keeping watch. Did you not hear the hyenas?'

Tears came into her eyes. 'You mean, you've been here all night in case the hyenas came?'

He simply inclined his head to her and reached up for his spear and blanket. 'Now you are here, I will go and sleep. You have the Bwana's gun?'

'No, grandfather, but the small gun is in the car. But, see I have this bad thing,' she replied in Chewa. She felt in her pocket and brought out the damaged bullet. 'What should we do with it? Will you show me, grandfather?'

She heard his intake of breath when he took it in his hand as if weighing it for the evil it had done. He looked at the grave of his old friend, then up at the tree. He bowed his head again, this time in thought, then carefully placed the bullet in the fork of the branches and, using his spear-haft, hammered it angrily into the shiny grey bark until it almost disappeared. 'That is what we do with such bad things, child,' he said quietly. 'It was his best gun – there is no need now to break it,' and he walked slowly away without looking back.

It wasn't until the following day that Vicky felt up to going out with Andrew on the kind of trip she'd been promising him. It hadn't rained for almost two days now, and the muddy tracks were drying.

'Remember the rules,' said Josh as they set off. 'No getting out without the gun, and no speeding.'

She let Andrew drive, once Josh had shown him how to get the heavy engine into reverse gear fast. You didn't fool around with three point turns when faced with an indignant hippo. By the time they'd stopped for a drink from the icebox, they'd already seen several kinds of buck, some zebra, and a couple of maribou storks, their balding heads looking sorely in need of sun hats as they bickered over something small and very dead.

'What a stench!' Andrew was gasping as he snapped the morose pair.

'That's one thing you don't get on the telly,' she laughed, brushing at the pestering flies.

'You're wonderful, you know that? You're trying so hard to make this holiday work in spite of everything, but let's find somewhere a bit more romantic away from this pong. I've got this thing about guns and elephant grass...'

'We always like to please our clients,' she said dryly as they got back into the vehicle.

'Hey – they're Josh's clients, not yours. Your clients are back in South Ken, and probably on their Christmas safari to Harrods.'

She smiled. 'Which reminds me – I'm glad I brought lots of presents, now Greg and Angela are coming.'

'Lucky old Greg. She's quite a stunner.'

Vicky gave him a sideways glance. 'If it's beauty you're after, how about this lot?' She pointed to where a family of warthogs were enjoying a good roll in the drying mud of a large puddle.

Andrew, passion temporarily forgotten, was delighted. 'Some cosmetic firm will go for these,' he said grinned, clicking away. 'For face packs, or something.' He wanted to go closer, but the boss male was getting fidgety. He called his harem to heel, and off they trotted primly into the bush, tails straight as pokers as if they'd suddenly remembered an urgent appointment.

'Let's follow,' said Andrew. 'I want the big fellow with some of the hoglets or whatever you call them.'

Vicky looked around. 'I'll take the wheel, you keep snapping.'

They bounced along keeping the warthogs in sight without panicking them. And then without warning, the peaceful family group erupted in panic. Dust flew, a colony of weaver birds wheeled up in alarm, and when Vicky turned off the engine, the horrible sound of enraged squealing reached them.

'Oh no,' she breathed. One of them was in trouble, that was obvious, but from what? If there'd been hunting dogs or jackals around, they would have heard them by now, but leopards were the silent killers.

'Please stay seated,' she said automatically, and swung herself onto the roof of the vehicle leaving Andrew blinking at the sharpness of the command. Clients had to be protected from themselves at times like this. Hadn't Dad said that often enough? And right now that's what Andrew was – a client to be protected.

What she saw horrified her. One of the females had a leg caught fast, in a noose of fine wire that tightened its searing grip the more the animal struggled. Poachers.

If she could cut the wire quickly, the animal would probably recover. The trick was to jump back the right way so that it didn't attack you. But maybe the poachers were still around, and in her rage, Vicky almost hoped they were as she jumped down and grabbed for the rifle and a machete.

Advancing on the trapped beast, she watched the way it was straining, and aimed a heavy machete blow at where the end of the wire should be. Damn! The warthog screeched as the wire jerked. Right place, but not hard enough. 'I'm coming, my lovely,' she said, tears in her eyes that she'd caused it more pain. With a quick look round, she set down the gun and put all her anger into a two-handed hack at the cruel wire.

With a final squeal, the little sow gave a leap and rushed off. Because she'd been quick, there wasn't much blood and with any luck it would soon be none the worse for its narrow escape. Backed up safely against the rough trunk of a mopani tree, she waited until the indignant noises subsided and then made for the Land Rover.

'The bastards,' was all she could say until she'd calmed down and was able to explain that it wasn't the villagers who had set the snare, but poachers. 'It's the leopard they're after, I know it.'

Back at the house, Josh was intrigued as well as furious.

'Maybe they reckon she's got the cubs round there. Dad thought the den might be over by Big Kop. There's plenty of cover there.'

'What about the bat caves?'

'Nah – I reckon the baboon pack's a bit aggressive for her with the cubs. Do you remember Scarface? Well, now he's king of the castle over there.'

'Is he still around? He must be older than I am.'

'Come on, let's go down to the village and see what they know.'

They sat with Kapemba, Foto and the others in the humid shade of the meeting tree, and it was soon clear that their own men knew nothing, but there were rumours of other snares on the Valley side. It all took a long time, and Vicky could feel Andrew's impatience as the talk dragged on. But if you wanted co-operation, you had to change down a gear and go with the drift. He seemed distant that night, as if it was all getting too much for him. Eventually she fell into an uneasy sleep, still angry that no one seemed to know what to do about the poachers, and only too aware that tomorrow was Christmas Eve and almost nothing had been done about that, either.

At breakfast it looked as if Josh and Maureen had been rowing again. By ten, Josh was on his first beer. In the kitchen, Vicky found a brace of guinea fowl and a few basics like tinned prawns and dried fruit. Nobody felt like the hundred-mile drive to the supermarket in town and it was obvious that tomorrow's Christmas dinner was going to be rather a scratch affair.

Maureen was listless and sulky, so Vicky ignored her and got on with it. She raided the drinks cupboard, soaked some dried fruit in brandy, added fresh mangoes and put the mixture in a shortcrust tart. She sent the children out after wild mushrooms, found the neglected herb patch and produced a stuffing that smelt of just about everything. By mid-afternoon, a fruit cake and something she hoped would be a chocolate sponge were baking. Even Andrew was doing his best beating up some mayonnaise. When he paused for breath, she stiffened.

'Listen,' she said.

'I can't hear anything.'

She put her head in her hands. 'Exactly,' she groaned. A strange hush had fallen. 'The generator's conked out,' she said briefly. 'Terrific!'

By six o'clock it was getting dark, but several things were clear as daylight. Even if Josh had been completely sober, he couldn't have fixed the generator. A rocker arm had snapped, and there was no way of getting another until after the Christmas break. They started the wood stove, but the cake was flat and the sponge more like ship's biscuits.

'An un-airconditioned Christmas by candle-light,' sighed an exhausted Vicky as they came back to the darkened house after the midnight service at the Mission and tumbled into bed. 'Adds to the ambience, I suppose.'

It was only then that she remembered Greg hadn't phoned. There could be so many reasons, but she went to sleep convinced it must mean a change of plan on Angela's part.

'It's no good, I just can't believe it's Christmas Day,' yawned Andrew over his breakfast papaw. 'Do you ever get used to it?'

'Used to what?' rumbled Josh. 'It's like this every bloody year.'

It was already ten o'clock, which was almost lunchtime by Kachinga standards. It should have been the cook's day off, but by the time Vicky had come out of the shower, Maureen had nagged Josh into going down to the village to get Agnes in.

Vicky thought this was unfair and said so. Just as it seemed as if a real clash was in the air, a large estate wagon swung into the drive. Greg and Angela had arrived.

Greg immediately apologized, saying the lines were down, the batteries flat – the usual. There were polite Christmas kisses and exchanges of gifts, and Maureen escaped to the kitchen looking very much the harassed housewife in spite of Agnes' help. Eventually Josh explained the rather obvious lack of the ceiling fan.

Greg suggested they try a temporary brazing weld for the rocker arm of the generator and asked if they had any brass rods. Josh blinked and went off to look.

Then everything happened at once. Angela asked for the bathroom and Vicky was left with just Andrew and Greg. Out of the blue, Greg said something to her in Chewa, then grinned at Andrew. 'Old Chewa saying. It's something like, *Machines are all female – you can never trust them – they're always getting sick.*'

Andrew laughed politely, while Vicky gave Greg an imperceptible nod and took a sip of her drink to recover. What he'd actually said was, '*I must talk to you. Think of something, fast...*'

'If you'll excuse me leaving you two together,' she said to Andrew as Angie returned and Greg went off to help Josh, 'I'd better give Maureen and Agnes a hand.'

She went quickly to her room and scribbled a note to Greg saying they could meet during siesta time in the kitchen as soon as the others were asleep, as they undoubtedly would be after a good meal in the afternoon heat. She gave the note to one of the children and asked him to find Greg down at the generator.

It seemed hours before the men came back, grubby with machine oil and ready for a shower, to announce that the weld might hold for a bit, as long as the machinery wasn't started until it had set properly.

It was a strange Christmas dinner, eaten in the thundery afternoon warmth at the picnic table under the jacaranda tree. As a meal, it wasn't too bad under the circumstances, and Vicky could feel Greg watching her as she did the hostess routine, filling everyone's glass cheerily whenever she could, except her own and his. To catch his eye could have been fatal.

At four o'clock, they listened to the Queen on the World Service as they always did, and it was a relief when eyelids began to droop, and at last and people drifted to their rooms.

As Vicky hoped, Andrew dropped off beside her almost immediately. Barefoot and in a loose cotton house coat, she crept out and tiptoed through to the kitchen.

Greg was already there. 'Couldn't sleep,' he said with a grin.

'Nor me.' And wasn't that the truth!

'Sorry about the undercover stuff,' he said awkwardly, 'but it was the only way. Listen, Vick, I think there's something going on over at my old place.'

'Not something political?' She was barely mouthing the words. 'Don't tell me – they're not plotting a coup!'

'No, Kazilimani's too well in with the President for that at the moment – and that's how he's getting away with it. It's poaching. I heard it from one of our old farm workers. Ivory, rhino horn – only high-priced stuff from the Valley.'

'And leopard?' Her voice rose in panic.

'Exactly. When I heard you talking about that snare, I knew they'd heard about her and had moved in here too. And the cubs would fetch a better price than even the mother's skin.'

Vicky shuddered. 'Oh Greg,' she said. 'What are we going to do? Does Angela know anything about it? Can't she help?'

'That's it, Vick. Much as I'd like to, I just can't trust her until I've got them cold and then maybe I can confront her father and get it stopped.'

Vicky simply stared at him.

'Listen,' he said, leaning forward, 'tell me exactly where you found that snare. Maybe if I go like the clappers, I could pick up a track and find the den. Then we could get Josh to post a watch and set up a trap for the poachers.'

'Okay, but you'll find it much faster if I come. I'll say I couldn't sleep and went for a drive. I reckon they'll be out cold for a couple of hours.'

'But you're not really dressed for it. And we'd need a gun.'

'We'll risk it. I can't get the keys to the gun cupboard from Josh anyway. Let's go.'

She found a pair of old riding boots in the cloakroom, belted in her cotton gown with a scarf of Maureen's and then they crept out like the couple of kids they once had been. When they reached the car, Greg slipped the hand brake, and they pushed the heavy vehicle down the sloping drive. It was a trick they'd learned as teenagers when Vicky hadn't wanted her sleeping parents to know what time Greg had left.

As the engine puttered into life, they both jumped in, and were still chuckling as Greg revved up to sixty. He slowed down for the bridge but was doing seventy by the time they reached the East Fork.

Hanging on tensely, Vicky guided him to the spot were they'd left the road. They bumped along in the Land Rover tracks, and soon found the empty snare. Now they were on foot in tearing thorn scrub as they followed a barely visible track towards the eastern boundary.

'I'm getting shredded, and I feel completely ridiculous,' she hissed. 'Like some wretched fashion mag's idea of what to wear on safari.'

'Actually,' said Greg. 'You look...' He stopped. 'You know, when we were young, I really had no one to compare you with. I suppose I just thought everyone was like you...'

He'd said it quite casually – as if it had only just occurred to him and might not sound as corny as hell. Vicky blinked and brushed a hand across her face but the words were still there, shimmering in the still air like heat off a tarred road.

'God, our dear papas must have thought I was a fool to go away from here,' she said.

They both started as a warning bark from a baboon sentinel sent a nearby troupe scurrying for cover. Now every creature, or hidden poacher, would know they were there. Biting her lip, instinctively she grabbed Greg's arm.

'I tell you something else,' whispered Greg. 'Douglas would never forgive me if he knew we were out here on foot without a gun.'

'I reckon he does,' she breathed sadly. They were very tense now. Ahead loomed a line of high rocky outcrops, with thick scrub concealing the caves where once, as youngsters, hand in hand, they'd disobeyed all they'd been taught and braved the dark – and the bats. Greg pointed to a great rounded boulder peeling sunburned layers of shale, which looked almost ready to crash down on them. Perched on it was a huge male baboon.

'Scarface!' mouthed Vicky, and almost waved. They were just close enough to see the aggressive blinking of white eyelids as he eyed up the intruders.

'Stay right there, old man,' murmured Greg. 'It's not your wives we're after.' Vicky felt her eyes stinging. Her father often spoke softly to the animals even at a distance, saying he meant them no harm. He said the San hunters did it, and curiously it often seemed to calm them.

A solitary locust flew up, its frilly pink under-wings catching the afternoon light. Vicky's eyes automatically went to where it had risen, then almost crushed Greg's wrist as she pointed to a wooden peg and more wire. Greg signed to her and immediately picked up some heavy stones and threw them at the snare. As the noose jerked up, they saw it could have sent a fair-sized animal to its death.

'So they know she's around here...'

Shaking with fright and anger, she nodded and they squatted down to listen. After five minutes they moved nearer the caves, and Vicky closed her eyes to hear beyond the clicks and chirps, distant bird calls, monkey chatter and endless rustlings of the bush.

They both heard it together – a muffled almost cat-like mew. Eyes wide, they stared at each other, hardly daring to believe their luck. Soundlessly they argued with frantic hand signals and nods about where the sound came from. Vicky indicated the large overhang to the right. Greg thought further over, in a small cave opening where a huge strangling fig had split the rock. The mewling came again, and Greg grinned as Vicky nodded her agreement.

He cupped his hand round her ear. 'They're calling. Mother's gone a-hunting.'

Her eyes queried his certainty as they crept forward at a crouch, stopping at some broken ground and very much aware not only that Scarface was still eyeing them, but that the leopardess might return from her hunt at any moment, silent as a shadow if she wasn't dragging a kill.

Vicky saw the tiny pointed tail first and almost fell over with excitement as she touched his shoulder and pointed. Then, in a magic moment that almost forced the breath out of her, she saw a small furry face peer quizzically round a stone, followed by another, round ears pricked. There was some squirming, a mew or two as the second cub chewed the first one's ear, and then with a glint of mischief in the amber eyes they were gone, hidden in the knotted fig roots by the cave.

When Vicky drew breath again, it seemed to scorch her lungs. Greg was still staring at the spot with a look on his face she'd never seen before. It transformed him.

Gently she shook his arm to break the spell. What they had to do now was get back as fast as possible and as they backed away, distant monkey barks of alarm galvanised Scarface and his gang. Something was drawing their attention, and any doubt as to what it might be was quickly dispelled by a noise that Vicky had never heard in the wild, only in TV documentaries at home. It was a distant grunting, sawing cough, not at all catlike, and just the way the books described it – the rare voice of a leopard.

She heard Greg breathe, 'Pray she's caught something,' as he grabbed her hand and they took off like a pair of frightened guinea fowl. In what was certainly the longest, swiftest five minutes of Vicky's life, they were back at the car, exhausted, scratched and panting.

'Greg Hamilton, you can't fool me,' said Vicky as she fought for breath while Greg crashed the gears. 'You're in love.'

'Yes,' he said as the vehicle touched eighty on the South Loop. 'I rather think I am. What are we going to do about it?'

'I'd say get a guard on the caves and tackle Kazilimani about those bloody poachers. The snares are so near the east boundary, they must be coming over from his place.'

Further talk was almost impossible at that bone-crunching speed, but as they neared the house Greg said, 'Vicky, have you really only got another three weeks? It's been so long...'

'I needed something like today,' she said. 'I've been in a kind of trance since I got back. I'm frightened, Greg. With Dad gone, how's it going to be? Suppose Kazilimani is just sitting there waiting to buy up Kachinga too? If I thought that, I'd never leave – not for anyone – ever.'

As they clattered up the drive they could see Andrew and Josh were already on the veranda, their faces a study in suppressed male wrath and curiosity.

That evening, Andrew, who never liked feeling out of his depths, was unusually quiet. Vicky wasn't even sure that he believed her explanation for taking off like that with Greg. The wrecked nightdress hadn't helped, and she'd quickly cut the fine white cotton into pieces for dusters and bandages and stuffed them in with tomorrow's washing. Nothing ever went to waste at Kachinga while her parents were alive. Eventually, Andrew had shrugged the whole incident off as just one more example of general weirdness about the place. He seemed more interested in getting some pictures of the cubs tomorrow, but both Vicky and Greg weren't very keen on the idea in case any more activity frightened the mother into moving them.

Maureen soon went to bed pleading a headache, but Andrew seemed quite prepared to sit up half the night rather than leave Vicky and Greg together, even with Angela present. Confused and tired as she was by the day's events, all Vicky could think about was that unless she took some action right now, tomorrow might be the last she would see of Greg. Glumly she went to get some water from the fridge. While filling her glass, she remembered the New Year trip she'd promised Andrew to get some shots of Victoria Falls, and an interesting possibility suddenly occurred to her.

Choosing her moment carefully, she worked it into the conversation, and Greg, who seemed to be pretending to be mildly sloshed, was quick on the uptake over the bit about wondering if they would like to come too. He reached over and took Angela's hand.

'Hey, Andrew – you wouldn't fancy a beautiful African girl to model for you, I suppose? What do you reckon, Angie? You could be famous. Should we make it a foursome?'

Angie and Andrew quickly agreed. Well done, Greg, thought Vicky, as the shattered group finally crawled off to bed. At least it was a positive note on which to end an extraordinary Christmas.

The mood next morning was one of slow recovery.

'If you didn't think much of an African Christmas Day,' rumbled Josh, 'you ain't seen Boxing Day yet. I suppose I'll have to go and check those lazy so-and-so's have posted the guard.'

As Vicky watched Greg and Angie drive off in the direction of what had once been the Hamilton farm, she couldn't help wondering how Greg would cope with being a visitor in his old home. And Mr Kazilimani was a force to be reckoned with, known all over for his wealth, charm, contacts and remarkable survival instincts. How did you tackle a man like Solomon Kazilimani?

'How about those shots of the cubs,' said Andrew hopefully, breaking into her thoughts. 'Couldn't we just try?'

She was very conscious that he must be feeling left out, but it was against her better judgement that she found herself on the track for the bat caves again. This time she managed to get the vehicle closer and called up the guard on the two-way radio.

To her great relief, he reported seeing the leopardess quite safe and heading for the Ngoma *dambo* without the cubs.

'It's your lucky day,' she grinned to Andrew, and asked the guard to buzz her instantly if there were signs of movement. Scarface and his tribe were off foraging elsewhere, which was no bad thing as they were rather unpredictable with strangers. With infinite care, she led Andrew to a good place within sight of the den and pulled him down beside her to listen.

But it wasn't at all like yesterday. Andrew simply wasn't the sort to stay still for long, unlike Greg who could sit all day in a hide if he had to, and Vicky was finding it hard to concentrate with his aura of restless energy so near her.

Crouching there, it crossed her mind that, while this side of Andrew had attracted her strongly, there were times when she felt quite exhausted by it. It wasn't so much that Andrew was one of life's takers, but he did demand a lot of attention. Yet if anyone had tried to explain this, he'd have been most put out – in fact Andrew considered himself the very model of concerned 'metro-man'.

They moved nearer the overhang, but she could hear nothing more than the usual bush noises. There was a strong smell of carrion from the remains of a small antelope half hidden in the fig roots, but no sound at all from inside, and some buzzards were lurking hopefully. Thinking the cubs might be sleeping, Vicky parted the leaves gingerly with a stick and then gasped in dismay. The den was empty.

Praying that it was the mother who had moved them somewhere nearby before leaving, she cast around for a while, and then went rigid with alarm. Someone had been here. On the ground was a wad of torn leaves streaked with blood. Shock and anger choked her as she noticed wisps of soft cub fur. There was even the imprint of a medium-sized flip-flop in a patch of soft sand.

'They've got them,' she hissed to Andrew, almost beside herself with rage. 'And they've either injured them or themselves in the process. Let's get out of here.'

For the second time in twenty-four hours, she covered the twelve miles back to the house in as many minutes, but this time she was driven by despair.

'Must have been last night,' said Josh, 'before the guard was posted. Bastards.'

'And what about the mother?' Vicky was almost too upset to speak. 'She'll be heavy with milk and very distressed.'

'And in no mood for visitors,' added Josh with heavy irony.

Maureen came back hot and tired from her weekly clinic round of the three Kachinga villages. It was a job that went with the territory.

'Worms,' she announced. 'Half of the kids at Chiyama have got them again, after all I said. And there's a dodgy measles case at Shingu that should really go the Dispensary.'

As Vicky got her sister-in-law a drink, she felt sorry for her. It must be like having a job you couldn't stick, with people you didn't like, and knowing you couldn't get a transfer.

'It's the skin ulcers I can't stand,' Maureen was saying. 'And cuts are always going septic in the rains. There's a kid at Chiyama in an awful mess with scratches. He'll need antibiotics if the saline solution doesn't do it. And a tetanus jab – I think we've still got some in the outhouse fridge.'

'What kind of scratches?' asked Vicky, suddenly curious.

'Mostly on the arms, fortunately, but deep and dirty. Said he fell off his brother's bike into a thorn bush.'

Vicky looked at Josh. 'I wonder,' was all she said.

They were at the village within ten minutes.

'Where's the boy with the bad arm,' asked Josh in curt Chewa of the women by the cooking fire. They seemed uneasy, and pointed reluctantly to a hut at the end of the compound, where a figure had emerged at the sound of the vehicle. It was Foto, and Vicky could tell instantly that something was badly wrong. He greeted them awkwardly then looked from Josh to Vicky as if trying to find the right words. Finally he said, 'You see, they are the children of my sister, but they were wrong to take them.'

Vicky was too relieved to be angry – after all, the lads might even have saved the cubs' lives. 'Just show us where they've got them,' she said. Of course, everyone had known. The women stopped work as Foto led them to a hut where a boy of about twelve was peering fearfully round the door. The sound of mewling greeted them.

The two pathetic little bundles inside made an attempt to reach her, thinking perhaps that their mother had returned. The boys had done their best. Two skinned rats had been put beside them, but the unweaned cubs hadn't managed to do more than play with them and lick the meat.

'Foto, could you please ask the women for some goats' milk and boiled water,' breathed Vicky, weak with relief. The urge to pick up them up and cuddle them, rub their furry little noses and whisper that everything was going to be alright, was almost unbearable. Her heart ached, but she had to resist touching them if the cubs were ever to be accepted back by their mother.

She diluted the goat's milk and let it dribble down her fingers. One cub quickly got the idea, and she could feel the desperation in the rasping grip of its tongue.

Andrew was taking snap after snap quite entranced, while Foto explained what had happened. The boys had been out at dusk catapulting bats by the caves – something they knew was forbidden. They were coming back to report another snare they'd found when they saw two men moving towards the Kazilimani boundary carrying a dead gazelle. So they'd taken the cubs in case the men came back and found them. One lad had been badly scratched, and then they'd been frightened in case they got into trouble. The problem now was how to return the cubs to the mother.

Back at the bungalow she rang Greg, anxious for a second opinion over what to do for the best, but was told the couple were out visiting. There was nothing for it but to sit up all night with the cubs. She tried raw egg yoke, beef blood and more diluted goats' milk, and eventually the youngsters fell into an exhausted doze.

The phone ringing by the couch where she'd fallen asleep woke her and she was overjoyed to hear Greg's voice. It was past eight o'clock, which was practically midday by rural African time.

'Can you talk?' she asked immediately.

'Not really,' said Greg wryly. 'What's the excitement?'

Quickly she explained all that had happened and asked him about returning the cubs.

She could hear him choosing his words carefully. 'I always say there's nothing like manure if you want things to grow properly,' said his voice.

There was a pause, then Vicky laughed delightedly. 'Got it. Rub the cubs with droppings to disguise human smells, right?'

'You mean the generator's gone again? What a pity. And I suppose Josh wants me to come over and fix it?'

'What? Oh yes, he does – very much.' The generator of course was still behaving perfectly.

Greg arrived an hour later without Angie, who was half-way though having her hair re-plaited. The cubs were given the necessary treatment with the contents of their basket and an old paintbrush, and seemed to enjoy the tickling game. Then Vicky called the watch, who said the leopardess was back at the den with a kill and probably sleeping 'because she too tired'.

It took a whole day of patient watching before Greg got the chance they needed to place the cubs back near the den. Andrew had fallen asleep in the back of the Land Rover and the minutes waiting for Greg to return were some of the longest in Vicky's life. When at last she saw him sprinting towards them waving the empty basket she could have hugged him.

Suddenly the bushes near the overhang moved and they saw her, amber eyes glinting in the evening sun. She scented the air and gave a low coughing grunt, pricked her ears sharply and pounced out of sight into the grass. A moment of blind panic grabbed Vicky by the throat as the grass thrashed again and they could see the magnificent dappled back and waving tail. Vicky closed her eyes. She couldn't be attacking the cubs – not after all this – no, please...

Greg touched her arm. 'Look,' he said as he passed her the glasses, and she saw there were tears in his eyes. There was the mother leading her bedraggled infants back to the lair, alternately licking, hauling and cuffing them along.

'Do leopards purr?' murmured Vicky.

'Do you know, I don't think they do,' replied Greg, rubbing his nose.

'Well, I would,' said Vicky, and burst into tears.

There was no doubt now in anyone's mind that the poachers were coming from the Kazilimani estate. But it was another matter altogether to confront Solomon Kazilimani himself on the matter. As Greg left, they agreed to say nothing as yet. The wily old operator could even have been in on it and passed the information to his men.

Now that the cubs were comparatively safe again, Vicky found herself lying awake beside the sleeping Andrew, quite appalled by the situation she was in. To have come out here like this with Andrew, thinking she loved him – to have put so much reliance on her father being immortal, on Kachinga always being there... . There was so much she'd got wrong. The years away now seemed like a holiday – a long holiday to give her time to grow up. But people could grow up in very different ways. Was Greg now the sort of man who could think of marrying a girl like Angela Kazilimani simply because it suited him? Maybe the girl was pregnant – it would have seemed perfectly normal out here – but then again, she seemed the ambitious type, and that would hardly have helped her modelling career.

As she tossed and turned, no answer came, and all she could think of as sleep drifted by her like a cloud across the moon, was Greg's face when he'd seen the cubs with their mother.

The next week passed more quickly than Vicky could have imagined, simply because there was so much to do. Andrew tagged along but his offers of help felt more like politeness than anything more substantial. He was like so many of the clients that passed through Kachinga. The majority treated it as just another interesting experience to add to their list. Only the rare ones got hooked, and if she'd ever hoped that Andrew would be one, she knew now that this wasn't much of a prospect.

They took a day out to drive into the capital to get stores, and Andrew found the place not quite as he'd hoped. 'Tacky 70s stuff, and that's the posh part – everything on wheels seems to be belching fumes or clapped out,' was how he put it. It was all true, of course, but for her father, the place was simply there to serve Kachinga – just a rather large, chaotic depot where visitors and new parts arrived, where they could sometimes fix things you couldn't fix yourself, like your teeth or your appendix.

With Maureen complaining of permanent backache, Vicky was beginning to worry about the amount that needed to be done around Kachinga before the next season. Everywhere you looked, something needed cleaning, painting, pruning, sharpening or oiling, and by the time they were due to leave for the Victoria Falls trip, Vicky was joking that they all really needed a break.

If it is possible to spoil an arrival at a place like Victoria Falls, Angela almost managed it. She took one look at the Baobab Lodge, where Vicky had booked because they knew the owners and always stayed there, and decided that a 'three-star, family-owned' was not for Solomon Kazilimani's daughter. When Angela suggested that they decamped to the nearest five-star international, Greg said, as tactfully as he could, that this trip was really for Andrew, but they could always eat there and use the pool, at which Angela sulkily caved in.

The Baobab Lodge was tastefully hidden in a riot of bougainvillea and shady cassia trees. Vicky had always liked its pleasant thatched chalets and the small breakfast terrace overlooking the lily pond. The owners said they were doing their special barbeque that evening, so by the time they'd settled into their chalets and were strolling down for their first close view of the Falls, even Angela had cheered up. The sun was already low over the distant escarpments and the mighty plumes of spray had a magical glow against the deepening blue. The thunderous roar drew them on and as the trees parted, they gasped at the nearness of the vast, tumbling walls of water. It always made Vicky feel as if she was on the edge of something far too huge to comprehend and wondered if the others sensed it too, like being there at the beginning of things – a shining moment.

Even Andrew was silenced by the power of it as they moved closer to the dizzy edge. In some places, there were still no guard-rails and the chocolate-brown rocks were wet and slippery. One wrong move and nothing could survive what lay below. A mile-long wall of water seemed simply to vanish in a great chasm of spray.

Angela broke the spell. 'This place makes me giddy,' she said.

'It always makes me want to fly. Just take off and...' said Greg, and spread his arms wide.

Vicky sighed. 'It makes me want the impossible. Dad named me after it, you know – maybe that's why.'

'Ha – that's so funny,' said Angela. '*Mosi-oa-Tunya*, the Smoke That Thunders – that's what we called it before you guys came along.'

'But that's Tonga, not Chewa,' retorted Greg, and was rewarded by a none-too-playful slap from Angela.

'Okay, you can call me Smoke-that-Thunders,' Vicky put in quickly, 'but you can name it what you like now. It's all yours again, so you choose.' This hardly seemed the time to mention the half-dozen other national languages that might also have to be involved in the renaming game.

Worn out by the long drive Vicky fell asleep almost immediately that night. She was dreaming of roaring water and an endless drop into the gorge below when a faint chattering noise outside woke her. For a moment she was back in the Kachinga of her childhood, with her pet vervet monkey called Chips chattering to be let in.

Without waking Andrew, she checked her watch – nearly half past three. The noise came again. Of course – monkeys often foraged round the hotel dustbins. Sleepily she thought about Chips, remembering the time she and Greg had tried to give him cough mixture when the baby monkey developed a chest infection.

The chattering continued. Damn, perhaps she'd better check the car windows – the little tinkers could be so inquisitive. Shuffling into her sandals, she reached for her gown and torch and quietly opened the chalet door. The chattering came again, louder, from behind the car. What were they up to?

'Shoo!' she hissed.

'Me Tarzan,' said Greg's voice. 'Who you?'

With a soft chuckle, he caught her as she fell into his arms, pummelling him. 'It's a good thing I haven't got a weak heart,' she whispered into the crook of his neck, remembering the scent of him.

'Oh, but I have,' he murmured. 'Vicky – just kiss me.'

Together they crept down to the river in the fitful moonlight, entwined, too happy to go back yet, but each very much aware of the partner they were having to let go.

Vicky was afraid that Solomon Kazilimani would be offended if he felt his daughter had been insulted, but Greg said it was more complicated than that.

'Solomon thinks it's just youthful rebellion on her part, I can tell,' he told her as they stood wrapped in each other's arms beside the moonlit river. 'But Angie's not keen on the way he treats her mother – that's his second wife. She never wants to be in that position herself, and she's always saying she needs to get right away, to Europe. I've always had a feeling that in one sense she sees me as her ticket out. Which is pretty weird when you think about it, because all I really want to do is stay here.'

'If only,' said Vicky, as the voice of the torrent thundered round them.

The atmosphere at breakfast was very strained. They'd agreed to say nothing until they got back to Kachinga, and if Andrew or Angela noticed anything, they weren't saying. In fact Angela was looking quite stunning in an ochre silk trouser suit that gave her skin a glow.

'Not exactly an outfit for roughing it,' said Andrew admiringly, and off they went to take some shots against a bed of giant silver aloes.

Looking at them, Vicky thought that Andrew would only have to mention the girl's modelling potential and Angie would jump at anything he offered.

They did all the usual things that day – got soaked on the Knife-Edge Bridge, tried to count the rainbows, and took the evening run along Riverside Drive as the setting sun turned the water to molten copper. Yet in spite of the prickly start to the day, the atmosphere between the four of them that evening had lightened and seemed more relaxed – as if some sort of unspoken understanding had been reached.

That night, Andrew said to her quite simply, 'You're not coming back with me, are you? Is it Greg or Kachinga?'

She shook her head sadly. 'I'm so sorry, Andrew, I suppose it's everything. I had no idea at all that it would turn out like this when we left London. But what would *you* do, if this was your home?'

'It's some kind of place, this country. But I don't think I'd want its problems.'

'That's fair enough. But, honestly, just leave me here, Andrew, and I'll be fine, one way or the other.' She tried to smile. 'I can always take on safari work elsewhere if it doesn't work out at Kachinga. Or maybe I'll become a harmless eccentric who talks to the animals – but this time I'll know what else was out there, and I'll have chosen to be here.'

The dry spell broke on the way back and it poured all the way to Kachinga. They waved off Greg and Angie at the fork for the Kazilimani estate, having already agreed to meet for drinks later that evening.

'M'mm – no cars around,' said Vicky. There was no sign of Josh or Maureen on the veranda – only Foto, looking very anxious, was waiting for them.

He put out both his hands to greet her in the local way and sighed in Chewa, 'Trouble has come to this house, my senior sister. Too much trouble.'

Vicky sank down wearily with him on the veranda steps and it was Andrew who went to bring them some water. Eventually she got the whole story straight. Josh had surprised two armed men laying a net near the den. Shots had been exchanged and her brother had chased the men over the boundary. He'd killed one and hit the other in the leg.

'And they're all over at Kazilimani's now? With the police? Let's go,' she said briefly, stunned by this new disaster. 'Do you want to be in on this?' she asked Andrew.

He nodded, with a cool, 'I guess showers often have to wait round here.'

Vicky's brain was going into free-fall. What on earth would Kazilimani do now? It was a terrific excuse to get Josh locked up – maybe it was just the excuse he'd been waiting for to get his hands on Kachinga. Her stomach heaving with fright, she hesitated only a moment before getting back in the vehicle and looked over at the flame tree where her father was buried. 'It's all right, Dad,' she said to herself quietly. 'I'm here.'

When they drew up outside Greg's old home, she hardly recognized the place. With all the improvements, it looked more like someone's idea of a country house than a farm. Solomon Kazilimani was seated in a large chair in the extended living room as if he was giving an audience. He greeted them gravely and waved for them to be seated. Josh was there, looking dejected and uncomfortable and Maureen, her head in her hands, was sobbing quietly.

'We have been discussing the future of Kachinga, have we not, Mr Carstairs. I myself believe that in view of this unfortunate incident and Mrs Carstairs's – er – health, it would be better if I made an offer for the place so that you could go back to town and find employment there. I have many friends...'

No! No! A soundless scream almost split Vicky's head, but Josh interrupted.

'I haven't got much choice, have I? You planned this all along, and I can't prove a thing, you old crook...

Desperation brought Vicky's voice back. 'Josh – stop it, please! Don't make it any worse.'

Then to everyone's amazement, Angela spoke.

'I have something to say to my father,' she announced, and addressed him in rapid urban Chewa. She sounded angry, accusing, as if issuing some kind of ultimatum. Vicky tried desperately to follow. She caught Greg's name, something about ivory, poachers, Angela's mother, Andrew, London and lots of very personal father-daughter stuff.

At last Solomon Kazilimani raised his hand to stop the flow. He seemed a little ruffled, but still in command.

'I apologise for my daughter's vehemence, but she has just explained many things to me,' he said. There was a heart-stopping pause as he collected his thoughts.

'First Gregory, may I say that I much appreciate your allowing my daughter to break off her engagement without embarrassment to either side.'

Greg inclined his head formally. 'I would never do anything to endanger your daughter's reputation or happiness,' he said.

Vicky almost fainted. How had Greg managed this? On the way back in the car, there must have been some very straight talking.

'I can see the non-Chewa speakers are at a disadvantage,' continued Kazilimani. 'It appears that Mr Charlton,' and he nodded to Andrew, 'has offered to sponsor my daughter for a college of fashion in London. The family will arrange a chaperone. We can discuss this later, Mr Charlton, can we not?'

Andrew took a deep breath. 'With the right qualifications and introductions, your daughter will be a great success, I'm sure, sir.'

A faint bubble of hysteria was rising in Vicky's throat. So that's what they been discussing on all those photo shoots. She almost clapped.

'But I'm neglecting my duties,' said their host. 'What would you all say to a large G and T?'

Talking about it afterwards with Greg, it appeared that Angela had accused her father of issuing illegal ivory export permits and said if anyone found out, he'd never be able to show his face among his grand friends in London, or anywhere, again. All she wanted was a chance to make something of herself. Why make a fuss about dead poachers? They were evil men, and couldn't he see it was better to claim he was supporting wild life than destroying it? And why did he need a poor estate like Kachinga? If the people who thought they could run it best wanted to lose money, that was their affair. No one had actually mentioned who those people might be.

In the remaining time until Andrew's return to London, everyone went to great pains to ease the tension. Angela went to her mother's family to make her arrangements for her London adventure, and Greg to Western Province to give in his notice. There was a brief enquiry about the shooting of the poachers, but no charges were brought, and when a relieved Josh and Maureen realized how things were with Vicky and Greg, they pulled themselves together to look for a place in town.

They had a farewell barbeque for Andrew, and there was drumming and some dancing for the first time since her father's death. 'All the luck in the world, Vicky,' he said as they sat for the last time on the veranda. 'You deserve it.'

'Need it, I think you mean,' she smiled, and touched his arm.

It seemed the best idea that Josh and Maureen should take him to the airport. 'Go on then,' Josh said gruffly to her as she was waiting to wave them off. 'Get on the phone. Who knows, you might even get through to Western Province.'

Two days and lots of phone calls later, Greg had let her know that Solomon Kazilimani had decided to be very generous over the release of his daughter from their engagement, since she had been the one to make the decision and that was the local custom.

Vicky almost dropped the phone when Greg told her exactly how generous he had decided to be. Doubtless he had his reasons, they agreed wryly. Greg joked that he'd get her an engagement ring that would make her walk with a limp, and she suggested generator parts, new welding equipment and spare wheels for the safari lorry instead. Or maybe their very own website, which she'd been wondering about, but there'd be quite a sum left, even after all that.

The sun was just beginning to go down when she heard his estate wagon take over the evening air from the buzz of insects. With all the cartons, crates and sacks, there was barely room for Greg. She flew into his arms as he bounded up the veranda steps.

'I still had to get you an engagement present,' he said, pulling out a box wrapped in some old Christmas paper. 'Best I could do on the gift wrapping.'

Inside was a cassette tape. 'I sorted this out before I left Kazilimani's. I won't say it cost an arm and a leg, but it might have done.'

She pulled him into the house and put on the tape. At first she could only hear some crackling, like dry grass, and faint mewling sounds.

'Greg! You didn't!'

'Call it scientific research. I put the recorder in the den when mother was out. Here's the best bit. They don't actually purr, but listen.'

There was a soft grunting cough and some excited mewling and rustling, followed by snuffling and gulping sounds as the mother settled down to suckle the cubs. After five minutes or so, things quietened down, with a bit more scuffling and mewing. And then, over the familiar noises of wild Africa settling down for the night, she heard it – a deep, throaty rumbling kind of a sigh.

'And that, my darling Smoke-That-Thunders,' he said, 'is the sound that leopards make when they're happy.'

A Long Way to Go

For one surreal moment, she saw the beach from seagull height, with herself walking ever more slowly while the other figure gained on her.

'I'm going for a long walk,' she said.

'Where?' he asked sharply, not moving from the bed.

'The beach. Where else is there?' she snorted, ducking unnecessarily under the ceiling fan, scoring a point that it was far too big for such a poky room. So far, so typical, along with the dribbling shower and variations on a theme of rice and fish every single day. And would he admit this trip had been a bad idea? *His* bad idea? She really had to clear her head or something in there might explode – and exploding anywhere near that wonky ceiling fan would not have improved the décor.

'Don't be daft – you'll only have the touts after you.'

She flapped the empty pockets of her shorts. 'See? I'm learning fast. If you haven't got it, you can't give it. I'll just have to out-run them.'

The thin chalet walls quaked as she slammed the door. If it hadn't been for the heat glaring off the whitewash and the feeble attempt at an avenue of palms, it could have been that dreadful holiday camp where she'd worked as a student. *Come and see the real Africa*, it had said in the brochures. Well, there were bigger palm trees in the shopping mall back home, which was where they'd normally be at this time on a Saturday – if *he* hadn't decided on a cheapie somewhere that was hot in February.

A half-hearted thorn hedge tangled with straggly yellow flowers and a low wicker gate tied with string were all that separated the hotel grounds from the beach. You could have broken in with garden shears. Hardly lion country. Or anything else country, except birds and crabs. They were pretty big on those. And kids. She took a deep breath as the first wave spotted her.

'Hello madam, which place you from?'

'England – Birmingham, big city, better than London. Yes, it's quite near Man United. My name is Anna. And your name is...'

A week of this and she'd got it off pat. No, she didn't want cocki-tails at the Pink Elephant Bar. Or to see the market very cheap. No money, see?

'I just want to walk. You know, by myself, okay .. ?'

Here, it seemed that none but the mad or the desperate walked alone. Clucking disapprovingly, the last hanger-on, a gangly youth with tombstone teeth and a faded *I love NYC* tee-shirt, finally abandoned her for a camera-festooned couple still in their winter pallor who looked good for a euro or two.

Peace at last. Ahead was a ten-mile curve of almost-golden, almost-deserted beach. She squinted against the glare from the sea at the far promontory almost hidden in a haze of heat, or maybe it was the spray from lines of breakers whipped by the warm Atlantic breeze. This was more like it; here the palms were not the gentle, swaying kind that dropped chocolate bars, but rustling, rattly things with ribby leaves and crippled trunks.

Gradually she began to relax. That airport transfer had really been an eye-opener. In spite of the rep's desperately right-on spiel about how poor this country was, someone had wanted to stop for pictures of a shack with fairy lights and an open drain, called Faith and Charity's Bar and Disco for All Your Bodily Comforts.

'I wonder what happened to Hope,' Matt had said. 'Probably caught something, I wouldn't wonder...'

She walked on for over an hour keeping to the firmer sand, flirting with the waves. They'd really needed this break. Matt was quite stressed out at work, what with the down-sizing and the new safety regulations, and as for herself... It was quite an effort to straighten up and take deep breaths of something that wasn't inner city air. You could get so tired of people always asking for things – saying there'd been a mix up and their giro hadn't arrived and the landlord was being difficult and they couldn't pay their bloody community tax or whatever. To be so weary of it all, when you'd once thought you could hack it and make a difference...

I'm losing it, she thought. And I'm too tired even to care. She kicked at a neat pile of sand by a tiny burrow. Crabs – the sort that waved their arms at you. The beach would be alive with them when the tide turned. Fiddler crabs – all on the fiddle. I'm getting crabby. I'm losing whatever it was that kept me going; that kept *us* going.

A jogger in a yellow and black local football strip jolted her, appearing suddenly from the dunes. He came pounding past, sweat-beaded, hardly glancing up. Perched against a scraggy palm stump she watched him dwindle like a hornet making for a distant ant colony, as the ants, brown and neat in tiny coloured swimwear, wriggled happily all unawares under cocktail-size beach parasols. She wasn't ready to go back there yet.

Heaving herself up, she turned into the wind and began to jog, feeling the drag of damp sand on her soft city muscles. Then she almost stopped in her tracks. Another figure had appeared from the dunes ahead. A child – a boy. And where there was one, there was always another. Damn! She'd have to go back without even time for a breather. Her feet were like suet puddings now and the breath dry in her chest as she crossly made the turn and, for one surreal moment, she saw the beach from seagull height, with herself walking ever more slowly while the other figure gained on her.

Soon the flip-flopping of his sandals on the wet sand was making her edgy. Better not look round. Perhaps if she slowed down he would overtake and leave her alone. But the footsteps slowed too. Come on, overtake if you're going to, she niggled, just like on the motorway, get off my tail. He was carrying something in an old poly bag and she could hear it swinging.

At last she caved in and half turned to face the silent, plodding figure. The child glanced at her warily, and she took in the shirt with no buttons, the ragged shorts belted with a strip of inner tube and the adult-size flip-flops that looked more like snow shoes on his well-worn feet. In the grubby plastic bag was something darkly purple, weighty, shapeless – and dripping what could only be blood.

'Hello,' she said. If this was the only child in West Africa who'd just beheaded his grandmother, it might be as well to keep it friendly. 'My name is Anna.'

'I am Audu,' he replied softly and fell in step a fraction behind her. Nothing more.

Okay, she thought, trying to forget the sodden bag as they padded on in silence. Children always wanted something. Yet this lad didn't particularly fit the beach-boy mould as he flapped along, dogging her steps respectfully like a warm shadow.

Eventually she cracked. 'Walk with me, Audu,' she said. 'Tell me, what is in your bag?'

She thought at first he said 'Coat'.

'Ah – *goat* – meat!' She flung a look at the vast deserted curve of beach behind them. 'Is there a market over there?'

The boy shook his head. 'From the village of my mother.' His voice had the huskiness of early teens, which meant he was small and thin for his age. 'They chop a goat today. My mother sent me to bring some for us.'

'So you will have a feast tonight?'

He nodded, with the beginnings of a smile. Beside her the huge soles flapped and sucked on the damp sand in the patient rhythm of some ancient, worn machine.

'How far have you walked today, Audu?' she asked, suddenly curious.

He seemed to be counting. 'Twenty-six kilometers,' he said at last. 'Ten more to home.'

She swallowed. Altogether, that would be nearly twenty-three miles.

'No bus?' she asked foolishly, knowing the answer. 'I'm sorry, I have no money with me.'

'It's okay.'

For perhaps another half an hour they walked along, sometimes speaking, sometimes not. Small things. He'd had three years of school; four brothers and two sisters. She told him she'd had sixteen years at school, and hadn't any children, but couldn't explain why.

Ahead was an opening in the dunes. 'That is my way,' he said.

'Oh...' It was still a good half mile to the hotels. 'I have money there,' she said. 'I could pay your bus fare.'

Audu squinted ahead to the crowded beach, then at the sun low over the sea. 'Is too far,' he replied. 'Dark soon.'

Then, without warning, he broke his stride and pounced on something in the sand with his free hand.

'I go now,' he said, and held out an unbroken, pure white cowry shell.

She cupped her hands for it, unable to say a word; desperately hoped he would smile, and thought perhaps he did, fleetingly. There was nothing to do but watch him go, flap-flap in the sand without a backward glance, the bloodied bag still swinging.

Carefully, she slipped the shell into her empty pocket. Would Matt understand all this? She thought perhaps he might.

Beneath her feet the soft sand stirred and shifted as the first fiddler crabs emerged to play out their secret lives. The tide had turned, and she still had a long way to go.

The Hand that Rocks the Cradle

*Two veiled figures appeared to be holding something like a tray between them,
although I couldn't quite make out what it was.*

I was hot and I was cross. I mean, having to share a coach seat with the
one person on the trip that I really wanted to avoid – Angela Moreton, and
I can tell you, she'd put on a bit of weight since our primary school days.

I knew the trip was a mistake – from the minute I'd heard myself saying,
'Okay, okay, count me in. I've always fancied a cruise down the Nile – just
as long as you promise I won't have to share a cabin with Angela Moreton.'

'You mean the Angela Moreton whose daughter married your son?'
asked Sally, dry as a pharaoh's sock.

Nothing much gets past Sally, which is probably why she's the one
running the Staynsthwaite and District Ladies' Choir. She's good, though.
So good we'd won the regional cup, and she'd decided we deserved
something a little more exciting than a day out in London and came up
with the idea of a block booking on a Nile cruise.

A faint sigh reached me over the top of her clipboard. 'Right, Jean – a
guaranteed Moreton-free cabin and plane seat. I think I can arrange that.'

Honestly, I couldn't pass up seeing the Pyramids at long last. Kevin, my
ex, was always worried he'd catch something. Angela Moreton apart, it had
looked like the perfect opportunity for the trip of a lifetime.

Except I'd forgotten about the coach excursions. Now, I don't think
it was deliberate on Sally's part, that by the time I boarded the coach
that day, the only free seat was beside Angela. But Sally is one of those
well-meaning people who really does believe that natural-born enemies
can become friends by being thrown together in exotic surroundings and
forced into a bit of bonding the hard way, like Sydney Poitier and that
other one, handcuffed together and on the run.

So far, the only bonding going on was between my skin and the plastic
bits of the coach seat. Angela was looking steadfastly out of the window
at the line between the bluest sky you ever saw and a white haze of desert.

'Turned out nice again,' I ventured cheerily.

'It's usually hot here in August, I believe,' she retorted, with a look a camel might have envied. It's the way she curls her upper lip.

I was about to reply that actually I did know that, since we'd both suffered our way through 'A' level Geography at the local high school. But that only reminded me that our teenage years had been no better than primary days. If anyone new to the district believed that the trouble between Angela Moreton and me had only started when our offspring, against all the odds, had decided to get married, they didn't know the half of it.

'I'm so pleased Tutankhamun's tomb is open again,' I said, determined not to be as squashed by Angela's sarcasm as I was by her thighs.

'Actually, I've already seen it,' murmured Angela. 'Some time ago, with Barry,' she added, fanning herself with her sunhat as if to waft away a distant memory.

I can't say I was surprised – that she'd already seen the world's most famous tomb, or about her wanting to forget it. She'd separated from Barry at about the same time as I'd split up with Kevin.

Maybe that was the trouble with Angela and me – we had so much in common, but somehow we'd always finished up in competition. I swear I didn't start it – it just happened - sports, exam grades, boyfriends...

When it came to offspring, we'd both stuck at one. But I'd beaten her by eleven months with a boy, and she'd caught up with a girl. With the age gap, our kids hadn't socialised much at school. But then my Jason had gone to uni, and her Karen had followed a year later – to the same town. Neither had said much about it, but then they sprung it on us. Within a couple of years of getting their first jobs, they were married. I'll spare you the details of the wedding, but let's just say that Jason, Karen and their friends seemed to enjoy it, having taken over the organising themselves.

And then of course there was the baby. What could I do? Stand back and just let Angela M. take over? I still think the fact it was a girl – her daughter's daughter as it were, made her think *our* granddaughter was more hers than mine. I felt cut out – excluded. Every time I offered to baby-sit, Angela got there first. Whatever I offered to buy, she'd already thought of it. She even trumped the lovely teddy I bought with a bigger one. I tried not to react badly, but I suppose I did, especially when they called her Alice. *Alice*, I ask you. *Her* grandmother's name, of course.

'By heck, it's hot,' said someone behind, and it certainly was.

'Not far now, ladies,' chirped Tarik, our guide. 'We don't set the air-con too high in case the contrast when you step outside is too much.'

There was some uneasy twittering, but Angela was still looking her usual aloof self.

'Our first stop will be the Mortuary Temple of Queen Hatshepsut, but don't worry – the security is excellent now.'

'Been there too?' I asked. This time, she didn't even answer, but she seemed to be remembering something – probably her trip with Barry, because there was quite an odd look on her face.

'That's never 3,500 years old,' said a voice from the back. 'Look at all those sharp angles and clean lines. It's more like a hydroelectric power station.'

We pulled up before a vast, sandblasted courtyard that ended in a sheer wall of glaring white rock, out of which two tiers of twenty or more plain, rectangular columns had been carved in deep relief.

'The condition is so good because it was covered by sand for many centuries,' explained Tarik. 'It is a monument to a very powerful woman who wore a false beard to show she was as strong as any man.'

'Sounds like my Great Aunt Flo,' said Sally's voice, to a general giggle.

'Ladies, please remember your hats and water bottles,' called Tarik as we got up to go. 'The walk to the first colonnade is longer than it looks.'

Now I don't normally feel the heat, being the tall thin type, but even I was beginning to feel like a wilted lettuce by the time we reached the colonnade. Waves of almost metallic air were bouncing at us from the bare ground and the rock wall beyond. I'd quickly left Angela behind, but I couldn't help a look round to see how she was doing. She was right at the back, and seemed to be flagging. Ha! I thought, almost automatically, I've got you on this one. Yet for once a twinge of something like sympathy caught me unawares. Or perhaps it was a tiny reminder, as a troupe of chattering Italian teenagers overtook us, that none of us was getting any younger.

We crowded into what little shade there was beyond the burning façade. And that's all it was; there was no cool, roomy interior like some of the other temples. In fact, it felt more like a film set. Yet we all agreed the frescoes were fascinating for their details of life on the Nile all those years ago. I loved the scenes of Queen Hatshepsut's emissaries returning from the Land of Punt, their boats laden with all kinds of goodies. It was like a child's painting of what an exotic land should be, with the gifts of fruits, strange animals and birds all lined up for the queen's inspection.

Then Tarik beckoned us further in. 'And here is my favourite,' he said. 'Especially for the ladies. See?'

He pointed with his torch to another panel. Two veiled figures appeared to be holding something like a shallow basket between them, although I couldn't make out what was in it.

'It's a custom you can still see today in the villages along the Nile,' said Tarik. 'When a new baby is born, it is placed in a winnowing basket, and on the naming day, the two grandmothers perform this little ceremony.'

'What are they doing?' I asked, thoroughly hooked by now.

'They pretend to snatch the basket from each other, first one way, then the other. Grandmothers are always rivals, yes?'

Feeling Sally's eyes hot on the back of my neck, I looked surreptitiously round for Angela, but she wasn't with the group.

'And as they tug, they chant to the assembled families, "See, I, your grandmother, your *father's* mother, loves you the best." "But no, it is I, your *mother's* mother, who loves you best."'

'No change there, then,' murmured Sally.

'And do you know what happens, ladies? With the tugging of the grandmothers, any badness in the baby falls from the winnowing basket like chaff, and the child grows up strong and good.'

There was delighted laughter and some clapping, and everyone had a good swig of water before facing the outside again. Hot cheeked, I turned to look for Angela, but she was still nowhere to be seen.

'Has anyone seen Angela Moreton?' I asked sharply.

Mild consternation broke out as we hurried outside. Angela was sitting on the stone floor resting against one of the pillars in a tiny patch of shade.

'I'm okay,' she said as I approached. She seemed to be scanning my face, which was odd, since she normally avoided my eyes. 'Honestly, Jean. Tell the others I'm fine.'

I gave the rest the thumbs-up sign, and with brief stops for more photos, they started the hot trek back to the coach.

'Are we getting too old for this?' I asked tentatively, preparing for another snub. She said nothing, so I squatting down beside her and offered her my water bottle.

'Maybe we are,' she replied, taking a swig and almost smiling at me as she passed it back.

Then it struck me. 'You've been here before, haven't you?' I said.

She nodded. 'Long before little Alice was born. I only remembered about that grandmothers' mural when I saw the place again.'

There was a pause. 'Tarik said you can still buy those winnowing baskets in Luxor market,' I tried, tentatively. 'They might make a nice souvenir.'

'M'mm.' Another pause. 'But I don't think I'd fancy going on my own.'

'We *could* go this afternoon.'

'After several cups of tea?' She was actually smiling, and so was I.

'Make mine iced coffee,' I replied, and when we instinctively held out our hands to heave each other up from the hot stone floor, it really did feel like a new beginning.

Not to be Opened Until Christmas

But what kind of present do you give to a boy who has nothing?

I think it was the flour bag that first made me take to Imbo. He was wearing it at the time, that day he turned up on our veranda looking for work as a houseboy. Someone had made it into a kind of smock by hacking out a neck and armholes – possibly his mother, or maybe he'd just done it himself – and it was probably all he had to wear.

There he stood, bare feet splayed like divers' flippers, the classical ebony features of his face marred only by a milked-over iris in one eye, and black enough to make even the caked-on grime look pale. His spindly legs were not quite straight – rickety, you might say. Rickets. We saw a lot of that at the clinic.

But the rest of him looked solid enough, and across the barrel chest, stencilled in red on the grain sacking, were the words: *A free gift from the United States of America, not to be sold.* It was love at first sight, if only on my part.

Boniface, our head cook and bottle-washer, was standing defensively by the front door, fairly steaming with disapproval as the negotiations proceeded.

'But there's Christmas, Boniface,' I said, risking rebellion in the cook-house. 'Please tell Imbo he can start tomorrow.' Boniface was brown ale to Imbo's Guinness – and I was the Pink Lady.

We had all tried dreaming of a white Christmas, but it wasn't easy. Was there really an Essex village where they would be out collecting holly? After three years in Kontogoro, I was beginning to wonder. But we had to try, Linda and I. That's what you got for being the only unattached females for hundreds of square miles – all the spare males looking at you hopefully for a traditional Christmas dinner.

Imbo had been taken on about a week before I left for town to do the extra Christmas shopping. It was only three hours away if the road wasn't too bad, and qualified as such only because it had a bank, a set of traffic lights and some shops with glass windows. Since he'd turned up every day and all seemed reasonably quiet on the cook-house front, 'present for Imbo' was added to the list. As I wearily turned the pick-up into the compound, I could see Linda's white coat winding along the narrow sandy path that linked our shared bungalow to the clinic like a slack tether. On particularly hot days, I could imagine it being pulled taut as our little brick home decided to drift away into the surrounding bush on a wave of heat like an absentminded nanny goat. In which case we'd have the only straight path in the whole of West Africa. But we'd still have been tied to the daily rounds – tablets and jabs, stitches and swabs, pink plasters for dark skin.

She heard the engine, and I returned Linda's expansive double-handed wave. Being Texan, she never did things by halves. Her whoop of welcome was answered by a faint cheeky echo from the cook-house. It was catching, and Imbo had caught it.

Linda greeted me as if I'd been away for a week instead of overnight.

'Tough day?' I asked, and we both mimed a laughing collapse into our not very well-sprung armchairs.

'Don't ask! But I'm not too bushed to sneak a peak at the goodies. Great! You got the pumpkins!'

In the interests of international goodwill, my opinion of pumpkin pie is best left out of this, but some of her compatriots were bound to come along on Christmas Day and help her eat the stuff. The uninitiated would have to make do with mince pies for dessert, which I was determined to make from Boniface's rather weighty pastry and the contents of two jars of Olde English mincemeat I'd found in town – very olde, by the look of the labels.

My musings on the suitability of roast vulture for fifteen (if we couldn't get enough guinea fowl) were interrupted by the arrival of Boniface. With one hand he was balancing a tray on which clinked a jug of iced lime juice, while the other had a firm hold on Imbo's ear. Its owner was following on in round-eyed confusion.

'This one drop a best plate,' he announced with his usual drama. 'You tell him go-go now, madam. Or shall I beat him small?' He was looking at me expectantly.

Imbo seemed to be getting the drift of the conversation and shot me his speciality, a one-eyed appeal from somewhere under Boniface's arm.

'But he can't have – they're not supposed to break if you drop them,' I said, remembering the set of best unbreakable plastic plates I'd brought back from my last home leave with the likes of Imbo and his band of brothers in mind.

'Ah, but you see, madam, he drop it in the fire,' was the outraged reply.

I could feel Linda swallowing her mirth along with her drink in deference to Boniface's wrath. There followed some delicate negotiations to satisfy honour all round. In return for continued employment, Imbo was to be docked the equivalent of one penny a week from his pay – which I would conveniently forget about after the first instalment. Boniface would then spare the rod and, in his opinion, spoil the child.

Linda gazed after the retreating pair. 'Poor little mite. I just don't know how you cope with these situations,' she said, with one of her helpless Sue Ellen smiles.

I said I thought I might have made a good memsahib in British India, if she knew what I meant. And she did. It came over me sometimes, playing Lady Bountiful – but reality usually came to the rescue.

'Funny,' I said, 'when I was doing the shopping, I just couldn't get that awful phrase out of my mind. You know: what do you get for the man who has everything?'

Linda nodded slowly. 'Yeah, here it's more like, what do you get for the kid who has nothing. So what *did* you get for Imbo?'

I pointed out a long flat box that I'd asked the shop to wrap in old newspapers. 'I got Boniface and Imbo some clothes of course, but when it came to Imbo, I stopped being practical. Okay, he may be the family wage-earner, but he's still only a small boy who's probably never had a decent present in his life. I just couldn't resist it. It's the biggest, noisiest play gun they had. It shoots caps and corks – the lot.'

Linda clapped her hands. 'Terrific! He'll really be able to crow it over the other kids with that. Hey, why don't we wrap it up real good.' And off she went to find some of the gorgeous wrapping paper and decorative trimmings her mother had sent in the last parcel from home. Making sure there were no watching eyes, we produced a gift wrapping extravaganza for the gun that wouldn't have disgraced Harrods, complete with ribbons, charity stickers, rosettes and a huge coloured label marked *Not to be opened until Christmas.*

'There now!' Linda sat back on her heels to survey our handiwork. 'That looks kinda special. We wouldn't want to spoil the surprise on the happy morn, now would we?'

'His or ours?' I asked. Not that Imbo could read, but we agreed it was the thought that counts, and we giggled like kids ourselves as we hid it on top of the wardrobe.

Christmas Day dawned on Kontogoro as it would on Roding Green and Fort Worth, only a little earlier and a lot warmer. The schedule for the day ran strictly to local time, with a midnight service at the mission which broke up rather late. Then, after a slow breakfast, we did the clinic rounds in heat that would have cracked the pavement, had there been any, and gave out sweets to the children. As usual, there were always more children than sweets.

By midday, everyone who knew anything about expatriate Christmas dinners was getting in an early siesta in preparation for what promised to be a hectic evening. At around four o'clock things began to move again, and I was in the cook-house slaving over the proverbial hot stove, a blackened ship's boiler of a thing that burnt wood when it felt like it, and I was roasting gently, along with half a dozen guinea fowl, two chickens, homemade stuffing (don't ask) and a mountain of yam-cakes. By this time, Boniface was well marinated in local gin but was doing his best to help, while Imbo did the stoking.

All things considered, the meal turned out quite well, and international relations had never been better. Our guests, mostly young volunteers with some local staff and their wives, had all brought along a little of whatever made them happy, and there was even some genuine

French champagne from Father Bazelaire who ran the mission and had a hot line to someone's diplomatic bag. Ignatius, the clinic orderly, declared that it was 'too weak and only for women, like Fanta', and we sat back to watch the results with interest.

The mince pies and even the pumpkin pie all disappeared and, over Afro-Gaelic coffee – another recipe peculiar to this part of the world – it was Presents Time.

There was the usual ribald exchange of items made specially for the occasion or not wanted from home parcels, including a loo brush for our household with the Papal Arms painted lovingly on it. Above the din, Linda called for Boniface and Imbo while I went to fetch their presents.

Boniface, pleasantly stoned and living up to his name, beamed as we applauded the dinner, and swayed off into the night with his arms full, leaving Imbo still standing holding his parcels and not sure what to do next.

'Come on, show us then, Imbo,' called Dr Hendrik, and they helped him remove the gaudy wrappings.

When Imbo saw what was inside the box, he gave a kind of involuntary gasp that seemed to come from deep inside his smock, but he made no attempt to pick up the gun.

A true Texan, Linda reached for it, aimed at the open door and pressed the trigger to give him the idea. The resulting flashes and clatter so startled Imbo that he almost dropped his other parcels. Several of the guests obligingly fell about miming death with mock heroics as Linda joyfully sprayed the room with corks. There followed a scramble to retrieve them and press the gun on its new owner, who stood there motionless as we loaded him up to the last ribbon.

Then, with a wild, unreadable look at me, and something that sounded like a sob, he fled into the darkness with his precious bundle.

'Peace on earth!' Linda laughed, and we raised our glasses.

'And mercy mild,' sang an Irish voice, and we finished the carol, even the high notes, and several others in some kind of harmony. Christmas – of a sort – had come to Kontogoro.

Boxing Day was best forgotten as the compound dozed in a hung-over haze of heat, and it was a couple of days before I remembered the gun. Imbo had been around the cook-house as usual, but there were no cork-popping or games of cops and robbers to break the dust-muffled silence, and the vultures sulked on unmolested in the silk-cotton trees. After some inquiries, I found to my surprise that no one had seen or heard the gun since Linda's impromptu Christmas dinner shoot-out, and I was more than a little puzzled.

Imbo had liked his new toy, I was sure of that. The look he'd given me, that sob in his throat – it must surely have meant that he did. Perhaps he'd been bullied out of it, or his family had decided to sell it. Even if he had managed to lose all the corks or break it so soon, which wasn't beyond the bounds of possibility, he could surely have used the bits and pieces for some kind of game.

My mystification deepened when I saw him a good week later with his usual crowd of cronies, happily catapulting a colony of weaver birds in the acacia tree behind the wildlife conservation area that passed for our back garden. Surely he couldn't possibly have thought the gun was real and been disappointed? No, that was silly. In the end I did what I should have done in the first place. I asked Boniface.

'Oh, he likes it fine, madam,' he answered, pausing from his floor-polishing. 'He keeps it in a cloth behind the firewood in the kitchen.'

So at least he still had it. 'But why doesn't he play with it?' I asked.

Boniface's bare feet, each wrapped in an old tee-shirt of mine, resumed their rhythmic shuffling. 'You see, it is the other boys,' he said in a tone that suggested polite resignation at my ignorance of such matters.

I put down the clinic coat I was mending. So that was it. Imbo had known, after one brief flash of joy at seeing the gun that he would never be able to play with it, and it was the pain of that knowledge that he had sent me in the strange look from his one good eye. The boy who had nothing had suddenly become the boy who had something – and that set him apart. When you had something, it could be taken away. Better to have nothing, just like everyone else who really mattered in your life.

'Thank you, Boniface,' I said, putting on the coat. I started off for the clinic feeling what Linda called, a whiter shade of pale. Three years, and I hadn't thought of that. I'd given the ultimate in useless presents – a toy that couldn't be, mustn't be, played with, and Imbo had known it straight away.

How long would it be before I understood that kind of harsh wisdom? And how long before Christmas really came to Kontogoro?

Those Far Away Places

They call me a dreamer, well, maybe I am...

(Those Far Away Places, popular song,
1948, Whitney and Kramer)

Ever let the fancy roam,
Pleasure never is at home.

(Fancy, John Keats, 1785-1821)

In Perugia

It is spring in Umbria, and three women from very different backgrounds are converging on Micheli's farmhouse near the ancient hilltop town of Perugia with one thing on their minds – Micheli.

What am I looking for? Julia asks herself, peering down at the earth-brown domes and spires as the plane comes into land. Maybe I should put myself on automatic pilot until all this is over and come down to earth without waking up – when I have to – eventually.

A couple of days in Florence – well, you couldn't miss Florence, and she had to convince herself that she wasn't in *that* much of a hurry. Then a bus pulling its way through the green heart of Italy, and up towards Perugia at last.

I didn't dream that any of this should be, she thinks, as the late sun on the ancient stones fills her eyes, but if I had, it would have been like this. 'Take the *scala mobile* from the bus station to the Piazza Italia, dear Julia, and follow the crowds. I'll be in the Bar Ferrari – it's quite chic enough for an English lady. It's on the Corso Vannucci, and serves the most wonderful coffee and chocolate cake in Umbria, which is to say the world.' Micheli, over the phone, cautious until she said she was alone, then persuasive, charming. Of course – or why else is she here?

If Peter had been home that night, she'd have said it was just a client, and no commitment would have been made. But he wasn't, and it had. Was it really that simple, after all those faithfully married years, so foolishly easy? One day, this dream of a man walks into the gallery, then the next, and asks you to lunch. When you accept, is it already too late? He says you must come to his farmhouse in Umbria – must. He works from home, so is always there, so simply email or phone. The spring is best. Why not come soon?

You ask yourself if it could actually be true – that there is such a thing as Romance. That there really is a Father Christmas. And if there is, how else should it be but – like this? Just so bloody *romantic*. Have I waited all my life for this? Me?

You email because he sent flowers when he left, to the gallery of course, not to home – where the heart isn't. He replies, several times. Finally, he phones the gallery. You tell Peter that you feel like a break and a friend of a friend has got this place in the Assisi area, oh you know, wonderful views, terrific museums, possible contacts. Might do Florence again, too – need some sun...

She'd started on the guide books, taken art histories to bed, and found herself reading bits aloud to Peter, sincerely, perversely, wanting to share this experience with him – what she could of it. 'Perugia – I don't believe this place.' Already it had taken on a life of its own. She could almost smell it. 'It makes Montagues versus Capulets look like The Archers. Three popes died there. One self–destructed from overeating, and they poisoned the other two. One gang of nobles was famously handsome, kept pet lions and went in for fratricide when not slicing up their rivals.' She was burbling now, but didn't care. 'And the rival gang? Well, their leader was murdered on his wedding day by the Abbot, at a surviving pope's request...'

'Well, you'd better watch your step then,' Peter had said. Oh God – had he guessed?

She'd pressed on blithely, not daring to miss a beat. 'Apparently, the Peruginos have turned out rather well.' Seemingly intent on the book, she'd been thinking that one of the statues had a mouth just like Micheli's, and no wonder half their artists were bisexual. 'A few centuries of direct papal rule was just what was needed, and now "the people of Perugia are famed for their politeness, urbanity, good taste, chocolates and shoes", it says here.'

'Maybe we should try it on the kids.'

'What, a holiday in Umbria?

'No, direct papal rule.'

'Oh, funny...' Or on you, Peter darling, you bastard. You think I don't know, but I do. Well, now it's my turn, and my turn will have *style*. I'd hardly bother otherwise. None of your nasty little London hotel rooms for me...

And before she'd even had time to dream about it properly, she is here – in Perugia, meeting in this oh-so-stylish way, in time for the evening *passeggiata* along the Corso. 'But do the English not take an evening walk like this, with all the family?' That's what they'd spoken about over the phone – just the meeting. Not feelings, not conditions, not past involvements, not the future. 'No, we don't do this,' she tells him. 'It must be the climate.' Yes, let's blame it on the climate.

Walking into the Bar Ferrari, and feeling so very English, so very *obvious*, having her hand kissed by this handsome man. Was there a pet lion around? A faint bubble of suburban hysteria rises in her throat. I don't normally do this, you know, she wants to yell. He'd never mentioned a wife – but then, he wouldn't, would he? Well they don't, men like Micheli. They managed things differently here. The climate again? Same old trite excuse. But if it wasn't, then what on earth was it?

Julia looks across the table at Micheli sitting there like some extravagant present, and sees a man who will age gracefully. Tall for an Italian, not inclined to fat, not too aquiline, evenly balanced. Skin just touched with olive, beginning of a new season's tan. Expensive glasses modified that liquid-eyed look and made him seem older which, at that age, was even an improvement. There's an age gap of – oh what does it matter if he's younger? If you wanted each other, that was enough. It wouldn't last, of course, she knew that, yet she could still appreciate a man who would never go bald if he lived to be a hundred. Micheli was basically a Jacob not an Esau. A smooth man.

To see all this over a chocolate-scented cappuccino, to remember the details she'd forgotten, as he says she looks wonderful and how was Florence – to describe the journey, her delight at the fruit trees in blossom like froth lapping against the hill-town islands – surely this was what it seemed to be.

What it is, is every cliché in the book and Julia knows it, but she also knows herself to be worth more than clichés, and that such things could be an art form if you have the right kind of soul.

Julia's nature is never to *assume*, so she tries one last pretence that all this is not so. 'I left my bags at the bus station – are the hotels full at this time of year?'

The light, that wonderful Primavera light, is fading down to indigo now and Micheli reaches for her hand. 'At Easter they come over from Assisi like locusts – to see the wicked town that locked up their dear San Francesco. But surely, dear Julia, you're not thinking of a hotel. My house is there for you, as I am.'

Even Micheli's accent is sophisticated. No hint of 'one Cornetto' here – not after a year in California.

She smiles, accepting. 'Is it far from town? I've already fallen in love with this wicked Perugia of yours.'

'To understand our roughhouse history,' says Micheli taking her arm as they make their way back to the bus station and the parking zone, 'you have to see it as the growing up of a very naughty child – a boy, of course.'

He pauses to greet a well-shod family on their stately *passeggiata* and introduces her faultlessly, 'a valued English friend and colleague', and chuckles as they move on again, drawing her that vital fraction closer along the narrow alleys. 'Do you know, just over there', and he points to a bulky rampart dark against an early moon, 'we built a huge catapult called the Priest-chaser to knock down the first papal palace.'

We. He said 'we'. It was seven hundred years ago. She laughs and warms to the game. 'And what about all those things you stole. The town gates of Sienna, the battle wagon of – where was it? That huge marble slab from the neighbours' cathedral. And you still haven't given back the wedding ring of the Virgin – now that was from Chiusi, wasn't it? Oh, Micheli, what would Mama say?'

'Remember,' he said, gently teasing a strand of hair from her temple, 'Whatever we do, Mama is always proud of us.'

Now they were standing head to breast on the *scala mobile* so that Julia has a compelling urge to blow a kiss to the hollow spot where the neck muscles taper inside his open collar. For some reason she has never understood, it is her favourite erogenous zone.

'I'll remember,' she murmurs.

As Julia and Micheli speed through the dusk with Venus rising, there are also stars in the blue English eyes of Cheryl Thompkins, *au pair* in another villa not far from Micheli's, belonging to the Bardi family. Cheryl got the job through an agency, but only just, because the clients specified a 'good' English accent for the children. Having glottal-stopped her way through school unhindered, Cheryl still forgets sometimes, but she's so pretty that most people don't notice. The men, anyway. Signora Bardi recognized the breed immediately when she'd picked Cheryl up at the airport, and given silent thanks that her husband was in Geneva on business until July.

At first, Cheryl had been a little disappointed that there were no men about at the Bardi villa except for the ageing gardener. She is not the kind of girl to break up a marriage unless she really has to, but likes to feel that most men would be tempted – in the right circumstances. That one day these will come along, is something Cheryl has never questioned. Having such expectations, she is also well primed to recognize what it will feel like, and on the day she saw her neighbour from the next farmhouse, Cheryl could hardly believe her luck.

It's him – it's true, she told herself. And he's only a mile away.

What Cheryl now wants is really quite simple. She wants to be Micheli's wife for ever and ever. First of course, they'd scale the dizzy heights of romance described for her in almost every book she's read since the age of thirteen. Sadly, a connoisseur of eyes might have noted a certain vacancy. It isn't stupidity, just an inability to analyse the situation for what it is. It really hurts, she tells herself with a kind of grim satisfaction, dreaming of the man in the other farmhouse only a mile away across the ridge as she gets the Bardi children's supper. But it's supposed to, if you want someone that badly.

Micheli had noticed Cheryl, of course, in the sort of way that fastidious shoppers notice a row of dresses or shirts they can easily afford as they pass on to something more exclusive. But as the Alfa zips past the Bardi villa, only the smallest flicker of her crosses his mind – the English girl up there for the summer. Ten years ago, he would have definitely made an attempt on her virtue just to prove that he could. Five years ago maybe, just for fun. These days? Well, if she were to make the first move, that would be different, but you had to be careful with girls as young as that, even foreign ones, and they were rarely worth the trouble. Maybe I'm growing up at last, he thinks, then takes his eyes off the dashboard glow for a moment to smile at Julia.

'If you are lonely, there's a little English nanny with our neighbours back there.'

The word 'nanny' reassures Julia, as he intends it should, but for an instant, a half-remembered flash of Cheryl's milky northern skin as her tight cotton top parted company briefly with her jeans distracts him, so that his gear change for once is less than perfect.

Micheli genuinely likes women and doesn't want to hurt them. He isn't the emotionally wounded type for whom there is some secret balm that only one woman can apply. Micheli has been adored since birth by women of every age, and has loved them all back. Julia's earlier caution in this respect is unfounded – there is nothing especially *wrong* with him, which is half his attraction to her. There is plenty wrong with her husband, and one could get awfully, cosmically, tired of it.

Cheryl, on the other hand, believes that seeking out that secret flaw, that hidden wound, is the key. Men were like that. You only had to find it, and the rest was easy.

Even as the Alpha turns into the drive of Micheli's farmhouse, and Julia is exclaiming how perfect it all is, Cheryl is determinedly scrubbing the Bardi offspring and working on a plan to see Micheli again soon. She knows, just *knows*, this is It, and so of course, in quite another way, does Julia.

Meanwhile, in California, and more specifically in the small but chic Bay Area apartment of Kimberley Studbaker, it is only Wednesday morning. Kimberley has already done her Alexander exercises, showered, and is getting her act together for an audition with the kind of energy and concentration which would have bemused even the bouncy Cheryl and made Julia feel like a fossil. Although only ten years separates Julia from the American girl, it is the same ten years that separates Julia from Micheli.

Kimberley's biological clock is ticking away, of course, the same as everyone else's – even Cheryl's. But Kimberley hasn't heard hers yet, while to Cheryl the term simply means that people get old, and therefore doesn't apply to her yet.

'Go for it, kid,' says Kimberley, inspecting her impeccable teeth. She blows herself a kiss in the mirror. 'Now, get this part or you're dead meat.'

Every day, Kimberley bombards herself with a formidable array of techniques for getting what she wants out of life. Just now, this consists of becoming rich and famous and having a terrific love life, in fact several terrific love lives, preferably set to run concurrently – but consecutively would do. The only thought she has given to mortality is that by the time it gets round to her turn, someone will have fixed it.

This was the kind of approach that Micheli had found so refreshing, yet ultimately quite disconcerting, when he and Kimberley had got together some time last year. Warned about West Coast Mellowspeak by cultural tentacles reaching even to Perugia, Micheli had soon found himself tangling with a language seemingly capable of redefining the emotions – an experience almost as novel and rejuvenating as tangling with Kimberley. Micheli now viewed his four-month affair with her as a valuable learning experience, but not necessarily one which he would care to repeat. For one thing, he had never been so artlessly and openly *pursued* by a woman he desired before, nor was he used to the sensation of being led in love-making.

Kimberley too had been impressed, more by a kind of indefinable class, as she put it, about her Italian lover than by any particular expertise. It was this very class that had enabled Micheli to conceal his relief that he could escape from California and Kimberley with some kind of dignity when his course on high-tech art printing came to an end.

That was six months ago, and bobbing in Kimberley's mind this Californian Wednesday morning is the half-submerged thought that if she doesn't get this part, some kind of drastic action will be needed to boost her confidence. There have been two other men in her life since Micheli, but one, a fellow actor, had turned out to like fellows too, which these days was living dangerously, and the other was married and developing a conscience. Lately, Kimberley had begun to regard Micheli as a brief stabilising influence in her life – more 'together' than her compatriots, more certain of what life was really about.

To ask Micheli and Julia at this particular moment what life is about would be both indiscreet and pointless, since they are now making love and have reached the point where nothing exists but their pleasure in each other and themselves that such pleasure should be.

Julia had been a little nervous at first. It wasn't the breaking of her long-held marriage vows that caused the problem, since she'd crossed that particular bridge on first making up her mind to come to Umbria. When the children were almost grown and her partner had broken the contract first, it did seem rather irrelevant. After all, she wasn't thinking of leaving Peter, and that's what counted, wasn't it?

It is more that she wasn't quite sure about the etiquette of this sort of thing. Micheli seemed pretty sure, she thought wryly at several stages of that delightful evening – so let him set the pace. After his experiences with Kimberley, this is something Micheli is more than happy to do, and he does it very well, with a combination of charm, humour and relaxed attention to detail that is sheer artistry.

Lying in the warm darkness beside this beautiful man at the deeply satisfying conclusion of their first evening, Julia surprises herself by thinking, it doesn't really matter what happens now. I know it's true, and she cries a few little tears when she is sure Micheli is asleep, because she doesn't want him to feel any kind of pressure from such emotion.

On the terrace before breakfast, Julia stretches her arms to the rising sun in a gesture as old as joy – then gives a surprisingly down-to-earth chuckle.

Micheli comes up behind her, stroking her soft stomach with one hand, lifting the hair at the back of her head high enough to kiss the nape of her neck, and says, 'What is that for, tell me?'

'I was thinking,' she says, 'I feel as if I've just been delivered by Harrods.'

Even as she speaks, and Micheli is laughing aloud at the peculiarity of this expression, Julia is aware of the discreet shuffling of Caterina, Micheli's ancient housekeeper.

My God, thinks Julia. That old duck must have seen some action round here. I wonder what she thinks about me. That I'm a bit old for him, I suppose, but she'll have worked out I won't be staying.

The thought doesn't depress her unduly. For a brief moment she tries to contemplate Caterina's life. What is it that Italian countrywomen *think* these days? she wonders, then gives up the unequal struggle against Micheli's expert touches.

'So what shall we do today to amuse you, my Julia?' he asks, and suddenly Julia, against all her will, is crying.

'Sorry,' she sniffs in her considerate English way. 'No one's ever asked me that. Not like that, anyway.'

Languorously, they settle for an art gallery or two before a late lunch in Perugia.

Over at the Bardi villa, the scent of the recently showered Umbrian hills and the morning light behind the red hibiscus trumpets is just as flagrantly erotic, but Cheryl has been doomed by Signora Bardi to accompany the children to a friend's pool – straight after the ironing. Right now, she's having her work cut out sorting breakfast for the little Bardis who get right up her nose sometimes, even though they're not bad kids, compared to some.

'Couldn't we have a party?' she asks her employer. 'We could invite some of the neighbours,' she adds hopefully. It's all she's been able to come up with as a way of seeing Micheli again, but Senora Bardi's attention span is always on the short side and she doesn't even pause on her way upstairs.

I need a crisis, decides Cheryl, pressing too hard on a pair of designer infant jeans. Perhaps when the old bag's out shopping for the day and the gardener's off, I could fix up something and have to ring Micheli for help. His English isn't bad. Maybe I could just call on my evening off and ask him to translate something for me. No – too feeble. I wonder if I could flood the washing machine. I read a story where somebody did that once...

Outside in the orchard the Bardi *bambini* – all three of them – are behaving in the way that children do when mother is dressing for a day with a socially superior neighbour and the *au pair* has her mind on other things. After making their new donkey a headdress of wild flowers, Lucia, the oldest, is practising inept ballet steps along the flagstoned path, while her two brothers are carefully tying a grasshopper to the donkey's tail with some thread from Caterina's sewing box. Perhaps weighed down by its heritage in these parts as the patient Brother Ass, the beast is standing up to this quite well. But with donkeys, you can never really tell.

'I'm only going to have two kids,' Cheryl confides to the Mickey Mouse on the front of the fifth wrinkled tee-shirt. 'I reckon they spoil them out here.'

But soon she is in a happy reverie about Micheli's first kiss which is totally unconnected with any thought of domesticity, or in fact with anything at all. It would definitely be evening and outside. Perhaps he'd suggest a meal in one of those little restaurants with absolutely no chips, and stop the Alfa on the way back at some glorious sunset view point. 'Cheryl, my angel,' he'd say, his voice choking with emotion, while his fingers are played havoc with her...

'Chereel!' calls Signora Bardi. *'Andiamo!'*

'Andy Armo yourself,' mutters Cheryl.

The precise moment when Kimberley lost the part she so badly wanted was when the casting director spotted a tousled-haired girl from Phoenix with breasts to make a strong man weep. The director was not a strong man, but knew the public was old-fashioned that way.

Kimberley herself didn't get the bad news for several days, and her primal yell of rage might have been even louder had she known that at that very moment, Julia and Micheli were enjoying the meal that Cheryl had so lovingly foreseen, but with Julia rather than Cheryl being served the asparagus tips on the moonlit terrace.

Mercifully unaware that someone else is enjoying her dream, Cheryl is in her room carefully constructing a substantial ball out of frayed wool, pillow feathers, fluff from under the bed, pieces of dry grass and a bar of Signora Bardi's very expensive Dead Sea mud soap. Seeing this, anyone might well assume that the sun has addled Cheryl's practical, if underused, brains. However, as with the donkey, who has now spent several days with an indignant grasshopper tied to his tail, appearances can be deceptive.

Meanwhile, what a distraught Kimberley needs now is for someone to tell her she is wonderful no matter what, and make love to her until she sees stars, short of which, only wildly impulsive action on a continental scale will do. Without even checking her credit balance, Kimberley flounces off to the nearest airline ticket counter.

'Florence,' she snaps at the clerk. 'And a.s.a.p. Leave it open – I don't know when I'll be back. No, Florence, *Italy*. You know, as in Michelangelo?'

Is Florence ready for this? thinks the clerk, making her out a stand-by for that night. A quick check on time zones convinces Kimberley that it would be unwise to phone Micheli just then.

She is absolutely right. It is 2a.m. in Italy and the fifth night of passion in Micheli's antique carved bed. Julia is beginning to wonder if she can keep up this kind of intensity until Friday, and if Peter will notice any difference when she gets home. It is the first time she's thought of Peter, but what has been happening seems to bear no relation to her normal life, and it is none the worse for that, she tells herself sleepily. Both are perfectly real – just separate, that's all.

Kimberley doesn't have time to phone before she takes off. Somewhere along the way, she changes her destination to Assisi because it's nearer Perugia. By the time she gets there, she was so jet lagged that she goes straight to the first hotel she sees and crashes out. When she comes to, still feeling a little rocky, it is again too late in the day to phone. Next morning she tries Micheli's number, but being unfamiliar with Italian phones she isn't sure whether she's getting an engaged, ringing or unavailable tone.

'Oh, the heck with it, I'll just show up,' she mutters to herself, as lone travellers often do. She heads for the Hertz office, vaguely aware that on the way her trim body is being undressed and rearranged in interesting positions by passing workmen.

It is only half an hour by car from Assisi to Micheli's villa – but long enough for Julia and Micheli to be planning on staying in today and lounging round the garden, and for Cheryl to decide that this is the day for blocking the washing machine. In fact, Kimberley's hired red Fiat passes Signora Bardi in her white Mercedes en route for an expensive day at a fashion show in Perugia. It is also unfortunate that while every other woman for miles around knows by now that Micheli has a house guest, Cheryl's embryonic Italian hasn't picked up this vital bit of information.

Right, Cheryl tells herself. I'll just make sure the flaming *bambini* aren't wrecking anything valuable, and then it's flood time. She is just about to collect her carefully constructed ball of washing-machine-blocking gunge from its hiding place on top of the wardrobe when a piercing scream from outside sets her clattering down the slatted stairs like a flamenco dancer on heat.

Sitting on the path sobbing and holding her foot is Lucia. Her older brother, aged six, is trying to comfort her, while the other is laying about the donkey with a garden cane. Fortunately he is only three and a half.

'*Che cosa c'è?*' yells Cheryl. It's a phrase she's got off pat by now. For the moment too flustered to appreciate that fate has presented her with a genuine crisis on a plate, she examines Lucia's badly bruised and swelling foot. There is something like a hoof mark, and the child is obviously in pain. As Cheryl struggles to remember the word for hospital, the smallest Bardi trips and starts howling, while the donkey continues to behave strangely, kicking its back legs, lashing its tail and braying forlornly. Somehow, she gets to the phone and dials Micheli's number.

'It's that little English nanny at the Bardi place,' says Micheli coming back into the garden where Julia is sunbathing. 'She seems distressed and I can hear a child crying. Maybe it is two children. Can you talk to her, *cara mia?*'

'I think we'd better go over there,' says Julia after a few minutes of Cheryl. She feels sorry for the girl, having had similar days herself when her two were young. 'It might not be as bad as she thinks. How heavy is a donkey anyway? I suppose it might just have crushed a foot bone.'

At the villa gates, they draw up sharply at the sight of a small red Fiat trying to turn in, from which a tanned arm is waving frantically.

'Dio mio!' breathes Micheli, and closes his eyes.

By this time, Cheryl doesn't know if she is glad or sorry to see both an Alfa and a Fiat drive up, and not just Micheli but two attractive women come hurrying to her side, one English, one American. The necessities of the moment temporarily suppress whatever turmoil each is feeling as Julia quickly decides that the foot should be X-rayed. Micheli already has the two younger Bardis on his knee and is hearing a rambling, tearful confession about grasshoppers and donkeys' tails. All three women have time to notice how good Micheli is with children, but the effect on each is rather different.

He'll make a wonderful father, thinks Julia fondly, who, of the three, is bearing up the best under the strain of the other two's presence. He's nearly ready. He'll choose carefully, and probably for the right reasons. She has quickly computed the situation with Kimberley and is determined to be dignified about it. She knows instinctively that Kimberley will not be The One, and that is some comfort.

He's so gorgeous, Cheryl thinks as they carry Lucia to Micheli's sporty little Alpha, but he's more *Italian* than I thought. They all love kids. That's nice. But he's bound to be a Catholic. Best not to dwell too long on how many kids Micheli might want, since they are all discussing who should do what, but the first wispy clouds of reality are beginning to streak Cheryl's wide blue skies. At least she might get to go with him to the hospital. But, bloody hell, why didn't things ever turn out the way you wanted?

Kimberley at that moment is going through the nearest she will ever get to the Dark Night of the Soul. What with her professional confidence in shreds, the travelling, the cool Englishness of Julia, wailing children about which she knows nothing, and the shock of seeing Micheli in his natural habitat, she has a sudden desire to yell *Get me out of here – I can't handle this!* and rush back to the good old US of A.

They all agree that the children are best kept together, and with people they know. Only one other person can fit into Micheli's car with them, so it has to be Cheryl.

'*Ciao!*' he says, blowing one elegant kiss towards the two remaining women. 'Please be comfortable until I return.'

Comfortable! The word starts to inflate like a hot air balloon between them – vast, laughable, uncontrollable.

As Kimberley, still slightly muzzy-headed from jet lag, drives Julia back to Micheli's place, she is dimly aware that stowing her suitcase in the boot would have been better than throwing it on the back seat for all to see.

But it was too late now. 'Will you be staying long or are you – on tour?' Julia sweetly inquires.

'On tour, I guess. You too?' retorts Kimberley with an edge in her voice that Julia doesn't quite like.

'I'm just enjoying a short break. Umbria's so glorious at this time of the year, and Micheli's being wonderful.' Julia is not going to say that she'll be leaving in two days, and for once Kimberley can't bring herself to ask. The English dame was obviously older than Micheli. Must be well over forty, calculates Kimberley, adding a few years out of pique.

Soon she is telling Julia all about herself and wondering if it is just because this woman is English that Julia isn't coming through too.

'You're married, aren't you?' she says at last, and it isn't a question.

'Yes,' smiles Julia. 'With two boys. Three, if you count my husband.' And she laughs. 'You should try it some time.'

'No *thanks!*' But Julia's casual reply has rattled Kimberley more than she cares to admit. Could she have got it wrong, and it's women like Julia who had really cracked it? She must have had her kids early enough to feel free now – but at least she'd got them, together with some kind of security. Oh God, thinks Kimberley. I'll be thirty next year.

'You've got terrific skin,' she says, as they take wary positions round the white ironwork garden table, almost adding 'for your age'.

Julia is quite touched. 'It must be all that rain.' Then, after a slight pause, 'Too much sun can be rather wearing, don't you think?'

Micheli came back that afternoon to find Julia reading in the shade and Kimberley asleep in the guest room.

'Forgive this, *cara*,' he says. 'I did not invite her, you must believe that.'

No, we just kind of turn up, don't we? thinks Julia without bitterness, like moths to the candle, like pilgrims to the sacred mountain, looking for God knows what.

They make love that night, but the illusion has gone. For some reason, this is less important than Julia would have imagined, and she feels more relaxed, perhaps because she doesn't need to feel grateful any more. Turning to sleep at last, she half-smiles into the silk pillow as she remembers something from years ago in a film about Eskimos. 'Lend your sledge to a friend and it comes back cracked. Lend your wife to a friend and she comes back smiling.' It's what you're used to, I suppose, muses Julia.

Kimberley has the grace to check in to a hotel in Perugia, at least until the coast is clear. Alone on her balcony she looks out over the town, hating it for its ancient, foreign self-assurance, its masculine strength and hard-won stability. Unbidden, her hate for the place turns into a wave of pure, intense, undirected anger that in the great cosmic crap game she might just have been backing the wrong number. When it passes, she feels physically weak, but knows she's experienced something she can use, can work with, both professionally and personally, and it cheers her up. Soon she is rewriting her own script. 'There's a price for what I want to be', her new lines read. 'I found that out in a place called Perugia.' She has also seen that she's got just enough time on her side to find out if she really wants to pay the price, but that putting so much store on Micheli has already wasted enough of that precious time.

At the darkened Bardi villa, the washing machine glints unflooded in the moonlit kitchen, little Lucia is sleeping like an angel with a bandaged foot, and even the donkey dozes in peace. Quite worn out by the day's traumas, Cheryl dreams of being back home where the rules aren't so complicated. Looking at her pretty, near-innocent face, it would be hard to detect that some change has taken place. Yet Micheli has now passed gently from being something attainable back into her fantasy world where for her, he truly belongs.

On top of her wardrobe, the ball of gunge lies forgotten. Ironically, it will later take on an even more sinister appearance when coated with dead flies and dust, and cause Signora Bardi's maid to believe that the English girl might be a witch. Fortunately, nothing much comes of that sort of thing these days round Perugia, except that the maid makes the sign of the cross a lot while Cheryl is around, thereby convincing the girl that continentals are just as weird as everyone says. In the back of Cheryl's mind, however, is a growing belief that spoiling children the way they do out here is better than not loving them enough, and that she'll only marry a man who really likes children.

At the end of the week, as arranged, Julia and Micheli part with tears, kisses and promises of discreet emails. For that moment, each believes that this is not the end.

Before her flight, Julia has a couple of hours to spare in Florence and goes again, as everyone does, to the Palazzo Vecchio where the replica of Michelangelo's David draws all eyes. But this time she watches the crowds as well as the statue and wonders what exactly it is that people have come to see. The perfect man. The belief made visible, tangible, that there could ever be such a man who is simply that, and not part god?

Well, she thinks, stirring a last chocolate-scented cappuccino, we can't blame him for being only a statue in the sun, nor for allowing us to see in him only what each of us is capable of seeing. He's still wonderful all the same. Then she blows the David a kiss, and with the sun warm on her back, she shoulders her bag weighed down with presents for Peter and the boys and strolls off to find a taxi for the airport.

Out of Season

The French, declared Mme de Sauvigny, were so much better than the British at arranging these things...

'More champagne, madam? Sir?'

'Why not?' Rob Patterson put on his best smile. At last – a legal opportunity to have a good look at the face belonging to the lovely knees beside him. That was the trouble with plane seats; you could never see your neighbour properly without making an effort.

Good – she was holding out her glass, and yes, oh yes, the old instinct was spot on. It was a face worth waiting for – nicely angled to catch the light; intriguing, yet warm. Silky hair to match the silky two-piece that rustled...

Watch it, whispered the department of his brain responsible for scruples in the cause of self-preservation. How dare you take mental liberties with this delightful person before you even know her name.

'Landing in ten minutes,' cooed the stewardess. 'Have a lovely weekend.'

It was natural she'd assumed they were together. This was a Lovers' Weekend Special to Le Touquet, for heaven's sake. He'd only turned up on stand-by and got a cancellation. Maybe his neighbour had done the same. You could always hope – and he had exactly ten minutes to find out, in the most subtle way, of course.

'Beats Eurostar any day,' he tried, raising his glass. Amazing – her eyes were Channel-coloured, but only because it was looking unusually blue down there today.

The silk jacket stirred. Rob could almost hear its wearer thinking... *We're nearly there. I won't have to talk to this idiot for too long...* So he was pathetically grateful when what she actually said was, 'Oh yes, flying's much better for Le Touquet. You must be meeting someone. How nice.'

This required some of the famous Patterson quick thinking. 'Um, no.' Here goes, he decided. 'I'm a writer. I'm supposed to be doing a book on *La Belle Époque* – you know, the *Entente Cordiale*, Naughty Nineties and all that.' Don't patronise her, you fool.

She smiled. 'I noticed the lap-top. I should think Le Touquet's got just the right feel. Are you staying with friends?'

Better and better. 'I've got a few contacts, but I needed somewhere quiet, so I've taken a flat on the front. It's pretty reasonable, out of season. How about you?' He knew he was prattling, but by now he would happily have told her his life story – even about Ginny dumping him for his agent, just as he'd landed the book contract, the sneaky, go-getting little...

'My mother's half French, which comes in handy. There's some cousins with this beach house...

The seat belt sign has now been switched on...

Damn! Just as this was getting interesting.

'Are you being met?' He held his breath and prayed.

She shook her head. 'The cousins live in Paris most of the time. But I've got so much junk I'm taking a taxi. I'm a commercial artist, you see.'

'Really? Landscapes or people?' Suddenly he could see her on a cliff top in a trailing white Monet gown and parasol, the lively, lovely lines of her body leaning into the sea wind against an endless sky.

'I do buildings,' was the surprisingly reply, bringing him down to earth with a bump as the small plane landed none-too-smoothly on the tiny runway. 'I draw people's houses, restaurants, town halls – anything they'll commission.' She held out her hand and he felt its warmth hitting him in just the right spot, like a good whisky after a bad week. 'Sophie Fuller. Greetings cards, personalised stationery, trade calendars a speciality.'

By the time they'd cleared customs, Rob had persuaded her that a shared taxi could cope with their combined paraphernalia. He had even dropped it modestly into the conversation that he could perhaps put some commissions her way. After all, he already had a couple of interviews fixed up with the owners of some rather grand houses in the area – ladies whose family memoires of Le Touquet's Three Rs – royalty, racing and roulette – made delightfully scandalous copy. Now he even felt confidant enough to joke about founding a writers' and artists' colony.

The idea clearly appealed to Sophie. 'Brilliant,' she smiled. 'My fiancé would love that. He's coming out next week. He's in advertising, but it's the creative side he really prefers.'

Well it would be, wouldn't it! With that one quaint, coy, sickening word, Sophie had shredded the intricate web of fantasies weaving away in his head.

Pulling himself together, Rob managed to grab a taxi. On the way into town, they chatted away about how nice it would be to have proper French bread again, not the imitation English supermarket stuff. Or at least Sophie did, until at a sudden word from her, the taxi came to a teeth-gritting halt outside a beach house that was pure *Belle Époque* – all blue-grey stucco, white wooden shutters and lacy iron balconies. At any other time, Rob would have reached for his camera or started taking notes.

'Good luck with the writing,' said Sophie, gaily over-tipping the driver. 'I'm sure we'll see you around,' and Rob was left alone in the taxi with only a hint of Chanel No. 5 and the memory of whispering silk.

Settling into the little studio apartment felt a bit flat after that. For several days, a fine spring rain blew in from the sea to scatter some petals from the chestnut trees. The famous white Le Touquet sands remained deserted by all but a few determined ladies with large, expensive dogs. The less determined ladies with pooches like hand muffs on wheels, stayed sensibly in town, sipping *tisanes* with their friends beneath huge scalloped café awnings. Put them in huge hats, thought Rob, thumping away at his keyboard in an attempt to concentrate, and little would have changed since *La Belle Époque* – at least, not out of season.

Then there was his appointment tomorrow with Mme de Sauvigny, one of the local *grandes dames* who'd agreed to an interview. Fortunately, when it came to it, the weather decided on something a little more appropriate for early May, and next morning the ladies of Le Touquet were out in force.

As indeed was Mme de Sauvigny. When Rob stepped out of the taxi, she was advancing down her velvet front lawn being decisive to the gardener in very *English* French.

'Mr Patterson, how delightful,' she greeted him, with scarcely a break in the flow. 'And so young. With computers writing everyone's correspondence, it's impossible to tell. Does one even write one's love letters on them these days?'

Rob assured her that one didn't, and this seemed to please the old lady.

An hour later he was already full of wonderful coffee and shameless *pâtisseries*, and Mme de Sauvigny had only got as far as her actress mother's third titled lover. She herself had married a French racing millionaire who had spied her, aged seventeen, in the royal enclosure at Ascot. The French, she maintained, were far better at *arranging* these things than the British.

She insisted on showing him round the lovely period house, and was clearly enjoying herself so much that Rob felt it no liberty to mention Sophie and how she painted people's houses.

'But I have a man for that,' said the *grande dame* vaguely, her mind still on some distant scandal.

'Ah, no, *pictures* of houses,' Rob explained gently. If he could get Sophie a commission, it would be an excuse just to see her again, fiancé-in-advertising or no.

'Oh, an *artist*. I knew an artist once,' Mme de Sauvigny exclaimed with a twinkling of her many rings. 'Dreadfully unreliable – but such fun.' She glanced back at the magnificent façade of the old house. 'For a Christmas card, do you think? Why not? My friends would be so jealous. By all means ask the young lady to telephone me for an appointment. Now where was I?'

But did she mean it? The question nagged Rob as he walked off the pastries along a boulevard fresh with the young green of plane trees. But of course, English-French ladies kept their word – and she certainly wouldn't forget, not with that phenomenal memory of hers.

Now all he had to do was let Sophie know as soon as possible – so why not call in on his way back to the flat? Just the thought of seeing her again made him lengthen his stride. In a brisk fifteen minutes he was in sight of the blue and white beach house.

Then he frowned. There was a car outside – something dashing and continental. And there, enjoying the afternoon sunshine and a bottle of wine on the front veranda, was Sophie herself and a man, also dashing and continental. Somehow, Rob had assumed he'd be English, and Sophie did say he wasn't joining her for another week, but obviously the wretched man couldn't wait. Rob hated him on sight.

Feeling too dejected to disturb the pair, he crossed over and mooched home along the beach, kicking at the sand like a schoolboy. He stopped for a while and glared at the Channel, knowing he was being cowardly. The Channel, steely grey today, glared back. Why couldn't he have just walked right up and delivered the message? Okay, better drop a note in later when it was quiet.

And quiet it certainly could be in Le Touquet out of season, and lonelier than Rob would have thought possible, especially in the evenings. How much writing was a guy supposed to do without losing the plot?

A couple of days later, he was rather listlessly making some notes on Edward VII's gambling losses at the local casino when the phone rang. He eyed it nervously, hoping it wasn't his publisher demanding to know how things were going.

It was Mme de Sauvigny, small pooch yapping imperiously in the background, wanting to know why the 'artist gel' hadn't called. Several of her bridge partners were interested too.

That was all the excuse Rob needed to stop work and jog down the promenade to Sophie's place. He perked up when he saw the flashy car wasn't there, but then maybe that meant Sophie wouldn't be there either.

To his great relief, Sophie opened the door, and she seemed to be alone. She thanked him for his note and apologised for not taking up the contact.

'Sophie, are you all right?' he asked, swallowing hard. She seemed different – pale and rather strained.

'Yes,' she said quite sharply. 'Why shouldn't I be? Oh look, I'm sorry. You've been to so much trouble. There's some fresh coffee. Or I've got some red wine open, if you'd prefer.'

Rob would willingly have drunk a whole bottle of red ink for just a few more minutes of her company, but settled for coffee instead. She waved at a chair as she went through to the kitchen, and he took the chance to check out the living room. All very French and charmingly in period, except that something sticking out of the waste bin caught his eye. It was a very touristy, gilded upside-down Eiffel Tower. On a plaque at the base he could just make out the French for 'We'll always have Paris.'

Sophie returned with the coffee and saw him start away from it guiltily.

'Didn't fit, so I binned it,' she said. 'Please don't think me ungrateful, but I've been so busy. In fact I should be sketching at La Carousel by now. Do you know it?'

Rob shook his head.

'That terribly expensive seafood place by the war memorial. It's a pain, but this phone is incoming calls only when the family aren't here. I'll phone your Madame de Whatsit from the restaurant, I promise.'

'Don't let me hold you up.' Rob swallowed his scalding coffee too fast. 'I could walk over there with you, it's on my way,' he lied hopefully.

She accepted almost absent-mindedly and collected her things, which Rob was only too happy to help carry.

On the way out, she hesitated by the phone, as if willing it to ring. Was it the call that never came? Had she delayed going out for it? Well, that was certainly something a writer could relate to. Walking along together, she asked how his book was going, more out of politeness, he felt, than any real interest. Determined to lighten her mood, he tried a new tack.

'I thought your fiancé had arrived,' he said breezily. 'I was just passing the other day for some croissants. Terrific car.'

For a moment he thought she hadn't heard him. 'Car? Oh no, that would have been Bertrand. He's one of the cousins – fairly local. He just popped over to see if I'd settled in and to show off his new car.'

Rob's quite irrational urge to jump up and kiss a passing seagull was quickly stifled by her next words.

'Matthew's due tomorrow. If he can get away...'

Her voice tailed off, leaving him crushed beyond words. The only reason Sophie was down in her beautiful mouth was that the rat-bag might be somehow delayed.

With La Carousel already in sight, he thought of suggesting lunch there, then decided not to make a fool of himself. Feeling very let down, and with no valid reason to stay around, he helped to set up her easel and left her there sketching the rounded roof with its art nouveau twiddles, and looking like a fine watercolour herself.

The next day was torture for Rob, every time he pictured some complete prat called Matthew being met at the airport by a rapturous Sophie. Except for a furtive dash to the boulangerie each morning, he couldn't bear to go out in case he saw them together.

After three days, even he was tired of living on bread smeared with week-old *pâté* and camembert. He gave himself a good talking to in the shaving mirror, determined to put on some very black coffee and get down to knocking his research into shape – which he managed to do for a good ten minutes before the phone rang.

It was all he could do to curb his impatience when a familiar yapping down the line heralded Mme de Sauvigny.

'Oh do be quiet, Hortense, you naughty girl,' she greeted him. 'Now Rob, I've just remembered something frightfully interesting for you. Shall I expect you at eleven?'

There wasn't much he could do. At half past eleven, he was still sitting on a very uncomfortable white ironwork chair with Hortense chewing his laces, wondering if Mme de Sauvigny was ever going to get to the point. So far, she'd done little except talk about Sophie's visit and what a delightful *gel* she was, well interspersed with observations about young people today not having enough romance in their lives, divorce being so undignified and true love being worth gambling for, scheming for and certainly worth waiting for, after all the time and effort one should put into it.

Rob began to feel his smile and his attention slipping. Thoughts of deadlines and doing something dreadful to Hortense were beginning to get the upper hand – until suddenly it dawned on him what all this was about.

'Take this dreadful man poor Sophie has been involved with,' she was saying, pausing only to call indoors for another pot of *tisane*. 'Married, wouldn't you know. Three children, some poor little wife, no doubt. Of course the wretch isn't going to leave them. They should teach them that at school – much better for them than all that netball and cookery.'

Rob forgot about kicking Hortense. 'You mean...' he began.

'She should have seen it coming. Such a cowardly letter – typed, if you please – and on the very day she was expecting him. She was so upset, poor girl – just had to confide in someone. This kind of thing is very bad for morale, don't you think?'

'Dreadful,' murmured Rob, his heart singing so loudly he could even have hugged Hortense.

'And away from home, too. I know she's half French, but it's not the same. She kept saying what on earth was the good of Paris. What do you suppose she could have meant by that?'

'Er, um...,' said Rob.

'I didn't like to press her at a time like that, but one has to rally round. So I'm going to find her lots of wonderful houses to draw to take her mind off it.'

And keep her here, too, you clever old darling, thought Rob. And keep her *here*.

'Madame,' he said when he could get a word in, 'have you tried that new place, La Carousel? I'd love to take you to lunch, if I may. This could be the beginning of a beautiful friendship.'

'I should certainly hope so,' said the old lady, admiring her twinkling rings with a far-away look in her eyes. 'Really, there's so little for one to do these days in Le Touquet out of season.'

Girl on a Donkey

She was a local heroine, but if her lonely statue on the hill top could speak,
what other story might it tell?

No, don't go. I could see you looking up at me as the guide was talking.
You have a thoughtful face, dear visitor, and that little story of his has
left you wondering.

Listen, it's me, not the wind – the girl you're looking at, cast in
bronze. See my name at the foot of the statue – Mila Gojsalic – here on
my lonely crag overlooking the valley. And the date – 1530.

You like my country, dear visitor, I can tell. You see a wild beauty
here – bare white mountains above a skirt of scented pines, against the
deep blue Adriatic. You smiled when the tour guide told you that we
have the same word here for 'visitor' and 'guest'. You liked that.

Yet from where I stand, the view is different. I see only rocks too
high for goats, slopes grazed to the bone, winter firewood, and a sea
where strange sails meant death. And did your guide also tell you that
our word for 'stranger' also means 'enemy'? Maybe not. Enemies, we
fear. It's only each other we hate.

Here I stand, heavy peasant skirt caught by some eternal wind,
headscarf squarely tied, looking defiantly towards the sea. Mila Gojsalic,
the goatherd, patron of that town down there – Omis, where I was born.
How I hated them once. Yet if saints weren't out of fashion here, they'd
have made me one by now. I'd have flowers and candles in the church
and a yearly procession. I would have liked that. Some joke that would
be.

So, dear visitor, you heard the guide tell how I got my statue – how
brave little Mila Gojsalic who was only sixteen, saved Omis from the
Turks all those years ago. You were only mildly curious at first, your eyes
still on the distant peaks of the Makarska as if you wanted to take them
home in your head. Then you began to weigh up the guide's story. My
story. Was it really like that – one young girl against all those Turks?

But of course, it's one of those quaint local folk tales, and none the worse for it being about a girl. Local heroine – that's nice.

That guide, by the way, he's not from round here. He's from Zagreb – got it from the books, I suppose. Now me, I never learned to read, although I wasn't stupid. If a goat was missing I always knew which one. When the storytellers came, I would creep in at the back of the circle hoping no one would send me away, and take it all in like hot soup you can taste a long time after. I could remember all the verses better than the boys.

But it was my eyes, you see. The left one was crooked. See-the-devil-round-corners, they called me. No, it's no good looking – they set it straight for the statue. Couldn't have a heroine with the evil eye, could we? Up here, I have the best view for miles. It's amazing what you can see when your eyes are straight. They gave me that, at least. But what I see is not as they would see it, nor ever was.

Let me say then, that the guide told you the bare bones of the truth, but bare bones need flesh on them, or a horse's skull could be a donkey's. Not my little Marco, of course. I'd have known him anywhere, dead or alive, by the halter I plaited for his bell. Marco, the copper bell, a sheepskin cover and a cooking pot were all my mother left me.

So it is quite true that one spring day a marauding band of Turks, part militia, part pirate, appeared along the coast, and correct too that, although the town was fearful, there was no outright panic. It had happened before, so the sea walls were in reasonable repair, and although the cannon were old, they made a great deal of noise when fired – just to show them. Preparations were made in the none-too-orderly fashion of our town, which is no bad thing if the enemy sees the fuss. The flocks were called in, weapons sharpened, grain stores checked, and the Council of Elders hanged one man for hoarding to show it was serious and got the prisoners out on the ramparts hauling stones. The men brushed up their moustaches and declared they were ready to die, and everyone cheered.

For six sleepless days and nights, the people of Omis, united for once, watched and prayed. Sails furled, the Turkish warships hung around the headland out of range. People said they could smell them on the wind – six ships, low in the water from the weight of cannon. A party came ashore with water barrels, but soon returned, and still there was no attack.

Then, miraculously, the town awoke to see the bay was empty. The watch said they had slipped away to fall on some other hapless town, but what was that to us if we were safe? Oh, the joy and boasting. Our preparations had made them think twice, our men were too fierce; our walls too strong...

The Council ordered a great feast with patriotic songs, and everyone danced in the market square – even me. I was not so much happy, as glad to be alive, which is not the same thing. But then, not to have been killed or sold in some heathen slave market was enough to dance for, wouldn't you say, dear visitor, even for a girl with the evil eye?

What happened next is as old as war, so they say. Before the month was out, a wounded shepherd crawled back into Omis to say the Turks had landed further up the coast and then done the impossible. Hauling their cannon with them, they had cut inland across the Makarska peaks into the Cetina valley, and were now dug in on the rocky plateau right behind us.

The men nodded grimly. Taking that position would be next to impossible. Worse, the shepherd said they were building rafts. Even the children could understand what that meant. The Turks were going to float their cannon down river and take Omis from the land.

This time the town was truly paralysed with fear. The seaward defences were strong, but since the people inland were our kind, the land walls had been left to crumble for years. Yet now the elders were saying that the inlanders were cowardly and corrupt, and we could expect no help from that direction. The men stopped boasting. The women hid their faces in their scarves, and kitchen knives in their skirts.

Then, as the terrified townsfolk huddled together, our brave Council came up with a plan. You heard the guide describe the scene.

'The town cannot be defended against cannon from the land side,' the elders declared. 'And it would be suicide to storm their camp so, like the Greeks of old, we must find a way by cunning. Someone must go into the Turkish camp selling wine laced with *raki* and poison. Someone the Turks won't suspect. A young girl would be best – innocent looking, but strong and brave. When the wine has done its work, she can set their powder store alight, and boom! The town will be saved. It's the only way. But where, oh where, can we find such a one?'

Picture the consternation. Mothers weep and hide their daughters' faces. Then up steps little Mila, so the story goes. Can't you just see it?

'I will do the deed, dear people of Omis,' I bravely declare. 'With my faithful donkey, I will walk fearlessly into the lions' den. I will load my little Marco with the wineskins and ring his bell as I go. The foolish Turks will take me for a whore or a simpleton. I'll say I'm an outcast, parentless, and only want to make a living. I will do whatever is necessary to stay alive until I fire the camp, and if I die in the attempt, what is that to me if I can save my beloved town?'

Naturally, they cheer my courage and the blessings of the town follow me as I set out, head high. Strong men shed noble tears and the women wail and pray as I set off with Marco into the cold dawn, the fatal wineskins bumping on his flanks.

It's a good story, is it not? And like all good stories it goes exactly to plan. At the camp, the Turks are at first suspicious, then greedy, then lecherous, but finally stupid. I have to surrender my virtue before the evening is out, that goes without saying. But what is that, compared to saving my people? When they are all too drunk or sick to care, I creep into the powder store with my lantern, and then there is a mighty boom they can hear right down in Omis.

The rest is just as neat. Next day, my little Marco limps back to town without me. Clearly I have given my all and perished in the confusion, but how great is the rejoicing! The men set out to chase the survivors around the hills and not one Turk gets back alive to the ships. Then the townsfolk weep for me and make up brave songs to my memory. What a lovely story to tell the children! In the end, I get a nice bronze statue. How pleasant it is to boast of such courage to the other towns, and these days, to our visitors.

Don't worry about the time. Stand in my shade where it's cooler. The others are still taking pictures. I won't let you miss the coach. I promise you won't need pictures to remember this place. It will come back to you clearly enough when you hear what really happened to turn me from flesh and blood into cold bronze.

It would be easier to say that the real story started on the night we thought the Turks had gone, but in truth it began a long time before that. You see, I think they were always a little afraid of me – the quiet orphan with the crooked eye.

I never knew which of them was my father, but he knew himself. My mother told me he had given her a donkey in foal for her silence. I liked to believe that he was an important man – maybe one of the Council, but try as I might, I could find none with a crooked eye. Marco was the donkey's foal, and when my mother died when I was about eight years old, he was all I had to love.

Yet from her I sensed that if I kept my eyes cast down, my face had some kind of beauty, even if the others wouldn't look at me. I should also tell you that this statue makes me look too sturdy, too square. By sixteen, I had long legs, a straight back, high breasts and narrow hips, and a newfound instinct whispered that, but for my eye, I would not have been unpleasing.

But who would take a dowerless goatherd? When I began to understand these things, I made up my mind that if I couldn't marry, no man was going to have me. Evil eye or no, there are many men for whom all cats are grey in the dark, but that wasn't my way – until I saw Gregor Pavic. The guide didn't mention him, did he? He was in the town guard, tall and straight in his boots of best calf leather. His hair had colours in it when the sun shone, like the coat of a good horse, and there never was a man who so filled my dreams.

And dreams were all – until that night when we thought the Turks had sailed away. The wine was free and everyone was drunk of course, even me, just a little. We know how to drink, our people – not like the Turks. Strong drink is forbidden in their country. But away from it, that's different.

So when, towards midnight, Gregor came and took me by the waist to dance the *kolo*, I didn't need more wine. His eyes and beard were dark as a Turk's in the moonlight, but his skin was clear and fine. I knew then that he would follow me later, back to my shack. And when he did, he took care with me so that it didn't hurt, although I'd been afraid from listening to the market women.

But after a while, I found a great delight in it, which the women hadn't mentioned, and so, I thought, did Gregor. It came to me then as something new and strange that merely being alive would never again be quite enough.

I knew he wouldn't marry me, but by then it seemed to matter less. One day he'd marry some whey-faced town girl, but still come to me in secret, and that way I would keep him. For now it was enough that we were together almost every night – until the news came about the Turkish camp high up the river.

Now let me say here that the Council elders never did announce their plan publicly to the town. The first I knew of it was when they came to my shack one night as I was waiting for Gregor. I never knew whose idea it was, but perhaps such ideas simply take hold when men are in council and they all feed off each other.

'There's no use sending a man. They'd just kill him and take the wine.'

'Definitely a girl then – but she can't be anyone's *daughter*, or we'd have a blood feud on our hands.'

'One of the whores, perhaps? But could we trust them?'

'We could give her a dowry – if she gets out alive.'

'But who would have her, after the Turks?'

The thought goes round – someone dispensable, disposable. Mila Gojsalic with the evil eye, perhaps? And as they say it, they spit to the side as usual, to chase away bad luck.

'And is she still... ?'

Discrete inquiries are made. Then not so discrete. Gregor told them about us, I know he did, to ease their consciences. I saw his face in the group when they came to find me, and I knew.

They didn't even have the grace to ask. They simply explained the plan and about the dowry if it succeeded.

'But suppose they kill me straight away for seeing the devil-round-corners,' I asked, staring hard at Gregor, who looked at the floor .

'The Turks are not particular in these matters,' said the Leader. 'And think, if they take the town, you'll be killed along with the rest of us anyway, or taken into slavery.'

I saw then that my only worth to them was as the scapegoat driven out into the wilderness. A goatherd has a feeling for such Bible stories. They were so certain of themselves that they'd even brought along the poisoned wineskins. I was told to watch and listen while they loaded Marco, as if I was an imbecile.

'Two skins of good wine first, so that they don't suspect – at the front on each side. Then two more laced with *raki,* here, on the donkey's left flank. Stay still, you foolish beast...'

'The poisoned wine goes behind on his right. Keep it away from them and serve it only after the raki wine, at the very last when they're getting drunk and careless. They mustn't get sick too soon.'

'Better save yourself some with the *raki* for when the Turks get fresh,' said another. 'But don't get it wrong, or you'll never find the powder tent.'

At that, they all laughed. I didn't hate them until then.

The rest of the town would not be told until they heard the explosion, in case there were spies. I should set off before dawn with Marco's hooves well-wrapped and his bell muffled. Once clear, I was to walk openly all day like a wandering peddler, and if I got within sight of the Turkish camp without an arrow in my back, I was to act boldly, even sing a little.

How can I describe that journey as I turned my face from Omis and took the path to the river? The sun was shining as it is now and there were bright yellow butterflies in the meadow flowers along the track edging the valley. The water of the Cetina had that strange colour of green glass beads against the blue of the sea beyond, just as you see it down there today. Such a morning might have gladdened my heart even then, but I had seen Gregor's face when they came. Now I didn't really want to live – but had no wish to die. I couldn't turn back, and my mouth was dry with fear.

In the hot part of the day, it crossed my mind to drink the poisoned wine there and then and have done with it, but Marco was thirsty too and led me to a place where the river water was cool on the stones. I drank it gulping as if to cure a fever.

It was only when I caught the glint of armour high on the crags above the scrub, that I realized I had only been pretending at fear. Although I was out of arrow-shot, I had to walk on knowing the Turkish scouts had seen me. To calm the shaking, I kept my hand on Marco's furry ears and tried to sing to him.

It was coming on for dusk before I saw any more Turks – just when I was almost ready to believe that a miracle might happen and I'd be able to walk right past their camp, and on to heaven knew where. But then I saw them – a pair on horseback riding towards me, white dust flying, lances high. They are *djins*, I thought in terror. If I cross myself and spit they cannot harm me. Yet from the pounding of the hooves, I knew these were no devils-round-corners, and all I had was my poor wits if I wanted to draw another breath.

Still as a rock, I waited until they lowered their lances for the charge. Then I jumped and waved like a puppet, arms over head, as if pleased to see them. Almost as their dust reached me, I grabbed a wineskin and held it out at arm's length. For an instant, I truly thought they would still run me through there and then, and in that moment it seemed that it was Gregor's face above the lance.

A great pain tore through me, as if my heart had indeed been pierced. Transfixed by it and pale as death itself, I'm sure, I stood my ground. At the very last, the rider swerved and looped the wineskin onto his lance. He swung it in, sniffed at it like a dog, and they started shouting to each other through the swirling dust in their thick, dark voices. The leader pushed me back against Marco with his lance at my ribs and gestured for me to drink.

Did I somehow manage to smile as I gulped the wine? I know I jangled some coins in my apron pocket, gesturing to the other skins, and ahead to where I thought the camp must be.

It worked, in that they decided they had better uses for me than to kill me there and then. It was getting dark, but I recognized the place when we reached it. There were steep drops on three sides with only one path up. The guides never mention it today. Perhaps it's been forgotten, along with so much else.

For the next part, perhaps you would say I was lucky. They pulled and prodded Marco and me up the narrow track to the camp, where an excited, babbling group were waiting for the booty to arrive. But they fell back as the Bey came from his tent at the disturbance. From his gestures, it was clear that I was to be kept for him first.

As he left, the others, leering and squeezing, let me serve them the wine. One squinted and turned his eye, pointing, and they laughed. It wasn't fear, but childlike amusement, and I wondered which was worse.

Some more arrived, smelling worse than goats, and from their tools I could see they'd been working on the raft down at the river. I also noticed the powder store was very near the path, and that the rest of the tents were in a rough double circle with the Bey's tent on the far side.

With the drinking, they began some kind of gambling game. I opened the third and fourth skins with the *raki*-laced wine praying that they wouldn't notice the new taste. Omis wine is thick and dark, but there'd been enough raw spirit added to those skins to drop a mule. I tried not to watch them, even as I realized that they were playing for their turn after the Bey had done with me, and my very skin felt stung by nettles.

Yet as a plan, it was working. For one thing, I was still alive. I didn't struggle as they led me through the maze of pegs and ropes across the open cooking space to the Bey's tent. I clutched one of the near empty wineskins to me like a child with a rag doll, but my see-the-devil-round-corners eyes were busy. Before they pushed me in, I spotted the horse lines at the rear, and also how the rest were at last pulling the poisoned wineskins from Marco's side and drinking freely.

Without his turban and armour, the Bey looked old. He was bald and fat, but he didn't smell as bad as the others. There was water in a big leather bucket in a corner, and he made a gesture for me to wash. Some instinct told me not to make it difficult for myself, so I tried to stop trembling and slowly took off my clothes down to my shift. In the bucket was a strange thing like a bread crust but soft and full of little holes. He seemed almost amused as I touched it nervously, then he signed for me to squeeze it and wash with it. He didn't look drunk enough, and I started to shiver, not knowing what to do.

On a wooden chest was a horn beaker, so I filled it from the wineskin and knelt before him, eyes down, offering it. That seemed to please him. He took the beaker, and the lust in his eyes gave me a strange feeling of power. Feeling suddenly as if nothing could hurt me, I rose like a dancer and let the shift slip slowly to my feet. As he drank, greedily eyeing my nakedness, I raised the wineskin to my lips and drank too, letting the dark wine trickle down my body.

He gave a kind of moan, pulled me to him and reached out to quench the lantern. I felt myself crushed under his writhing bulk and let myself go limp. I tried holding my breath, then bit into my hand so as not to cry out and anger him. After that, it was over quickly. It could have been much worse from what I'd heard of their customs. He spent himself quickly, and was soon snoring like an old dog on his mat.

The snoring was so loud that I was afraid the guard would come in for me, but when I risked a peep outside, I saw, to my amazement, that both guards were in a dead sleep. One was twitching and his face looked a strange colour. A bonfire was flickering in the open space and some were dancing while others reeled about. Somewhere, I could hear vomiting. But not all of them would be too drunk to guess the deadly truth.

Feeling round in the dark tent for my clothes, I came across one of the Bey's silk tunics and pulled it on. There was a good moon, and moving like a bobcat onto sheep, I stole the purple-faced guard's dagger and crept towards the horse lines. I longed to see my poor little Marco, but he was back by the path near the powder store.

For one great long moment, I looked up at the moon, and knew I didn't have to die. With any luck, I could have found my way over the steep edge and hidden in some caves that were only an hour's walk away until they tired of looking for me. Then I could have crept back to Omis, or maybe to some inland town. But there were shouts of alarm now, and I knew I had looked too long at the moon.

Whispering to the horses to calm them, I cut their halters, hoping they wouldn't bolt too soon. How I wanted to leap on one and ride free. But to what – failure, even death, in my own town, or fear and loneliness in another? For what, after all, had I so far achieved but to make a few Turks drunk or deathly sick?

I thought of them all back in Omis under the same moon, shaking with fear – of Gregor, of whichever one was my father, of the whisperers and the spitters, and the one who said 'Don't get it wrong, Mila Gojsalic,' and I thought, clear as a bell, to the devil's horns with all of you. You don't deserve it – but I'll save you anyway. I'll *make* you remember me.

There was only one plan now, and that was mine. This was my will, not theirs, and I would do it, not from love or hate, but simply because I knew I had the power in me. Keeping the dagger, I ripped off the flapping tunic and ran, naked as the moon, full tilt towards the campfire. I moved so fast that they didn't see me until I was amongst them. It wasn't too difficult to dart through the lounging bodies and snatch up a burning brand. Slashing at their grabbing hands, I leapt over the tent ropes, in and out, until I could see Marco and the powder tent.

Without pausing in my stride, I threw the knife to hit Marco on the rump, yelling like a wild thing in a voice that wasn't mine, 'Run, Marco, run!' and when he started away, I shouted, 'Tell them – remember me.'

They were after me now, any that could still move, and this time it wasn't for lust. The less befuddled had seen where I was heading.

I reached the leather tent of the powder store with the brand still burning and tried to set it alight, but they must have kept it damp in case of sparks. They were almost on me now, yelping like wolves in the dark as I darted inside. There was nothing for it but to hurl myself at the nearest keg and overturn it, then plunge the brand into the gritty, yielding powder.

That was my last act on earth before a dozen Turks, a great roar and the blinding, searing flash of eternity overtook me. Yet all I could think of as my spirit joined the wind was that my little Marco was safe, and that I, Mila Gojsalic, who never did see the devil round corners, had beaten them all.

So what do *you* think, dear visitor with the thoughtful face? Does it make more sense to you now – more than all that virtuous self-sacrifice, that virgin-martyr courage? What you see depends on where you're standing, does it not? And they did remember me, didn't they – after their fashion?

Good, you're nodding, smiling a little, glad you stayed awhile and listened to the wind. Better go now. They're getting back into the coach, and this is a lonely place when the sun goes down. But you will remember me?

The Trumpet Vine

Suntaree was as beautiful as the day she'd arrived in Bangkok from the north looking for a brighter future - but the simple life was all Vipak had to offer.

It was the splash of a coconut falling into the klong which woke Vipak that morning. Beside him, his wife stirred and asked sleepily, 'Shall I get it?'

'Go back to sleep,' he told her, all the more irritably because he knew he was being unkind.

The breath of her hill-country voice was sweet, even in the mornings – yet the question irritated him. Surely Suntaree had lived down here long enough now to tell the difference. The older ones made a much heavier splash.

'I only thought, if it was a green one...'

He heard her sigh as she pulled the quilt more closely around her. For a green one, she would have got up quietly, found her long-handled frog net and rescued it without even waking his mother or next door's cockerel. The old ones were hardly worth fishing out these days, but fresh green coconuts sold for ten *baht* to the hotels and bars because the tourists liked them filled with fancy cocktails, orchids and tiny parasols. At least Suntaree knew that much.

Vipak lay there in the perfumed dark pretending to be asleep, knowing that his wife was awake too, but unwilling to explore his troubled feelings too deeply. Suntaree had given him no real cause for anger, so how could he feel angry? She was still as pretty as when he had first seen her at the central bus station, just down from the North, bewildered and looking for work. Everyone said the girls from Chiang Mai were the prettiest, and he'd soon found that Suntaree had a quick brain without the sharp tongue that so often went with it.

He'd found her a job in the factory where he worked, but his mates had teased him. 'A girl like that could earn good money in a bar or shop

– even in a hotel. She'll be off when she learns some English. She's too good for you.'

Suntaree said the close machine work made her frown and squint, and she didn't seem to mind when they had to move south back to Saduak because his mother's sight was failing. At least there were no fares or rent to pay and the family plot beside the klong was still producing vegetables and coconuts.

'How the trumpet vine has grown,' he'd said to his mother, for it was the one good thing to say about his old house when he saw it again. The massive creeper had claimed one of the main timbers as its jungle tree. 'It looks like it's the only thing holding up the house.'

'It's the same with you, son, now I'm old,' replied his mother. 'But there are so many changes here, so fast... I'm almost glad I can hardly see much these days, although I can hear the noise. You won't recognize the Floating Market. The long-tail boats are full of tourists now, all taking pictures, even at monsoon time. My old friends don't go there now. We just trade quietly in the back *klongs* where I know they won't cheat me.'

It was true, thought Vipak, as the cracked voice of next door's cockerel started the day. Motorised long-tails had made life easier for the traders and guides at first. Now there were just too many of them, churning the muddy waters of the *klongs* into waves that ate into the banks where the stilt houses grew like mangroves.

He gave up trying to sleep. Soon it would be light, which meant less than an hour of peace before the first long-tails roared by. The cargo was always the same – big, pale *farang* with their zoom lens and camcorders that cost a good year's income from the farm.

At first, Suntaree had seemed content in her new surroundings, with a mother-in-law who was kind and needed her help. But lately, Vipak had seen his wife gazing into the water as if looking for something else beside her own delicate reflection. She never talked about her own home, but once, just once, she said she missed Bangkok – which Vipak took to mean the wages from the factory.

'But this is your place now,' Vipak told her, 'and we have enough to eat. When my father was alive, this was the best coconut grove on the klong. If we both work hard, we can live well enough here.'

'So please, Vipak,' murmured his wife, 'will you mention to your respected mother that now is not the time for a baby? Every morning she asks if I am feeling well, but I know what she's thinking.'

They'd agreed that they should wait a while before starting a family. After all, the boat needed mending and getting a motor scooter would take most of their savings. Then there was last season's banana stock that needed replacing.

'I'll explain to her that this is the modern way,' he'd told his wife. But of course, he hadn't.

The thought of all the work to be done made Vipak turn restlessly on his side of the mat. Maybe he should see about getting some big stones to bank up the foundations. If the long-tail traffic went on like this, they'd soon have no house left.

Quietly, he wrapped his sarong tighter and got up. At the side of the house, he had a drink from the rain butt beside the trumpet vine and paused, as he had often done as a child, to measure one of its dark, shiny leaves against his hand. The scent of the heavy cream flowers, large as soldiers' bugles, was strongest in the night hours. Even in Bangkok, Vipak had never seen a finer vine than this one.

'Aiee!' He jerked his hand away as a large spider dropped onto it from the inside of a flower. He didn't kill the creature although it was the stinging kind, since all living things were there for our enlightenment, but as he watched it scuttle off, he knew what his lesson was this morning – that with such beauty comes fear and danger. It was a lesson he was learning fast.

There was no one about as he went down the wooden steps to the *klong* and had his morning wash in peace. The water didn't look very clean, until you held some in your hands, up to the light. Then it looked much better.

Somewhere in the distant maze of waterways, the roar of a long-tail shattered the quiet. Soon it would begin. Vipak gave himself a final, despairing sluice with his bath scoop as if it would wash his bad thoughts away, then straightened up. But his fears clung like engine oil to a shirt.

At first, he'd hardly noticed that it was often only outside his own home that the long-tails stopped for photographs. It was the trumpet vine of course, hanging so gracefully over the old wooden house, hiding its decay. He hadn't minded then. After all, it was an obvious place for a picture, and what could you do? The *farang* usually looked happy enough, in spite of their hairy legs and funny hats. You got used to it – even the women. They'd take their shots, smile, wave, and then roar off in a flurry of water and exhaust fumes. And then he'd begun to notice how often Suntaree would just happen to be down on the steps doing the washing, preparing vegetables, straining rice, combing her long wavy hair...

But he wasn't always there. You couldn't watch your wife all day, that was the worst of it. A man had to work, and work hard – hoeing the vegetables under the palms, checking the fish traps, splitting coconuts on the iron spike his father had used before him and hacking out the fibre, red as *farang* hair. And then a man could get to thinking.

Vipak felt the spring of the wooden floor inside as Suntaree got up. In no time she would have the bowls of tea steaming and the breakfast rice ready. Then he would have to leave – leave his pretty wife, guarded only by his near-blind mother, to the procession of long-tails and the endless photographs.

'Just one more, honey, by those big white flowers.'

'Can you ask her to lean over a little more?'

'Isn't she a picture?'

They both knew enough English now for all that.

'I'm going to walk to the road depot to ask for some big stones,' he told her. 'Our house is not safe.'

'So early?' asked his wife with her lovely smile as she gathered the dishes into the washing basket.

'It's a long way.' He set off along the bank until he found the path that led behind his neighbour's house and back through to their own land. There was no one about. Feeling like a thief, he crept along until he could see the back veranda, and then froze. His mother was already up and sitting there as she often did with her pan lids ready to bang in the direction of monkeys when they noisily raided the vegetable gardens. He felt ashamed of his smile of relief that she could not see him.

But his mind was made up. Moving quietly as a jungle cat he reached the side of the house where the trumpet vine grew and took up his position behind its dense screen.

Several times he was stung by insects lurking in its shadows, but it wasn't long before he heard the first long-tail approaching. And then, just as he'd feared, Suntaree appeared on the steps, still in her flowery night sarong, hair loose, the basket of dishes balanced at her slim waist.

'And here is a typical old-style house of the *klongs*', he heard the guide say. 'With one of our charming girls about her daily work. Time for pictures, please.' He was a very smart young man in a clean white shirt and dark trousers.

'Oh, it's so quaint!' The word was new to him. What was *quaint*?

'Did you get the flowers in, George?'

'Isn't she a doll? What's your name, honey?'

Then he heard his wife's voice say quite clearly and in English, 'My name is Sunny. One day I like to go to Bangkok. You can help me, please?' Risking a look, he saw her choose a clean bowl from the washing-up basket and pass it shyly to the guide.

They'd been well prepared. Coins clinked and notes floated in like leaves. Almost too shocked to draw back into the shadows, Vipak fought a dreadful surge of anger struggling to the surface as the idling engine picked up speed and a wave of muddy water swirled against the bank. He felt as if he was drowning, choking, in a tide of jealousy and fear.

He had to wait until it was time for Suntaree to take his mother to the clinic in their tiny boat before he could come out, but he knew what he had to do. He went to find his panga and hacked and chopped at the trumpet vine like a madman until not a single leaf was left, and then he started on the root.

'We saw the first pieces near the Danong Bridge,' sobbed his wife, holding a damp blossom to her cheek.

'I had to do it,' said Vipak sternly. 'It was destroying our house,' he added in a gentler tone. Now that his rage had died down, he did not want it to be disturbed again by the look in his wife's eyes.

'I shall miss it,' said his mother, clinging tightly to Suntaree's hand. 'The scent made the whole house sweet. Especially in the mornings...'

There was heavy rain that night, enough to set the house timbers creaking. Vipak slept eventually as the storm died away, but in the quiet before dawn an unmistakable light splash awoke him.

'Now *that's* a green one,' he said in a kindly way into the darkness. 'But you stay in the warm, Suntaree. I'll fetch it out.'

There was no reply.

Puzzled, he reached for the soft warmth of her body, for the scent of her, but the room smelt only of mud and dead leaves – and beside him, the sleeping mat was empty.

Love is Like a Butterfly

Stephanie was taking her singles holiday in Crete like medicine after the divorce...

Stephanie didn't much like waking up in the morning these days, now there was no one else in the bed. And what was that appalling noise? It sounded like a punctured klaxon just below the window.

Of course – it had to be a donkey. She'd seen some yesterday on the road from the airport.

'Go away!' she murmured, and buried her head under the hotel sheets to muffle the insistent braying. Had it all been a dreadful mistake, this holiday alone? It was the boys who'd talked her into it.

'Go on, Mum, just book it, we'll be all right at Gran's.'

And good old Mum had said, 'It's just what you need – and there's bound to be a few others in the same boat.'

They'd meant well, of course. The boys had taken it better than she'd feared and were adjusting in their own way, as teenagers do. For her, the shock, after the first shattering blow, had been finding out, not so much that she missed Ian, but that she was afraid of her own company – of going out alone, of facing herself in the mirror each morning...

Then her alarm started pinging – she'd set it quite early so as not to give way to just lying there pretending things weren't happening. Maybe if she threw it a biscuit or something, it would keep quiet.

But no, just getting out of bed was part of the process, they said.

Up! she commanded. That's all over now – isn't it?

She padded barefoot over to the shutters, then gasped as they swung open. It was like walking into a film; the light was so different. The very air was butterfly blue and smelt of warm bread and honey. In the pines, a thousand insects buzzed and whirred a greeting, and beyond the spread of rosy pink and white bushes that reached almost to the sea, she could see her early morning alarm call, tethered near the beach café, head back and still going strong.

'Ssh!' hissed Stephanie. It must have woken half the hotel by now, but at least it would be something to talk about at breakfast.

Breakfast. The thought of having to walk alone into a room full of strangers filled her with dread. Now don't get silly again, she told her pounding heart.

Suddenly the desperate braying stopped. She peered across the greenery and saw a little old lady in widow's black making her way slowly across the stark white sand. There had been women dressed like that in the brochure, spinning outside white-washed cottages, but this one was dragging a sack, had a bag over her shoulder, and was collecting litter. Stephanie felt a surge of indignation tinged with pity. At that age, it didn't seem right that she had to be clearing up after the tourists, just so they could say how unspoilt it was.

The donkey, on the other hand, seemed to have cheered up at the sight of her, and now that he'd stopped his serenade, she could hear another sound – a kind of high-pitched chant. And then it all fitted in – the stooped, head-scarfed figure was actually singing to the donkey. She put down the rubbish sack, rummaged in what Stephanie had taken for a shoulder bag and took out an apple. Then she looped the leather contraption over the donkey's nose. Wiping the apple on her skirt, she took a bite, patted the donkey's rump and headed off towards the café dragging the litter sack and munching. It was breakfast time down there too, and somehow it didn't seem such a big deal any more.

The worst moment was standing there with her tray from the buffet and finding there wasn't an empty table on the terrace. She felt like dropping everything and running, but just in time, a friendly female voice behind her came to the rescue.

'There's room over there with me and Aileen, if you like. My name's Rita.'

With a grateful smile, Stephanie followed the statuesque red-head to a table where her friend was trying out her Greek on the waiter. By her third cup of coffee, Stephanie knew all about Aileen's separation and Rita's 'ex', and was already beginning to feel a bit more in touch.

'Men, who needs them?' Aileen was attacking a croissant, then immediately clapped a hand over her mouth. 'Oh lord...you've not just lost your husband, have you, love?'

'You could say that,' said Stephanie and explained, without the worst parts.

'Ah, a member of the S.S.,' said Rita. 'Suddenly Single,' she added sympathetically, seeing the 'excuse me?' look on Stephanie's face. 'Vell, vee have vays of making you smile. Still hurts, does it?'

Stephanie nodded bleakly. 'Think of me as convalescing. But I'm not here on the look out.'

The women chuckled. 'I wouldn't worry,' said Rita. 'There's only one man in the group who'd be anyone's idea of a rest cure. He's not quite tall enough for me, and he says he collects bugs or something, which definitely rules him out for Aileen.'

'A pity,' agreed Aileen, 'otherwise he might be quite therapeutic. Sort of springy and enthusiastic. But bugs – ugh!'

'I'm sure this place will keep him busy,' murmured Stephanie, carefully removing a small winged green thing from her coffee. 'It must be a collector's paradise.'

For the next few days, Stephanie was happy to let Rita and Aileen choose the best spots under the tamarisk trees and what to eat at Giorgio's beach taverna. By Thursday, her freckles had joined up into some sort of tan and she'd even swum out of her depth with Rita yelling encouragement from a lilo. Not far away, cutting quite a dash at windsurfing was the elusive bug-collector. At that distance, with his fairish hair licked down and darkened by the spray, he looked a bit like Ian...

Rita must have noticed her gaze. 'M'mm, very agile. You said you liked dancing. I bet he does, too. It's always good for the soul, dancing.'

To Stephanie's dismay, a telltale catch came into her voice. 'Ian never liked it,' she managed to say. 'He preferred squash. That's where he met *her*.' Quickly she turned her face to the waves. Suddenly Single – it had a kind of sting to it, and it did still hurt.

Back at the beach, there was a welcome distraction. The old lady Stephanie had seen on her first morning, who they now knew was Georgio's mother, and was called Eleni, was taking her grandchildren down to the water, still fully dressed in her widow's black, right down to the thick stockings and head-scarf. Stephanie was so intrigued by the scene as Eleni ploughed into the water in full gear and started to give swimming lessons to one of the toddlers, that she hadn't noticed developments out in the bay. Approaching fast was Aileen with the windsurfer in tow. Close up, he didn't look a bit like Ian, which was a relief. He seemed very self-contained and pleasant, yet lacked Ian's air of confidence.

'This is Richard,' announced Aileen, with just the faintest note of triumph. 'I'd be heading rapidly for Turkey now, if he hadn't fixed the bar on my pedalo.'

Oh heck, thought Stephanie. What are they up to, after all I said...

She wasn't quite sure at what point Richard also realized that he was the victim of a none-too-subtle plot, but it was probably when Rita shamelessly lassoed him into coming to the hotel disco that night. Stephanie herself had already half-agreed to come, but suddenly found she couldn't face the thought of dancing, of being close to anyone again. It was time to break lose.

'Look,' she said as they reached her corridor, 'it was a nice try, and I do appreciate it, you two, but I'm just not ready yet. I'm going for a moonlight paddle instead.'

Single. She kicked at the damp sand as she walked along the calm tidal edge under an almost-full moon. This is what it meant – no one to share such moments with. Except those chirping things in the pines. What *were* they called?

She stopped by the beach taverna, and one of Eleni's numerous sons brought her coffee and an ouzo. As Stephanie sipped at it cautiously, he asked her with a dazzling smile if she was interested in a 'special walk tomorrow, with many butterflies, very fine scenes. Very cheap, if you book here, not at hotel.'

She booked. It seemed an ideal opportunity to stand on her own two feet for a change, and get in some serious walking. It was a very early start, mainly because of the two-hour, white-knuckle ride in Georgio's pick-up to find the place. With her were three serious Swedes wearing boots impeccable as expensive luggage, who informed her in beautiful English that the Samaria Gorge was one of the finest walks in Europe, famed for its rugged scenery, fabulous displays of butterflies and a famous retreat by the tattered remnants of a British force from the German parachute landings on Crete in 1942. It was ten miles long, during which it dropped 4,000 feet to the sea. Stephanie looked at her unserious trainers and wondered what she'd let herself in for.

Waiting for them at the start, were two cheerful brigands who said they were guides, and another group, among whom was – Richard. Damn!, thought Stephanie. Would he have come if he'd known I'd be here too? Would I?

They nodded to each other warily as the group set off down the path. 'I'm here for the butterflies,' he said. 'How about you?'

'Just the walk', she replied. 'You don't actually *catch* them, do you?'

He tapped a bulky professional-looking shoulder bag. 'Don't worry, it's not killing bottles in here, it's camera gear. Where I work, the European collection is complete anyway. No, the photography's just a hobby. I do orchids too, and there's a supposed to be a few rare ones round here.'

After that he went quiet, as if he felt he might be boring her, but the path was occupying all their concentration now. It was single file and plunging deeper into the winding cleft ahead. As the morning sun caught the rocks, the buzzings and chirpings grew to a heady chorus.

The group straggled on in companionable silence, stopping sometimes to look at the view as the last mist vanished into the blue. The butterflies were a delight, dancing in clouds above the scented scrub.

Richard snapped away happily and swapped notes with the guides. She heard him telling one of the Swedes about 'The Institute', and thought it sounded not at all boring. He was never far away, although he didn't crowd her. But it was when he was most intent on his work, that she suddenly saw something in his face. It wasn't pain – but it could have been the memory of it, and she remembered what she'd read somewhere about what the Greeks said of the sting of a scorpion – only those who had been stung themselves could understand what it was like. Was that why she found his presence here not as an intrusion, but as something vaguely soothing.

The thought made her quicken her pace a little. What was the point of all this hurt? Of all this humming, vivid life around them, if there wasn't some way to use it positively?

'Richard,' she said, just behind him. 'I'd love to see one of those buzzing things – don't know what they're called. What do they look like?'

He looked over his shoulder and smiled. 'Cicadas,' he said. 'Hang on.' He listened. 'I think there should be one up there'. He stepped off the path and advanced on a pine sapling, then beckoned her.

'Not too long, please,' called the guide.

'See, there's one. Watch.' He took off his hat and held it over a fork in the tufted branches. After a minute the buzzing stopped. 'It thinks the sun's gone in,' he said with a grin.

Thoroughly curious now, Stephanie peered in to the shaded spot as he lifted the hat. 'Wow! It's more like an overgrown bluebottle. I thought they were a sort of grasshopper.'

'Actually, they're related to greenfly.'

'Well, at least *they* demolish the roses quietly,' she smiled as the buzzing started up again.

He laughed as he jammed his hat back on, then started – 'See that? It's very rare. I'd have missed it if you hadn't stopped me. I won't be a moment.' Dumping his bag at her feet, he shot off after a small blue butterfly.

She looked round. The others had dropped out of sight, and the view was stunning. She was completely alone and, for once, the time seemed precious in this extraordinary wilderness of bright wings, wild flowers and soaring cliffs – utterly peaceful yet invigorating. So when a distant sharp cry of pain brought her round, it was all the more surprising.

'Stephanie, are you there? I'm stuck!'

'Keep calling,' she yelled hard in the direction of the sound.

'Nothing like a twisted ankle to take your mind of things,' he said when she found him with his foot in a crevice. 'Just didn't see it. I think I'll have to give up chasing butterflies.'

She helped him get his foot out of the fast-stuck boot, then pulled the boot out. But it was obvious that he would find it very difficult to walk without help because the ankle was already swelling.

'I'll get the guide,' she said, and patted his arm. 'Don't worry, I'll be back. Can you look after my bag? I'd better run.'

'Be careful,' he called after her as she got back to the path which, if anything, was getting rougher. She set off at a cautious jog. Ahead was the narrow entrance to a gorge which turned out to be so narrow that in places it was almost possible to touch both sides with arms outstretched. Beyond it, the view was so clear that it was like looking into a bowl of pure crystal.

As she plunged on, a wild exhilaration took over, so that she lost the sense of her pounding feet and was unafraid of falling. That runner who'd raced from Marathon to Athens, had he yelled crazily into the wind, feeling that he could fly like that buzzard up there – and did he have blisters like I'm going to have tomorrow, wondered Stephanie, suddenly sobered by the sight of the others ahead and a sensation that several toes were about to drop off.

Then there was the coming back with the guide to show him where Richard was. They saw him at last, hobbling towards them on a makeshift pine branch crutch. She thought it made him look tremendously brave, and told him so.

Between them, they got him down to the end of the gorge, where an anxious Georgio was waiting with the Swedes beside the pick-up. Richard's group had gone, but it hardly mattered as there was room to make him comfortable in the back.

'But there is a festival in the village tonight,' yelled Georgio above the labouring engine, grinding gears and bumps. 'How will you be able to dance?'

Propped up beside Richard in the back of the pick-up, between baskets of watermelons and sacks of oranges, she joined in the laughter and groans. The sun was setting over the mountains and she felt wonderfully tired, but also happier than she'd been for months.

'But everybody must dance,' insisted Georgio. 'You know my mother? She eighty-two – oldest lady in village. It is she who start women's dance every year. She show them – she very good.'

An image of Eleni in the village square, hands on hips, with a red shawl over her widow's black, leading the women into a swaying circle swam into Stephanie's mind.

'Do you think,' said Richard quietly, as a wild lurch brought them closer, 'that we might manage a nice quiet little number – if I promise not to stand on your blisters?'

Stephanie smiled in the darkness. It was surprising how close you could feel to someone when you ached in all the same places. 'Your ankle will be safe with me,' she said. 'Maybe just a little soft-shoe-shuffle.'

Villa Rosa

The woman staying at the villa wore no ring and was of considerable beauty.
There was an air of experience about her and to Luis, she looked like a woman
who had known love...

The water tanker laboured along the coast road from Port Mahon to Binbeca, gears grinding as Luis eased it over the speed bumps by the hotels. Several pairs of short shorts and tanned legs abandoned the middle of the road, while their owners looked around at the honking, clanking invasion of their afternoon stroll.

Las touristas everywhere, as usual. All that untouchable flesh, well, since his marriage, anyway. It was too much for a man.

Luis sighed as the near-empty tanker picked up speed again. He was trying to remember the last time he had seen his wife naked. Teresa was a good woman. She had done her share of clucking with the other women at the topless invasion of their beaches, but the men – they had managed to survive it somehow. The last baby had not improved her figure, and there were stretch marks. Did *las touristas* not have babies? Well, said Teresa, they'd never get to heaven for all their blond hair. That his wife could confuse fair looks with fitness to join the choirs of saints and angels was no surprise to Luis, and he felt shame at it. Shame at her lack of sophistication beside the worldly, sleek foreigners – and sometimes at his own.

His face brightened as Villa Rosa came into view on the next rise. It was the last on his list, and he called there every week during the season to deliver water. Even as a boy, he had always liked it. The view was good and the garden was like an English garden, so they said. In fact, so much water had been used to plant the rose beds and the hedges of hibiscus that sea water had seeped into the well.

Such extravagance with good water – yet now it was a pleasure to call at Villa Rosa, with its climbing scented roses almost concealing the crumbling pink plaster. Usually, it was let to English or German families in the summer, and sometimes they invited him in for a sangria and to practise their Spanish. But this year, and Luis's smile broadened, Villa Rosa had only one occupant, an Englishwoman of some dignity and education – and considerable beauty. There were a lot of books in the house this year, and a laptop on the sitting room desk. He thought perhaps she wrote poetry. She was soft and rounded and always smelt very good. Indeed, she seemed a perfect resident for Villa Rosa.

Would she invite him to join her on the front patio again for a sangria and an almond biscuit? Her Spanish was good for a visitor, and she had a notebook for jotting down phrases of the Minorcan dialect. Last week, she had asked him about local dishes. 'So you really do say *grevi* for meat sauce? My book says that dates from when English sailors used the harbour in the 19th century.'

Luis was able to tell her that their Lord Nelson had stayed here, and been flattered at her interest in the island. 'He was a very romantic man, I believe,' he'd added rather daringly. 'Ours is a romantic island, is it not?'

She'd smiled at that, rather sadly, he thought. She wore no wedding ring, but there was an air of – experience – about her. The experience of one who had surely known love...

'Romantic? For the lucky ones, perhaps.' She'd stumbled a little over the words, as if caught unawares. 'Is that how you say it?'

He had nodded encouragingly, hoping that the blue gaze would once again meet his, and thought of sea and sky, and scented petals against his cheek. Her next words had stayed in his mind all that week; 'Romantic, but not for me, I think. You see, my –er– friend has not arrived. I was expecting him to join me.' She had looked down, almost as if speaking to herself. 'He was going to leave his wife, you see. Perhaps they...'

Her voice had trailed off and she'd quickly poured him some more sangria. Did she think that he, Luis, a good Catholic, would be shocked? But Luis was a tolerant man. The visitors had different rules. No rules at all, Teresa said. But he felt angry at this man, whoever he was, to leave a woman so! His sense of chivalry was outraged. It was an honour to be taken into her confidence.

His chest swelled as he turned the tanker into the drive at Villa Rosa. All the shutters were open. So English! He parked under the clump of date palms and bounded up the steps between the tubs of lavender.

'*Hola!*' he called, with a rap on the door. 'Luis the waterman is here.'

Inside the house he could hear water draining. Had she been taking a shower? The mere idea made him giddy, and he thought he could hear white-crested waves beating against the rocks.

'*Hola!*' answered a soft voice. 'You are early this week, Luis. I won't be a moment. Please come inside out of the sun.'

He stepped awkwardly into the living room, feeling dusty in his dungarees. As his eyes adjusted to the shadows after the glare of the road, he could see a photograph on the desk among the books and papers. A man's face, good-looking, casually dressed, worldly, surveyed him from the expensive brass frame – the face of a man who could leave a woman lonely.

At last she came in, dressed in a light pink silk robe and her hair was gleaming. 'I'm glad you've come, Luis,' she said, and smiled. The smile seemed to last an eternity. He could think of nothing to say. The eyes were so blue, her skin so soft and fresh.

'There was enough water left for the shower, *señora?*' he managed to say.

To his amazement, she went to the shutters and began closing them one by one. 'There should be enough left if you would like a shower, too, Luis,' he heard her say. 'Will you stay a while...?'

The woman lay for a long time in the shuttered room watching the shadows of the palms dance across the bed, across the robe on the floor, across her body. She was smiling. Beside her on the pillow lay a full-blown white rose from the garden. How perfectly romantic, she thought. If I touch it, the petals will fall. Let it be. She had not planned that such a thing would happen. Not this afternoon, not ever. And yet there was that rose. A wordless touching of two virtual strangers. Perfect.

That morning, she'd woken to find the sky overcast and the Tramontana wind from the north rattling the shutters. It had been such a summer – a lonely summer, and now the season was changing.

At home, the blackberries would be ripening on the heath, and spiders spinning cobwebs from the curtains of her flat. Here, it was the wind that spelt the change. People did strange things, the local people said, when the Tramontana was blowing. It could make you restless, even drive you mad. A whole summer of waiting and wondering. Waiting for another letter, the call to say that Steven had settled things with his wife at last and was free to join her. What had gone wrong? She hadn't realized how tired she was of waiting.

All these things were true, but they couldn't explain that rose. She must leave soon, whenever she could book a flight. He wouldn't come now. Would he even call? Or even write? It was like waking up from a dream of her own choosing, the dream where she and Steven could be lovers for ever and his family did not exist. Romantic and foolish. And it had taken one afternoon to make her see it. Oh goodness – she should really have told Luis she'd be leaving.

There were fewer short shorts around now as Luis steered the tanker round the last bend to Villa Rosa. This time he didn't spare them a second glance. All week, he had thought only of today, and the lady like a rose who would be waiting. Teresa, occupied with the baby's cough, had not noticed his distraction, for which, he noted wryly, he'd probably got some of those angels of hers to thank. He'd missed Sunday mass, pleading a stomach upset, but there were penances a man could do – afterwards. The villa was booked until Christmas, and so, Luis could only hope and pray, was he.

Turning into the drive, he noticed the garden looked dry and lifeless. Someone had cut all the roses. He frowned as he saw that the doors and shutters were closed. Of course, it was cooler today. He leapt up the pink steps and knocked anxiously.

He knocked again. The very sound of it told him the house was empty. It could only mean been one thing – that she, a lady, was ashamed of making love with a water man.

Too disappointed to be angry at her betrayal, he forced himself back to the true purpose of his call. She would still need water. He must not fail her, even if he meant so little to her. Pulling his dignity together, he went round to the side of the house and found the loft door open. He returned to the tanker, unhitched the hose and as he trailed it dispiritedly up the steps, he noticed a scattering of white on the loft floor. Rose petals. Perhaps the wind had blown them up there. And then he remembered the roses. Who would have picked them, every last one? While the tank filled he sat on the steps and held some of the fading petals to his cheek.

Then Luis received the kind of jolt that only those who have stolen an afternoon rose can really understand. A pair of feet stood before him – large feet, in espadrilles, belonging to strong, golden-haired legs; shorts, a beach shirt and a towel over the shoulders, more gold on the chest and head. And he knew even as he blinked that this was the man in the photo.

'*Buenas dias,*' said the flat British accent. 'You speak a bit of English, don't you? You're early, but I'm glad I've caught you.'

'*Caught* me?' gasped Luis, hearing a roaring in his ears, not of waves, but of the crowd at a bullfight. If he knows, he'll kill me, hissed a voice in his head.

'What?' The man seemed more puzzled than angry. 'No, sorry, wrong word. What I meant was, there was something I wanted to ask you. When you've finished, could you come in for a minute?'

He is English – a cool one, thought Luis frantically. He will wait until I've filled the tank – and *then* he'll kill me. But I must see her. Not to speak, but to know that she is happy.

His work finished, he went back up the front steps like a young matador who, foolish with fear, enters the bull's stable to ask after the animal's health. The door opened, but no cruel horns rushed out to embrace him.

'Ah yes, *gracias,*' said the bull who, to Luis's surprise, seemed almost embarrassed. Luis risked a glance beyond him into the room. The books and laptop had gone, and the place seemed untidy in the way men are when they are alone.

'I'll be wanting water for one more week,' said the man. 'Is that okay?' He had changed from his beach gear but, for all his expensive clothes, seemed ill at ease.

'For one, or two, or family, *señor?*'

'For one. *Uno*,' was the curt reply.

'And the *señora* who was here before – she has gone? She did not tell me of her departure.'

'She didn't even tell *me*!' The tall Englishman sounded bitter and defeated. 'I don't even know why she left. I called, but it must have been too late. Actually, that's what I wanted to ask you about.'

'*Señor*?' The bull is confused, thought Luis the matador, and doesn't know which way to charge. But I too am confused. I must not stumble now. Maybe I should just make a run for the tanker.

'I'm rather worried about her. When you saw her last, did she seem okay? I mean – was she *well*? Look, won't you come in?'

Was it a trap? The man gave a weary shrug to the side of the room Luis hadn't seen from the door. No, not a trap. Luis blinked and stared. Lined up against the wall were roses – all the roses from the garden, in pots, vases, jugs, even buckets.

'You see' said the Englishman, 'she left no message – just these, and in such a crazy place. I really don't know what to make of it. I thought I'd better move them down here. I did wonder though, whether the strain of being alone for so long had been a bit much for her.'

Now I have him, thought Luis the matador as the crowd threw rose petals. But I will spare him the death cut. 'The lady was well when I saw her, *señor*, but sometimes when the Tramontana blows it makes people do strange things. Lonely for such a woman is not good. It is better she left, no?'

'What? No – I mean, yes...' muttered his wounded opponent, still staring at the banks of roses. 'I just can't understand it. For heaven's sake, she'd put all this lot in the loft, beside the water tank!'

Luis made a hurried departure, but as he honked his way back to Mahon he was smiling and thinking of perfumed petals soft against his skin – and thanking all Teresa's angels and saints for the safety of home. After all, he was only a simple water man. He couldn't really be expected to explain the romance of the rose.

Travel Writing: People & Places

Wherever you go, there you are.

(Attributed variously to Buddhist philosophy or
an unknown Native Australian)

*Like all great travellers, I have seen more than I remember,
and remember more than I have seen.*

(Benjamin Disraeli, 1804-1881, British Prime Minister and author)

Travelling Women

Neither the Royal Geographical Society's list, or any other, of articles necessary to travellers in tropical climates makes mention of husbands.

(Mary Kingsley (1862-1900), responding to criticism of herself and other women travelling alone)

To awake alone in a strange town is one of the pleasantest sensations in the world.

(Freya Stark)

Out of Africa
In the steps of Karen Blixen

'If I know a song about Africa... does Africa know a song about me?'
Every year, thousands of fans of 'Out of Africa' visit her old haunts to find
out.

'I had a farm in Africa at the foot of the Ngong Hills...' To write a book
that has become a much-loved classic is one way to be remembered, but
when it is made into an Oscar-winning film with Hollywood stars and
wonderfully evocative music, you are well on your way to immortality.
Something like 60 million people have seen *Out of Africa*, and the book
has sold over 1½ million copies. Of the thousands of people who visit
Kenya each year, many are hoping to recapture a little of its magic by
visiting some of the places associated with its author, Karen Blixen. But
how much is there left to see, and what would she herself now recognize
of the Africa she wrote so movingly about?

In January 1914, Karen, or Tania to her friends, arrived in Mombasa's
Kalindini harbour after a 19-day voyage from Europe, as did all would-
be settlers at that time. There was no dock, and the steamer anchored
among the trading *dhows* to be immediately besieged by a mini-armada
of canoes offering everything from shells, trinkets and fruit to trips
ashore. To get the flavour of that experience these days, it has to be
from a small cruise ship visiting the tiny ports of lesser-known places
in Madagascar, the Comoros or Mozambique. The Dhow Harbour is
still very atmospheric, and can be easily reached on a walking tour of
Mombasa Old Town or by taxi from the city centre. There might even
be a few *dhows* at anchor (where once there would have been hundreds),
but Kalindini Creek hasn't changed that much, because most of the new
port development is not visible from here.

The passengers were then rowed ashore, often risking a soaking, to the
Leven Steps, and escorted to Leven House to complete the formalities.

Looking at it now, it's hard to believe that in those days this venerable building was both the Customs House and Government House. To send word home of their arrival, the newcomers would have visited the Post Office, which has survived largely because it was built very solidly to reassure the Indian railway workers that their savings would get home safely. Meanwhile the luggage, which in Karen's case included her fine china and glass, would be dispatched up the hill to the Mombasa Club beside the Fort by an ingenious rail-and-trolley system, and some wonderful pictures of it in use can be seen in the Fort Museum.

The Mombasa Club, where Karen Dinesen was married to Baron Bror Blixen the morning after her arrival, has been much enlarged since, yet retains its air of exclusivity. Opposite the Club, the original Coffee House where the Swahili traders would do business continues to serve refreshments, but is now more of a gift shop. Many of the Old Town streets have been partially restored, especially the finer merchants' houses with their brass-studded, heavy wooden doors, balconies and fretwork screens for the women's quarters. Some of these are now small hotels or antique shops selling Out-of-Africa-type souvenirs, but there's still enough original ambience to deflect charges of theme-parkery.

After their wedding luncheon, the Blixens' party took the famous Uganda Railway to Nairobi and apparently drank champagne in their pyjamas before settling in for one of Africa's most interesting train rides. Unofficially called the Lunatic Express, the train still somehow manages to chug its way from sea level up a series of scenic escarpments through the Tsavo National Park to the main plateau height of around 6000ft/2000m. Most visitors now make the journey by air, but on a fine day when there's a view of snow-capped Kilimanjaro and the high plains, it's possible to capture some of what Karen Blixen herself said of flying in Africa with no intended pun – that it was the most transporting pleasure of her life.

In smaller planes going directly to the game parks from Nairobi or Mombasa, the experience can be even more *Out of Africa*, as her words come back: 'You may at times fly low enough to see the animals on the plains and feel towards them as God did when he had just created them…'

Before leaving the Mombasa connections behind, however, and especially if travelling north to one of the coastal resorts, it's worth mentioning that Denys Finch Hatton, Karen Blixen's lover after her marriage foundered, had a small estate at Takaunga near Kilifi Creek. He would sometimes fly her down there, landing on the beach, for a weekend by the Indian Ocean. One night, she wrote of how 'a row of Arab dhows came along, close to the coast, running noiselessly before the monsoon, a file of brown shadow-sails under the moon.' You could be as lucky. Even today Takaunga is slightly off the beaten track (the new coast road to Malindi) but the beach is beautiful and was used for both *Out of Africa* and *White Mischief* which features the goings-on of Kenya's 'Happy Valley' set, some of whom were their friends.

But it is of course the scenes of her life on that coffee farm at the foot of the Ngong Hills, only twelve miles from the centre of Nairobi, that stay longest in the mind. In fact the couple did not move to the stone-built house seen in the film for nearly five years. Their original, more modest, bungalow is now incorporated into a hotel in the suburb of Karen, named after her when she eventually had to sell the estate. But the house, now the Karen Blixen Museum, is a must for all her fans. It is much as it was when she left it so regretfully in 1931. Many fascinating photographs with some of her belongings are there, and the film company has donated the copies of her furniture designed from original photographs specially for the film, including the white mosquito-netted bed and famous gramophone. The elegant panelled dining room is set as if for one of her sophisticated candle-lit evenings, and the stone fireplace by whose light Karen and Denys would dazzle their friends, or each other, with their tales is still in place. Outside, along a covered way, is Kumante's kitchen, re-kitted out with period utensils – all of which makes it rather disappointing that no inside photography is allowed.

Perhaps the most evocative spots to pause for a quiet moment, are the side veranda with a view of her beloved Ngong Hills, and the back, as seen in the film, where her belongings were laid out for sale when she left. Other photo opportunities include the drive where she would light a lantern to let friends know she was at home, and a collection of old coffee farm machinery.

As for Nairobi itself, once a morning's horse ride away, but now around 30 minutes by car from the house, depending on the traffic, little is left that Karen Blixen would recognize. Imagine her amazement, and perhaps dismay, at the way the town has grown, from a population of tens of thousands when she first arrived, to the bustling, jostling one and a half million people of today. Many of the roads and tree-lined avenues have been renamed, but there is of course, the once infamous Muthaiga Country Club, which opened for business (and pleasure) on New Year's Eve 1913 and is still going strong. Its modern amenities include acres of fine tropical gardens with an excellent golf course. Only 15 minutes' drive north-east of the city centre through the wealthy suburb of Parklands, it is unfortunately for members only. In the Blixens' day, things were more relaxed, with settlers coming in by ox-wagon for a hot bath or taking the odd pot-shot at the fixtures and fittings, and occasionally each other. So exclusive is it that some maps and guide books omit it completely.

Instead, try the Ngong Races, held every second Sunday for most of the year. The course is easily accessible by bus, matatu (minibus) or taxi (shared or otherwise). And for pure nostalgia, close to the summit of the Ngong Hills at Point Lamwia, there is the grave of Denys Finch Hatton, marked by an obelisk.

In *Out of Africa*, the woman who loved him, and Kenya, so dearly, memorably asks:

> *If I know a song of Africa, of the giraffe and the African new moon lying on her back... does Africa know a song of me? Will the air over the plains quiver with a colour that I have had on... or the full moon throw a shadow on the gravel of the drive that is like me?'*

Her drive may be rough tarmac now, and her dream gone, but Africa certainly does know of song of Karen Blixen. A suburb of Nairobi is named after her, and the emotive music from the film wafts from hotel lobbies all over the continent. Maybe she would have approved of that.

Agatha Christie's Other Career

The world's best-selling writer of detective stories was also a great traveller with a passion for the archaeology and lost cultures of the Middle East.

With over two hundred million books sold world-wide, few would dispute that Agatha Christie is one of the most successful novel writers of all time. With her books translated into over one hundred languages, she remains the queen of detective fiction, while her famous play, *The Mousetrap*, is still enjoying the longest-ever run of any play in London's West End Theatreland. Such is her fame that some of her devoted fans in far-flung places still inquire about her 'latest' book in spite of the fact that Dame Agatha died in 1976.

What her readers love is not just the ingenuity of her plots, but her evocation of a particular kind of Englishness – the lost world of the drawing room, rose garden and library; the ladies' maids hovering nervously in the background; the so-correct butler (who might possibly be the murderer); the eccentric detectives, wealthy widows, and the importance of trains running on time. But it is only since two of her most famous books, *Murder on the Orient Express* and *Death on the Nile*, were made into Hollywood blockbusters that her other great passion - the archaeology, people and magnificent desert landscapes of the Middle East - has received much attention from her adoring public.

'How much I have loved that part of the world. I love it still and always will,' she wrote in her autobiography.

Agatha Christie was always capable of springing surprises. She was born in 1890 in genteel Torquay, amid the lush and quintessentially English countryside of Devon, but few biographies mention that her father was a wealthy American expatriate. Educated at home, as were many girls at that time from her background, she was always fond of reading and puzzles. It was a comfortable world, soon to be comprehensively shattered by the outbreak of the World War I. Again, along with many women who had led sheltered lives until then, she became a nurse, and took to it with a determination born of a previously dormant inner strength of character. Having to administer all kinds of medicines and drugs gave her a huge interest in the subject. By the end of the war she had become a dispensing chemist with a thorough knowledge of poisons and forensic matters.

Her lively mind quickly found an outlet for such experiences, and the result was her first crime novel, *The Mysterious Affair at Styles* published in 1920, which introduced the 'country house murder' and her bristly little Belgian detective, Hercule Poirot, to a world badly in need of some entertainment and escapism.

At this point in her career there was no hint of the heat and exoticism of the Middle East in her books. But then, for a brief period in 1926, Agatha seems to have experienced an intense emotional crisis. Possibly this was brought on by her mother's death, followed by her husband's bombshell announcement that he had fallen in love with someone else and wanted a divorce. The double shock was too much for her, especially as divorce was quite unusual and socially shocking at that time. Her reaction was strange and dramatic. She went missing – simply got into her car and drove off, leaving no clues as to her whereabouts. There followed a national hunt by both press and police, in a mini-scandal that has become the subject of several films, the best known of which stars Vanessa Redgrave as the distraught novelist, in a series of spectacular hats; Agatha herself was a tall woman and always cut an imposing figure.

On her recovery, or perhaps as part of it, she gave way to another impulse and bought a ticket for the famous Orient Express to Baghdad, citing no other reason than that she'd read an article about the recent excavations of the ancient city of Ur, conducted by the famous archaeologist, Sir Leonard Woolley. She had, she was to explain disarmingly later, always been fascinated by the glamour of 'The Orient' (which in those days to many European minds seemed to start somewhere around Istanbul) and the Orient Express was simply the only way to get there. This was the start of a life-long love affair not just with the countries of the Middle East – Syria, Egypt and Iraq in particular – but also with a man fifteen years her junior who was one of Woolley's assistants. This man was Max Mallowan, himself a rising star in the world of Middle Eastern archaeology. They seemed, at first acquaintance, to be an unlikely pair, but their mutual love of the area gave them a lot in common. Their marriage, in 1930, proved to be a happy one, particularly as Agatha was able to accompany Max on his digs where she took to expedition life with gusto.

While still finding time to work on her detective stories, she quickly learnt to catalogue and photograph finds, to match and mend ancient pottery and how to clean precious objects buried for centuries in the desert sands. At Nimrud, in what is now Iraq, she was particularly successful in conserving a unique collection of carved ivories dating from 850BC (now in the British Museum). Her decision to clean them with her own face cream turned out to be an inspired emergency move which protected the brittle material from further deterioration.

Agatha proved herself an excellent expedition cook and could whip up specialities such as chocolate éclairs and soufflés from local ingredients in the most unlikely circumstances, to the appreciation of her husband and colleagues who always took pride in dressing for dinner, wherever they happened to be. With her background as a nurse and chemist, she also became the camp 'medic', all of which provided some interesting material for her famously elaborate plots. It was no secret, for example, that Leonard Woolley's wife, Katharine, was heartily disliked by the rest of the team. So in *Murder in Mesopotamia*, the unpopular wife of an expedition leader is murdered with one of the finds – a weighty Neolithic corn grinder – thus giving rise to an innovative type of crime story where the murder weapon could turn out to be something very unusual. She also appears to have been the first to hatch the kind of plot where absolutely everyone around has both the time and inclination to do the deed. Yet ironically, it was Katherine Woolley who had brought Agatha and Max Mallowan together (perhaps to get her out of the way) by asking the young man to show her the desert countryside around Ur.

It was as if her marriage to Max had suddenly breathed new life into the whole genre of detective/crime writing, and indeed into Agatha herself. Each year the pair would spend several months in yet another exotic location. Spring was the best time for digging. It was then that the stunning desert landscapes were at their most attractive. Agatha revelled in the difficulties and uncertainties of desert travel. The couple had the use of a huge Ford car specially converted for rough conditions and affectionately christened 'Queen Mary', and there are some wonderful snaps of her wading across a flooded *wadi* near Nimrud, voluminous skirts hitched up decorously and stout stick at the ready.

Only once did she complain of hating a dig – in northern Syria, when a plague of mice got everywhere, including the bed, but she also wrote to her agent about rain and storms where 'we all huddle in quantities of jerseys and woolly knickers...'

Her output rose steadily. *Appointment with Death* was set in Petra, the famous rose red city in Jordan, while *They Came to Baghdad*, *Murder on the Orient Express* and *Death on the Nile* speak for themselves. There can't be many visitors to the great temples at Karnak and Luxor who don't look up and remember one of those huge stone lintels crashing towards a would-be victim beneath and wondering if it just might happen to them. Did it fall or was it pushed...?

Wherever she travelled, she made sure that her most enduring creation, the prickly, portly Belgian detective, Hercule Poirot, came along too in her fertile mind and got his share of the action. She had already realized that successful archaeologists had a lot of the detective about them, and so, not content with the meticulous Monsieur Poirot, she introduced a seemingly absent-minded example of the sleuthing species into *They Came to Baghdad* – the outrageously named Dr Pauncefoot Jones. Of course it was no surprise to her fans that this charming, if vague, archaeologist would turn out to be just as well equipped with 'those little grey cells' as the great Poirot, or indeed Agatha herself.

Apart from her crime novels, Dame Agatha, as she became in 1971, wrote movingly in her largely autobiographical *Come, Tell Me How You Live*, of her love of the Middle East and its people. 'Here, some 5,000 years ago *was* the busy part of the world... I am thinking it was a happy way to live.' She loved the romance of suddenly finding 'big stone Assyrian heads poking out of the soil' or 'a dagger slowly appearing with its golden glint, through the sand'.

When Max was posted to North Africa during World War II, Agatha returned to her original career as a dispensing chemist. After the war, Max was given a professorship in Western Asiatic Archaeology, and it was only Agatha's ill-health which forced them to abandon their desert explorations.

The exotic and authentic backgrounds of Dame Agatha's plots must have introduced generations of readers to whole areas of the Middle East which were largely inaccessible to most Westerners at the time, and gave many the urge to see its majestic desert scenery and fascinating archaeological sites. It's not unusual to find tourists wandering around with one of her books at sites like Ur, Luxor or Petra, and armchair travellers can always try one of the numerous web sites devoted to her. There's an amazing amount of information about her life and work posted by her true devotees, with everyone from primary school children to college kids and graduate students studying her plots, and asking each other eagerly for some particular piece of information to complete their assignments. Meanwhile the conservation of the delicate Nimrud Ivories stands as a further enduring memorial to the painstaking care and attention to detail which she always applied to everything she did.

Paddling Her Own Canoe:
Mary Kingsley's 'Travels in West Africa'

*'There is nothing like entering into the spirit of a thing like this if you mean to
enjoy it, and after all that's the wisest thing to do out here,
for there's nothing between enjoying it or dying of it.'*

In 1897, a young woman, thirty-five and single, published a book that
became an overnight sensation. She was Mary Kingsley, born in the
staid London suburb of Islington, a doctor's daughter and niece of
Charles Kingsley of *The Waterbabies* fame. Yet her book had nothing
to do with polite Victorian society's preoccupation with fairies and the
innocence of childhood that might have been expected from someone
of her background.

Travels in West Africa is an account of two journeys she made between
1893 and 1895, quite on her own, to the coast of West Africa and along
some of its rivers. Every page of it is shot through with astonishing
facts, memorable scenes and a cavalier attitude to danger and hardship,
tempered with throw-away lines, a sparkling curiosity, wry humour
and sound common sense. For two years upon her return she'd been
pressed into giving talks to various worthy societies and institutions
around the country. There she stood, according to contemporary reports
of such events, 'slender, upright', hair parted in the middle topped by
her signature little pillbox hat, 'blue eyes, humorous mouth', 'less like an
explorer than anyone I ever saw', drawing her audiences into a world
they could scarcely imagine – confiding in them:

> *When you have made up your mind to go to West Africa the very best
> thing you can do is get it unmade again, and go to Scotland instead;
> but if your intelligence is not so strong enough to do so, abstain from
> exposing yourself to the direct rays of the sun, take four grains of quinine
> every day for a fortnight before you reach the Rivers* (The Niger Delta
> in today's Nigeria), *and get some introductions to the Wesleyans; they
> are the only people on the Coast who have got a hearse with feathers.*

All she had to do was write it down to reach a vast readership eager to hear about exotic places and experiences. And what Mary had to tell them was extraordinary, not simply in itself, but because it came channelled through a fine, wide-ranging intellect free of any formal education. Along with her accounts of learning to paddle a dugout canoe solo over rapids, dealing with hippos (alive or very dead), the habits of crocodiles, cannibalism, deaths by witchcraft and climbing Mount Cameroon, all 13,760 ft of it, almost straight up from sea level, she aired her forthright views on a range of issues – missionaries (mostly against), polygamy and the uses of trade gin (mostly in favour) and British colonial policy (mixed – although she was a firm believer in what she regarded as the true ideals of imperialism). She had a born naturalist's curiosity and attention to detail combined with an artist's eye for the beauty of these untamed regions and, very importantly, the knack of communicating all this to her audience or readership in a way that was lively, accurate and quite poetic.

She was also a boat person. Years before the joys of 'simply messing about in boats' entered the language via *The Wind in the Willows*, Mary Kingsley declared, 'Ah me! Give me a West African river and a canoe for sheer good pleasure.' The fact that she was steering a heavy trading dugout with a bed-sheet as a sail, by moonlight while the crew slept, only makes her statement the more astonishing. She took the tiller of several small coastal steamers on various occasions, and her diversions into boat engineering and navigation are still read with enjoyment by boating types today.

Camping at night on an island in the Ogowé River (in what was then French Equatorial Africa, and is now Gabon), she writes:

> *In the darkness round me flitted thousands of fire-flies, and out beyond this pool of utter night flew the white foam of rapids; sound there was none save their thunder. The majesty and beauty of the scene fascinated me and I stood leaning with my back against a rock pinnacle watching it. ... If there is a heaven, that will be mine...*

In that last phrase lies one of the clues to this fascinating woman's philosophy of life – one that would bring her into conflict with some of her admirers. Querying the existence of heaven would have shocked her famous, late author uncle, Charles, who had been the Canon of Westminster, not to mention the bulk of the populace. It also helps to explain why a woman from such a background might choose to go to West Africa in the first place, when the area was still very much regarded as a death trap for Europeans. Her doctor father, whom she idolised, was not only frequently absent on exotic collecting trips to the Americas, he was also absent-minded, so much so that he managed to marry her mother only four days before Mary was born, omitted to have her christened and made no provision for her education. Inspired by his stories of strange customs, wild places and the specimens he brought back, she set about reading everything in his extensive library that interested her. Natural history, anything to do with the sea, rivers and sailing, and engineering fascinated her, as did the religions of other cultures, but she never felt the need of a religion for herself.

She seems to have had a very free but lonely childhood, followed by many years of looking after her by now ailing, elderly parents in Cambridge where the family had moved. When they died within six weeks of each other, she had no outside contacts or experience of life, yet the following year she was on her way to Freetown, Sierra Leone. Later, when asked why she'd chosen West Africa, she replied rather mysteriously that she had gone there to die, but when she hadn't, found she'd rather got to like the place.

As to *how* she did it, her extensive reading and new liberty to question everyone around her in Cambridge led her to some intelligent conclusions. She had very limited means, and was neither a missionary, a true explorer, a government or company official or a wife of any of those. So she decided to become a trader, which she now realized would be well understood in the region, but also a scientific collector of freshwater fish species, for acceptability at home. To these ends, she befriended a fish expert for identification books and collecting equipment to bring home anything new (in fact she discovered five new fish species), and then bought up a small stock of trade goods that were popular in the area.

Added to these was a reason of her own – a wish to continue her father's interest in the religious beliefs of other cultures. In West Africa that amounted to getting to grips with voodoo and the various cults associated with it in different areas. In particular she wanted to record beliefs around fetishes (objects imbued with magic power), and was particularly pleased when a witch doctor presented her with a basket for catching souls. Summing it up, she said she was travelling for fish, fetishes and trade.

But when it came to how to dress and what to take for her own comfort, Mary Kingsley's preparations had a simplicity that, for us, borders on the eccentric, but to her seemed like common sense. She went just as she was, in her stays, a good thick skirt, long-sleeved, high-necked blouse, buttoned boots and fur pill-box hat. The boots, she confesses, were on one excursion not removed for a spell of three weeks because mosquito bites on the feet were so troublesome. A pair of cotton slippers is mentioned almost as an indulgence. Whatever else she needed fitted into a black portmanteau which often doubled as a pillow, doorstop or writing desk.

Beneath the stays, skirts and petticoats must have been a constitution like an ox and a good pair of legs, considering the amount of walking (or marching as she called it) through dense forests, mangrove swamps, across rivers, and up and down ravines in humid heat that would have melted a lesser mortal. Lots of strenuous paddling, capsizing, camping in the open or sleeping in mud huts where the air, as she put it, was often 99% mosquito, were all taken in her stride. Overnighting in a chief's hut, she wonders what the awful smell could be, and by the light of a firebrand, traces it to a bag hanging on the wall:

I shook the contents out into my hat, for fear of losing anything of value. They were a human hand, three big toes, four eyes, two ears and other portions of the human frame. The hand was fresh, the others only so so, and shrivelled.

Without so much as a squeak, she carefully returns them to the bag and goes outside for some air, reflecting that 'although the Fans will eat their friendly fellow tribesfolk, yet they like to keep a little something belonging to them as a momento' and is happy to find 'a perfect night, with no mosquitoes', and the village sleeping peacefully 'walled in on every side by the great cliff of high black forest'.

It's understandable then, that much of *Travels in West Africa* is concerned with trying to understand traditional religions and the mindsets behind them. Three chapters, entitled *Stalking the Wild West African Idea*, *The World of the Spirit* and *Gods, Devils and Secret Societies* contain details that intrigued and horrified her readership in equal measure and were directly responsible for creating huge interest, and not just in the budding discipline of anthropology. They were also instrumental in galvanising debate about government policies and missionary attitudes towards native beliefs and customs, such as attempting to stamp out polygamy and 'heathen festivals'. But about the endemic and ubiquitous beliefs in voodoo/witchcraft, she had no doubt:

> *The belief in witchcraft is the cause of more African deaths than anything else. It has also killed more people than the slave trade. Its only rival is perhaps smallpox...*

Her descriptions of witchcraft beliefs and the misery and suffering they caused to the innocent, especially women and children, are quite blood-chilling. While she could see no point in replacing voodoo with certain Christian beliefs, which to her mind caused only confusion, she was a great supporter and friend of that other famous West African Mary, the Scottish missionary Mary Slessor, with whom she'd stayed in Calabar. Mary Slessor lived completely alone among the local people and won their trust, which encouraged Mary Kingsley to do the same. Mary Slessor's work in abolishing the killing of twins (and often their mothers), and teaching by example rather than preaching, became a model for more enlightened missionary attitudes to local beliefs and customs.

More upsetting to some sections of the public was Mary Kingsley's criticism of government policy in West Africa, which to her seemed inherently based on the notion that anything European had to be superior to anything African, and that included people. Her admiration and liking for Africans, to whom she entrusted herself completely for most of her travels, shines through all her writings, in an age where such feelings, if they existed at all, were mostly accompanied by patronising remarks and behaviour.

As a highly independent and free-thinking woman, Mary was no stranger to this kind of behaviour herself, and so kicked out instinctively against it. When attacked in the press for being a single woman with no business to be out on her own and criticising the government, she simply replied: 'Neither the Royal Geographical Society's list, or any other, of articles necessary to travellers in tropical climates makes mention of husbands.'

Yet for all her independence, Mary Kingsley always remained truly feminine rather than a feminist. Possibly she didn't openly support the women's suffrage movement in case that would have jeopardised her other causes. But how endearing it is to read that her main concern when tramping through a rainstorm along a jungle path near Libreville, was that she'd had to replace the broken laces of her stays with black bootlaces, and that the men behind her might spot this indelicacy thorough her soaked white blouse.

At the end of her epic ascent of Mount Cameroon, (Mungo Mah Lobeh, the Throne of Thunder) in appalling weather, she asks herself: 'Why did I come to Africa?... .Why! who would not come to its twin brother, hell itself, for all the beauty and charm of it?'

But that was Mary Kingsley – quirky, controversial, always her own woman, and author of one of the most influential, knowledgeable and humorous travel books ever published.

Travels with my Daughter: Backpacking in India

'Come on, Mum, it'll be fun,' she said. 'You know you want to.'

When it's the fourth time that you've had to get out and push your broken-down taxi from the airport, in the middle lane of the Mumbai morning rush hour, certain voices come back to taunt you.

As the gritty slipstream from an overloaded lorry almost forced us into a nearside bullock cart, the first voice said, 'India? *Backpacking?* Are you mad?'

Easily recognizable, that one – the voice of my husband suddenly realising I might actually mean it.

Then there was Catherine, our daughter, saying, 'Come on, Mum, it'll be fun. You know you've always wanted to.' But, since Catherine was right beside me pushing, and we were both laughing helplessly, there didn't seem much point in mentioning it.

'Sorry, Auntie,' puffed the embarrassed driver.

For a moment, I thought one of his elderly female relatives had turned up to give us a hand. But then, one of the nicest things about India is the way strangers are quickly popped into categories of some vast extended family. I was that Auntie, and I rather liked it.

Two months previously, Catherine had suddenly handed in her notice and announced, as they do these days, that she was going round the world – by herself, first stop India. Somewhere between me wishing aloud that I'd seen more of the place than I'd managed from that air-conditioned coach trip round Rajasthan last year, and her father predicting instant kidnap by *dacoits*, we reached an understanding. I would go with her as far as Mumbai, Goa and Kerala. We'd make no advance bookings except for major rail trips, and simply see how far south we could get. After that, she'd be on her own.

Next there was the question of a rucksack. Catherine's, when fully packed, was the size of small sofa, but then she was going for six months or more, depending on when the money ran out. I tried lifting it, but with a wonky back from years of childbearing (only three of them, but sometimes it felt like six) I could hardly move the thing, and almost cancelled my ticket. Then, thumbing through a shopping catalogue full of things like nose hair clippers and foot spas, I saw it. A lightweight backpack – with wheels, and a retractable handle. Saved! Furthermore, it was the first clue that I wasn't the only middle-aged woman wanting to be foolhardy with a wonky back. And we soon found we weren't the only mother and daughter team around, either.

So there we were, my new nephew, my daughter and me, with the bullock cart definitely gaining on us. It was getting too hot to think, let alone push. Yet when an air-conditioned tourist coach swept snootily past, I actually felt quite sorry for them.

The Colaba hotel district was within spitting distance of the Gateway of India – a metaphor taken rather too literally by my new nephew and many more potential relatives around. We eventually decided on a small hotel that was better on the inside than it looked from the street, having been warned that in India it is usually the other way round. For all the peeling paint on the art deco ironwork and creaking Gothic lift, the *en suite* rooms were clean and cool.

It made sense to go a bit over budget in Mumbai, if only to recuperate from the overnight flight, and to tweak our perceptions around to the Indian way of things. As we collapsed onto the beds, Catherine said, 'I'm so glad you're here, Mum,' which was quite undeserved, since she'd done all the negotiating so far, and I was very glad to be there, too.

We soon perfected our technique. Catherine would go up to the hotel counter, ticket office, or whatever, beam at the incumbent, introduce herself and then say with a flourish, 'And this is my Mum.' It worked every time. I was often promoted to Mummy, never mind Auntie, which inevitably made Catherine someone's honorary sister or cousin instead of just another young, single western female.

There were plenty of occasions when we were particularly glad of each other's company – like the time we took the Malabar Night Express. It arrived already full beyond imagining. Since the sleeper wagons weren't where they should have been and the thing was starting to move, we jumped on anyway, and then had to stumble the entire length of the moving train over sleeping bodies, mountainous piles of baggage, laundry, rice sacks and mail, in almost pitch darkness. We found the only two spare bunks on that train by Braille, I swear, while somehow avoiding arrest for groping lines of sleepers' sticking out feet.

When a glorious dawn finally broke over this swaying snake of humanity, our sleeping companions, two Sikh businessmen who'd been dead to the world when we'd staggered in, blinked a little when they woke and saw us. Catherine's head popped up and she went through her routine. Smiles broke out, hands were shaken across bunks and they bought us beakers of *chai* from the corridor vendor. It tasted exactly like English rice pudding, which is to say, delicious.

We had been travelling non-stop for nearly twenty-four hours when we arrived in Margao, the capital of Goa. It was about 10:30p.m. and we were looking forward to a shower and beds that didn't move. The very latest guidebook had showed some budget hotels not a hundred yards from the station on the main street, the inevitable MG (Mahatma Gandhi) Road. Out we trundled from the garishly lit platform, wondering why there was no one around to check our tickets – and straight into a darkened, rubble-strewn, completely deserted building site.

Our first impression was that perhaps we'd arrived in the middle of a power cut, although the station lights were on. The second was that it was deadly quiet – like no Indian town we'd so far come across. Finally it dawned on us. They must have moved the station. We'd been travelling on the recently opened Konkan rail link from Mumbai to Goa, and this was a completely new station, probably miles from the old one in Margao town centre. The map was useless, we had no idea where we were, and neither had the solitary taxi driver who emerged from behind a pile of barbed wire and rusty pipes. After twenty minutes of frantic, cross-town night driving, we arrived on what looked like MG Road, and found our chosen hotel where they told us that the old station had in fact closed down a week ago. The rooms were somewhat less 'airy and pleasantly decorated' than described, more like mosquito-splattered, with ingrained grime and live-in cockroaches. But at least there was a dribble of water in the shower and the beds were stationary if you didn't turn over too quickly.

My main contribution on the trip was as beastie repeller – preferred weapons, a knotted towel or well-aimed sandal. I tackled anything from ants to stray dogs. One night we found a column of ants had come in through the cracks in the floor and were cutting up and carrying off neat portions of some chewy peppermint indigestion tablets from my medicine bag, having first removed the wrappers. Catherine soon lost her Buddhist tendencies and joined in the nightly swatting routine.

At Trivandrum we met a mother and daughter from England who'd started in Nepal and were heading for Singapore. They told us that on one train, they'd come across not just one body, but two, quite unrelatedly deceased. One was a poor soul on her way to hospital who had died in their carriage, and two hours later there turned out to be a dead beggar under the seats. They said that it had given them a new perspective on complaining.

We made it to the southern tip of India, via Kerala, and loved every minute of it – the startling green vistas of palm-fringed paddi fields and sleepy backwaters, fishing boats with their bobbing lights out to sea, and the tropical moon above it all. We even liked the part where we were woken up at 2a.m. by voices and the thuds of a pick-axe on the cracked earth right outside our ground floor window and a familiar ghastly smell wafting into the room. Then we remembered that at breakfast we'd mentioned the smell and blocked drains to the proprietor. A gang of *dhoti*-clad workmen had arrived to clear out the septic tank. So were they late, early or the night-shift? Reclining in the moonlight on our balcony wall and directing operations was the foreman in a loin cloth and turban. 'Soon finish, auntie,' he said, seeing my face at the window and waving cheerfully.

The next morning all that remained was a patch of clean sand, and the air smelt of neem blossom. But soon it was time to head back to Goa for a few days of relaxation before leaving Catherine to continue at her leisure to Delhi and eventually Indonesia, Australia and New Zealand.

A friendly Irishman at a beach shack recommended a place run by a lovely man called Edwin who'd been in the British merchant navy before returning to his native Goa.

'One big family – that's how I like it,' beamed Edwin on my last night, bringing over a huge plate of prawns sizzling in garlic butter to the communal table. 'God bless our food and all who eat it.'

'Amen,' agreed the 'family' – a couple of antique dealers from Zurich, two Londoners, a Canadian trucker called Chuck escaping from the Ontario winter, and a Dutch mother and daughter team.

When my taxi for the airport arrived, I felt quite weepy when the Swiss couple (who were actually very bald, very gay and very caring) said not to worry, they'd look after my daughter as their own, and when I left Catherine there smiling and confident, I knew she'd be fine. It had all worked out so well, and one day we're going to do it again. South America, maybe. I'll swat the ants and anacondas, and Catherine can do the Spanish...

Expect the Unexpected

I was a stranger and you took me in.

(NT, Matthew 25:35 – said to be the work ethic of
'unofficial guides' the world over)

And that's when I knew I wasn't in Kansas any more.

(Over-used reference from Wizard of Oz, applied to anything
from ants in the sugar bowl to being arrested for taking photos)

Hands Across the Sea

And now it's time to share some of those 'touching' personal experiences.

If you've read *A Passage to India*, you'll know what I mean. Maybe nothing actually happened to poor Miss Quested in the Malabar Caves but since those far-off days things have got much worse for the female traveller. When it comes to a friendly welcome, expect to be given a warm hand – often in the most unexpected places. Not even HM the Queen is safe these days, especially when visiting Australia. Unless you have hips like an ageing rhino, or take Arnie Schwarzenegger along as an escort, the chances are that sooner or later you will be subjected to the exotic grope.

But was it always like this? Was there really a time when the British girl abroad was known to be frigid, and a tickle on the torso was just to see if she was real? Oh, those school trips to Calais in the days of reinforced underwear, bobby socks and neatly-buttoned blouses – English daisies tripping down the gangplank for their first experience of, well, just about everything, really. We needn't have worried. The butchest members of staff always wielded umbrellas on the sunniest of days with cries of *'Va t'en, salaud'* (Go away, you nasty man) at the first sign of the handy foreign male.

Personally, I blame the mini for what happened next – the skirt, not the car. Suddenly every young female decided she had a body after all, and there hadn't been so much exposed flesh around since woad was in vogue. And when the mini-wearers went travelling, the average male south of Dover thought his luck was in.

As it happened, I missed most of this because I was teaching in West Africa, where foreign women were treated like Mary Kingsley even if they behaved like Girls Aloud.

In Zambia too, they kept their sense of humour. When one of the Peace Corps volunteers took a fit of feminism and went bra-less in a loose smock, no one actually touched her, but she never found out that her African name meant 'free film-show'.

Holidays back in Europe came as a bit of a shock. When in Rome – well, we all know what Romans do, but I thought I'd be fairly safe when pushing a pram. Not so. In Italy, the best solution is to have a husband related to the nearest Mafia boss. Failing that, he should be handy with a stiletto, and definitely not be having a siesta while you're out shopping.

Tunisia was interesting. We got several offers for our daughter, then aged seven – well-meant, I'm sure, but what would we have done with all those goats? The new baby was nearly abducted several times, but as this was usually by women intent on breastfeeding him, this doesn't really count. Meanwhile, it was my husband's turn to be tweaked – by other fellers. Me, I took to wearing a long beach robe wherever I went, which helped a bit.

Every year, more women in Islamic countries go back to traditional layerings. While the northern shore of the Mediterranean goes topless, the southern and eastern parts worry increasingly about ankles. There are Australians who can get away with hitch-hiking round North Africa in shorts, but who wants to pack a punch like a kangaroo just to be left in peace? I've taken to carrying a huge cotton scarf which can be slung round offending parts. It seems to act as a sign that you respect the rules. If trouble looms, head for the nearest mosque gates, scarf over head. No one will defile the precincts of a holy place by goosing an infidel.

If it hadn't been for one quite recent 'hands-on' experience, I'd have thought I was getting past that sort of thing. It was at the Pyramids – right inside the middle one to be precise. I had asked Ahmed the friendly taxi man to take us to Kephron's pyramid because the queue for the Great Pyramid was half way to the Sphinx. Husband had decided to sit this one out with the Diocalm and bottled water, (mine's like a policeman, never there when you want him), while the attentive Ahmed led me, bent double, down the steep ramp to the central chamber. He said he'd wait in the recess so that I could commune with the spirit of the dead pharaoh, and that was fine by me.

Having communed, I got back to the recess again, where Ahmed politely waved me on ahead of him, 'in case you fall, madam'. Oh, I fell for it all right. Off I went, clambering, almost crawling, towards the postage-stamp-size patch of sunlight ahead. In the darkest, narrowest part of the tunnel, his hands went round my waist. They ventured higher, lower, everywhere. I didn't stop, but neither did they.

'Not so fast, dear madam,' puffed Ahmed. 'I will make you very happy.'

'This is for hands,' I said, patting the side-rail firmly, head down and gathering speed. 'Now behave yourself, Ahmed, it's Ramadan.'

There was a languorous desert sigh, but the hands obeyed. Who could tell what the tourists really wanted? It was always worth a try.

On the way back to Cairo, Ahmed proudly showed me pictures of his first grandchild. With my own children now old enough to be travelling on their own, I found the whole thing, well, rather touching, really.

One Night in Lagos

Gladys, the owner of the A1 Tourist Hotel, greeted us with a hug,
at which the electricity gave an ominous flicker and almost died.

Nobody goes to Lagos unless they have to, and we had to – it was the only way out of the country that my friend Mags and I could afford after three fascinating weeks looking up our old teaching haunts in central Nigeria. After a heart-warming send-off from our former students, we'd been provided with the college vehicle and driver, a large bunch of bananas and two sturdy convent girls as escorts to get us as far as Enugu for stage two of the trek home.

Things had already gone a little awry at Enugu airport (strictly Domestic), because nothing seemed to be flying directly to Lagos where we were hoping to catch our homebound flight. So we'd spent the last nine hours bribing and hustling our way there via Abuja, which wasn't part of the original plan. Stage three was surviving the landing in a very small plane at Ikeja Domestic and a night in Lagos itself so that we could get to Murtala Muhammed International bright and early for the London plane.

There's a theory about travelling in this part of the world: however bad a time you've had getting there, getting out again is even worse, but actually *being* there, with people you know and love, makes it all worthwhile – and this seemed a good time to put it to the test.

By the time we finally touched down at Ikeja, sweaty, grubby, thirsty and shattered, it was eight o'clock and dark. Very dark – the city was having one of its power brown-outs. In the simmering gloom we managed to convince the nearest sober taxi driver that we couldn't afford the Intercontinental, and were therefore not worth robbing (gales of laughter all round), so he agreed to take us somewhere near Murtala Muhammed that was 'fit for ladies', i.e. not a brothel in its spare time.

He said he would come back for us at 6a.m. next morning, and, still in great good humour, warned us not to oversleep.

We had mixed feelings at our first sight of the A1 Tourist Hotel, an unlovely two-storey concrete block with loose tile-work and dangling wires, but Gladys, the owner, greeted us with a hug, and said our 'en soot' room would be clean in twenty minutes. She told us to help ourselves to drinks from the fridge, which was chuntering away to itself in a corner of the bar, but as the door closed behind her the electricity flickered and almost died. Then it pulled itself together and reverted to a kind of gloaming that wasn't quite enough to revive the fridge or the tiny TV. We made ourselves comfortable on something that had had the stuffing knocked out of it some time ago – as indeed, by now, had we. Nevertheless, we congratulated ourselves on finding somewhere that felt friendly while not being the Interconters, and knocked back several tepid Fantas straight from the bottle by the light and smell (a hallucinatory mix of fumes, badly trimmed wick and incinerated insect wings) of a kerosene lamp left burning on the tiny bar for such emergencies. Finally, the power gave up completely, to yells of consternation and annoyance from many in the neighbourhood.

An hour and four Fantas each later, we were shown up to our room by torchlight. It smelt of lamp smoke, damp, bleach, insect spray, and something Mags swore was goat, although we hadn't actually seen any about at that point. The naked light bulb chose this moment to flare briefly back into life, revealing the kind of room that looks better in the dark. There was one iron-framed double bed, a table-top fan reluctantly beginning to stir the smells around, and Gladys was right about the 'soot' – everything was quite imaginatively filthy. We'd have preferred single beds, but you can't have everything.

While Mags brushed dead (mostly) insects off the bed so she could roll on it laughing with hysterical relief that we'd actually found somewhere to sleep – so she fondly imagined – I plugged the fist-sized holes in the window mozzie mesh with a scarf. There wasn't much I could do about the missing panes, broken locks, and an air-con unit that clearly hadn't worked since Independence. Then off went the power again without even a blip, at which the general racket coming from the street outside actually increased as pedestrians, cyclists and dogs bumped into each other or fell into the storm ditches.

The bathroom, for want of a worse word (we were, after all, 'en soot') had one tap stuck in dribble mode, and a bucket which soon proved its worth in galvanised zinc. The only way to flush the loo, or achieve anything ablution-wise, was to let it fill from the leaking tap and use it as creatively as the space and darkness allowed. The drain was a hole in the floor about the diameter of mature cobra, with no grill but, as Mags remarked, at least it wasn't blocked and it stopped the place flooding. There was no door on the 'en soot', and in the middle of our clanking and splashing, Gladys brought up supper – cheese (tinned) and chilli (very fresh) sandwiches, washed down with half-pint enamel mugs of Lipton's tea with condensed milk, all of which tasted wonderful as we'd only had a few bananas and some groundnuts all day. When asked about the chances of a wake-up call, Gladys seemed a little vague as to what this might involve and bade us a warm goodnight and sweet dreams.

Propping a chair against the door and setting both our alarms for 5a.m., we doused the smoking lamp and collapsed onto the fetid bed in our underwear, thinking it would soon go quiet. Up country, where we'd just come from, nothing much had stirred after ten o'clock except mozzies, but here we had a late evening class chanting the Koran next door and several high-life bars at full belt. Opposite was an all-night panel-beater's/garage whose car-washing hose was apparently the only running water in the street. Judging by the racket, it was also doubled as the community bathhouse and dating agency.

The power was still off, so the fan was useless and the air was dark and thick enough to be cut into slabs and served with custard. Mags, a gifted sleeper, had just started to snore gently when the taxi driver's claim about being near the airport proved to be unnervingly accurate. With a tile-shattering roar, a large jet tried to land on the roof. It missed, but the bombing-raid din woke up not only the goats in the yard outside (Mags was right about those, there were about half dozen) but every dog, chicken and baby around.

Things settled down again, but not for long. The power suddenly came back on, including the light we'd forgotten to switch off and the fan, which fell over with the shock. At a stroke, the street sprang noisily back to life – until, at around 1a.m., the entire district blacked out again. Clearly this was it for the night, because the emergency generator in the yard cranked into life, filling our room with diesel fumes and waking up all the goats, chickens, dogs, babies...

There were mozzies, of course, and annoying small, flittery things – and that strange itchiness you get when, with a start, you remember where you are. Sunrise was a long time coming. By then, four more jets had tried to land on the roof and the car-wash hosepipe opposite was back in business. What finally got us up, though, was a lot of shouting which developed into a nasty fight right outside the window, involving several taxi drivers, one of them ours.

We watched aghast through the gaps in the mozzy mesh. Gladys said as she kindly brought us tea, (with goats' milk this time) that our man was being beaten for not paying his 'toll' to the local gang boss. To our relief, he won on points.

'I see my ladies did not oversleep,' was his smiling greeting, as we, bleary-eyed, met him, bloody-nosed, on the doorstep.

Nepal - End of an Era

In the market, I bought a Kate-Adie-type waistcoat with lots of zips and pockets, and someone whose grandma must have been a seer asked me what disaster I'd been parachuted in to cover.

The trip was billed as 'A Short Walk in the Himalayas', which suited me fine as I'm not really the Sherpa type. A thirteen-day holiday in Nepal, including five nights in Kathmandu with the chance of a flight to see Mount Everest; three days walking in and around the old hill-station of Nagarkot; two days in Pokhara, the base camp town for lots of treks with its tranquil lake and views of the Annapurna Range. Apart from rumbling Maoist insurgents, blistered feet, Nepal's notoriously unhealthy water supply, a completely irrational fear of dodgy rope bridges over precipices and a tendency for trouble to follow me around, what could possibly go wrong?

As it turned out, quite a lot. Our chosen dates happened to be 23rd May-4th June 2001, and on June 1st, Crown Prince Dipendra, heir to two thousand years of Nepalese monarchy and known to his old Etonian friends as Dippy, went crazy and shot eight members of his family including his parents, the King and Queen, and two of their retinue.

Until then, things had been going remarkably well for our little group. Having been otherwise occupied with teaching and child-rearing in various parts of Africa for most of the hippie era, I'd rather missed out on experiences such as the obligatory overland trail to Kathmandu, smoking dope on Kashmir houseboats and fasting in ashrams run by bearded, chubby, chanting gurus in swaddling clothes. A surprising number of us felt the same, and while we agreed that, although the Kathmandu experience would have been much more authentic then, there was enough left to get the flavour of what it must have been like for the really adventurous in the 60s. Admittedly, some of those who'd stayed on after running out of steam or money didn't look too well on it, and serious doubts were expressed about how they'd get on without the NHS and a pension when the wheels finally came off at the end of their search for themselves or the meaning of life.

We strode off to do the sights, haggled a bit, got lost in the Old Town (doesn't everyone?) and wondered whether it was okay to take pictures of the Burning Ghats on the sacred Bagmati River, ('No, not *Bas*mati, Malcolm, have you got that thing switched on?'). The guide said that it should be fine, from a respectful distance, so we did, except for two women friends who still didn't think we should. He also pointed out the deserted Royal Burning Ghats, the only ghats not doing a roaring trade, as well as several dead dogs and great wodges of suspiciously dark garbage almost choking swathes of the sacred river. There was smoke and ash everywhere – in fact one lady said she felt quite ill with it all.

Suitably reminded of our own mortality, we were bussed off to various Buddhist stupas and more temples than you could shake a joss stick at, eventually to arrive at Nagarkot for our three days of short walks in the Himalayas, foothills thereof. Nagarkot, and especially The Fort Hotel, reminded everyone of Pankot and Rose Cottage in *The Jewel in the Crown* which every single one of us had seen. At the briefing that evening round a huge log fire, the group had bonded well enough to accept that the short walks were going to have to be split into three tiers of capability. The A-team, or Show-Offs as they were quickly dubbed, consisted of a retired wing-commander, a whippy young Indian lady doctor, my husband and someone else who didn't say much but mentioned marathon training. With them would go the chief guide, a Sherpa who'd been up Everest and whose idea of a short walk turned out to be running up and down rice terraces all day without even breaking sweat.

I plumped thankfully for the B-team with most of the others, to be shepherded along by Number Two guide. Firmly in the C-team were a couple from somewhere in the Fens who shouldn't really have been allowed out because they'd interpreted a short walk as on a par with nipping out to their corner shop for a packet of ciggies. There was also a spare husband who'd already sprained his ankle, and a very overweight widow who was quite sweet but in denial about almost everything. The C-team was put in the charge of the driver, a burly Tibetan, in case any of them needed a piggy-back, yak, taxi or air ambulance.

Both the scenery and the rural poverty were humbling. There were tiny distant paddi fields gleaming like emerald cloissoné, and underfoot paddi squelching with frogs; bedspreads of red peppers and garlic laid out to dry, thin women bent double under avalanches of firewood, thinner children clutching goat kids, and far, snowy horizons. There were even yaks, and we stroked one. The air was essence of mountain pine you could have drunk with ice and a tonic.

On the last night in Nagarkot, just before dinner at eight, the family A-team member let out a strangled yell from the shower. Intrigued, I grabbed a shoe to help swat whatever it was, only to find him clutching a towel and staring at his feet, which appeared to be bleeding profusely from several places, right across the white tiles and down the drain hole.

'Christ,' he said, short-sighted without his specs, but rather appropriately in the circumstances, 'I think I've got the stigmata.'

I pointed out that he didn't like animals or poverty enough to make like Francis of Assisi, and that his hands seemed immune, so becoming stigmata-ised (or whatever you called it) didn't seem a likely explanation for the *Psycho* scene in the shower. Then I spotted a large black swollen wiggly creature attached to the back of his ankle where he couldn't see it, and another one sneaking off down the drain, probably the one that had recently abandoned his gushing left instep. Leaches hadn't figured prominently in first aid training for teachers, and neither of us could remember much about them, apart from something to do with blood coagulation and having to burn them off, although that might have been ticks. But we had no matches, which was probably just as well, because the hangers-on (there was another on the other side) dropped off with a swipe of a towel and also disappeared down the hole.

There were now four places bleeding away copiously on hubby's feet. 'No, they don't hurt. But when's it going to stop?' he asked plaintively. 'Um,' I replied, helping him hobble to a chair, and grabbing wads of toilet tissue to staunch the various flows. My husband has always been a bit of a bleeder, so I soon ran out of loo roll and cotton wool pads. We were already fifteen minutes late for dinner and the last two were still leaking. In desperation, I fluffed out my emergency tampon and stuck it over the biggest seep with some blister tape just to get his socks and shoes on. Finally, leaving the room looking like a field dressing station, we tottered over to join the others and mumbled our excuses.

They were already on the main course, but a B-teammate next to me was curious, so I quietly told her all about it, including the tampon part. She then told her husband, and the ripple spread up the long dining table like Chinese Whispers. In the always inevitable lull in polite conversation, a voice, clear as a York Minster bell from the other end said, 'What? Kate had to use a *tampax* on a leach bite? Eee, I never knew the holes were *that* deep!'

The table went into spontaneous convulsions. Soup was spluttered, thighs slapped and eyes wiped with napkins as the assembled waiters looked on in bewilderment. The only way out was to blame the outburst on the English sense of humour.

Next morning, on the nine-hour drive to Pokhara, the A-team doctor explained that leeches use both analgesic and anti-coagulant chemicals to keep the blood flowing, but that after a while these wore off and the bleeding stopped. We'd somehow thought they were supposed to seal things up after they'd had enough, and that we'd knocked them off before they'd got around to it, hence all the wadding. Oh, how we laughed...

The journey was further enlivened by a game of dare involving a rope bridge, below which raged a torrent in fetching shades of milky turquoise. Perilous pit-stops at village café loos; getting stuck in exhaust smoke belching from over-laden lorries painted and tinselled like elephants going to a festival; a vast number of landslides-waiting-to-happen, mainly on hairpin bends – we took it all more or less in our stride.

After one not over-hygienic pit-stop, someone quoted Dame Edna Everage's memorable song-line: '*The Black Hole of Calcutta was a pretty dreadful place / The curries were disgusting and the loos were a dis-GRAYCE.*' This set off more quoting, including a fine Edwardian-style attempt at *The Green Eye of the Little Yellow God* – the one that starts, '*There's a one-eyed yellow idol to the north of Kathmandu*'. But no one could get further than the first verse. There was mention of Mad Carew and the Colonel's daughter, which caused some confusion with *Eskimo Nell*. Only one person thought *The Green Eye* wasn't by Kipling, and he turned out to be right. Apparently it was written in 1911 by someone called John Milton Hayes – who was definitely *not* to be confused with John Milton Keynes, John Milton and especially not John Maynard Keynes .

It was Thursday May 31st, although by now most of us were barely aware of the day or date – only that we had four days left and it wasn't enough. After the final white-knuckle series of bends and almost sceneried out, we reached Pokhara and the Bluebird Hotel, to be rewarded by the very last of the sunset catching the stunning peaks of the Annapurna Range. The guide just had time to point out the great peak of Machapuchare (near enough 23,000 ft/7,000 m), named after its fish-tale shape and sounding interestingly similar to Machupichu in Peru, named for exactly the same reason. He said the best time to get pictures was at dawn, because the goddess who lived up there would veil her face with cloud soon afterwards at this time of year, so you had to be quick.

Naturally, we slept right through dawn and woke up on Friday morning of June 1st to see nothing of the mist-shrouded peaks then or for the rest of the day. We spent it in rowing boats, oared and coxed by the dominant males, on Pokhara's magical mirror lake, and generally wandering round the town. From the boats, the guide had pointed out a flag on a high-walled lakeside compound belonging to the Nepalese Royal Family, and said it meant some of them must be staying there, but it wasn't likely to be the King and Queen at this time of year.

After lunch in town, we pottered about the muddy market devoted mainly to trekking gear, shawls and instant food. I bought a putty-coloured North Face gilet/waistcoat with lots of pockets and zips, thinking it would cure me once and for all of losing essentials such as pens, batteries, peppermints, hankies, sunglasses and string. They instantly renamed me Kate Adie, and someone whose grandma must have been a seer asked which disaster I'd been parachuted in to cover – the curries or the loos.

Much of the afternoon was spent amiably trying on the snake charmers' pythons for size, drinking *chyia* (like Indian *chai* with a dash of spices) and avoiding duck-pond-size puddles, bicycles, livestock of all sizes and the more grubbier and grabbier *sadhus, gurus* and similar frequenting the bazaars and temples. The old India hands said they couldn't be proper *sadhus* if they grabbed you, and it wasn't done to touch the real ones anyway. The men said that wouldn't be a problem for them, and so did the two woman-friends, to smiles all round, as their orientation had been quietly acknowledged and accepted by the group in the usual middle-aged, middle-class British way:

'Ooh, do you really think so?'

'Trust me on this one.'

'Well, you never know, do you?'

'We were next door to them in Nagarkot.'

'Oh, I see...'

Not much happened in Pokhara or in the Bluebird Hotel after 9:30p.m. A mixed group of a dozen or so Nepalis arrived and introduced themselves briefly as agency workers. Everyone had been saying what a bad season they'd had this year, and until their arrival we'd been the only ones there. I sorted out the camera and set the alarm for 5a.m., determined to catch Machapuchare at sunrise, and we went to bed nicely tired after a thoroughly enjoyable day.

I'm not a heavy sleeper at the best of times, and that night I kept hearing intermittent odd noises from about 2:30a.m. onwards. Doors were being banged upon, there were raised voices, phones ringing, some wailing, even sobbing. Eventually I went to the door to look for signs of sudden illness, secret police, Maoists insurgents or smoke, but our downstairs corridor looked perfectly normal. Hubby, who could sleep for England and in fact has slept through, on various continents, the night feeds of three babies, a hurricane, the tail-end of an Indian Ocean cyclone, a small earthquake and two burglaries, slumbered on. By now it was 4:45a.m., and I noticed the sky seemed to be lightening. Determined not to be caught out by the shy goddess and not wanting to wake him, I put a sweater on over my nightie with my new Kate

Adie waistcoat on top, pulled on some trousers and boots and grabbed the camera.

Hair awry and hoping no one else was around I slunk down the corridor to the outside back veranda and was almost stalled in my tracks by a truly memorable view. It looked like several days of creation out there, all at once. Dawn's rosy fingers were doing their bit on all the Annapurna glacial peaks, and Machapuchare herself was positively glowing. Unable to believe my luck I was snapping away, when the view suddenly became a lot more memorable. I jumped like a rabbit, as a soft male Nepali voice behind me said, 'Good morning, ma'am.'

'Good morning to you,' I replied gaily. 'Isn't it wonderful?' But there was something about the way he hesitated to agree.

'Have you not heard the news?' He must have seen I hadn't a clue what he meant. 'Last night, the Crown Prince, you know, the heir to the throne, went mad at the Palace and shot his mother the Queen. They say he shot her first, then the others.'

Now it's possible he actually said *our* news, or *our* crown prince, but by now both hands were over my mouth with the still-open camera dangling from its wrist strap, because I'd actually thought for one barmy moment that he was telling me Prince Charles had shot *our* Queen, followed by lord knows who else, back home in Buckingham Palace, where royal family relations hadn't been too good of late.

Thankfully, before I made a complete idiot of myself, he added, 'And then Prince Dipendra tried to shoot himself – we think...' and his voice trailed off in a sob.

It would be churlish (a favourite word of our own dear Queen) to say I felt almost weak with relief that my own fears had been unfounded. Also piling in were suspicions that he was the local fantasist (quickly dismissed), sympathy for the Nepalese and dark thoughts about what effect the ensuing mayhem would have on our getting home on schedule. Which is how I found myself in my nightie making sympathetic noises and taking the hand of a weeping Nepali gentleman in the glory of a chilly Himalayan dawn. At least I was able to offer him a tissue from one of my many Kate Adie pockets.

Watching this scene from their balcony were the two woman-friends, who had also been determined to catch the dawn. The first I knew of their presence was a call of, 'Hey, Kate, are you okay? Is everything all right?'

I said that I was okay, but some other things weren't, and suggested we meet for coffee with my companion, Nawang, who would explain. The waitress had her face covered, and two more of their compatriots were crying into the hotel phone in the lobby. Even Machapuchare had covered her face. The TV was on, blaring solemn music and showing formal pictures of the late King and Queen with titles announcing their deaths at 9.15p.m. the previous evening at the Palace, none of which got us any further. Nawang said that he'd been phoned at about 2:30a.m. by his brother who lived above his office near the Palace. He'd heard some shots and suspected the Maoists. He had eventually got hold of his cousin, a Palace guard who'd been on duty at the time, from whom he'd got the story. Nawang had been so upset that he'd woken the other members of his group who'd also been very distressed, and spent half the night on the phone trying to get more information about the tragedy.

The best consensus was that Crown Prince Dipendra had gone crazy at a family dinner. He'd shot his mother dead first because she was objecting to his choice of bride, followed by the King, a brother prince, three princesses, an aunt and an uncle. The next fatality was a guard who'd tried to stop the bloodbath, and then Dipendra had turned one of his three guns on himself. He was now unconscious on a life-support machine, and no one was sure what might happen next.

As it turned out, Nawang's version was the nearest to the truth (as revealed weeks later by an extensive inquiry), that we heard all that day from any other source. It was Saturday, and our last day in Pokhara. The guide was consulted about whether it would be polite, or indeed safe, to go into town. He said he knew we would be respectful, and it should be all right if we stuck to condolences and didn't mention politics, which seemed very reasonable. Hubby kept insisting that I should never have bought 'that Kate Adie flak jacket', implying that, as usual, the whole thing was my fault.

We set off in twos and threes rather than a posse, having mooted a discreet rendezvous at the market juice stall around noon to swap information. Most shops and cafés remained closed; even the snake charmers had given up. Three of us found a tiny place run by a Tibetan which was open, with what looked like the entire 'ferengi' population of Pokhara asking what the hell was going on in a variety of languages. When Kipling mentioned rumours in the bazaar, he wasn't kidding. By lunch time, we'd been variously assured that:

- The Crown Prince was already dead
- He'd flown to the Seychelles
- All airports were closed
- International phone lines had been shut down
- The dead guard had done it, and was a Maoist.
- The Maoists were going to take over anyway.
- The funerals would be that evening at the Royal Burning Ghats.
- The late King's own brother was obviously behind the whole thing because he was the only notable royal who wasn't present, dead, or nearly so.

In the event, only two of these turned out to be true – the ones about the airports and the funerals. No one had been able to phone home in that largely pre-internet, pre-mobile-phone era, not because of government intervention, but because the lines were jammed by anxious Nepalis and news agencies from all over the world, and no one official was answering anyway. It was also true that the late King's brother, Prince Gyanendra, hadn't been in town – he'd been the one staying at the royal lodge by Pokhara Lake, and had flown back to Kathmandu at dawn on hearing the news.

The airport news caused most concern. Two of our group had chosen to fly from Kathmandu to Pokhara because they'd missed the flight to Everest. On rejoining us at the Bluebird Hotel, they'd defused some good-natured teasing about being too scared of heights and hairpin bends to go by road by a plea for sympathy, since low cloud had stopped them seeing anything at all, but they had a return ticket. Then someone said they'd heard from a lorry driver that the road to Kathmandu, and there was only one road, had been blocked by a massive landslide after heavy rain at around six o'clock this morning.

Over an early dinner to allow the whole staff to watch the funerals on TV that evening, insurance policies were checked for acts of god, missed flights, Maoist uprisings, landslides, advanced dysentery, lost work days and additional fees for dog kennels. All in all, it was agreed that there were worst places to be stuck if it came to it. We had enough clean underwear (one dissenting voice, male) and socks to get by, and anyway, there wasn't a damned thing we could do about any of it. Rather subdued, we went to join the weeping staff round the TV, where the Royal Burning Ghats we'd seen only days ago were fulfilling their ancient role against a midnight-blue sky filled with the writhing breath of dragons and eerie lamentations.

The guide had said to be ready an hour before the set time for departure anyway, because even if the landslide had been cleared, there would be delays with so many people trying to get in or out of Kathmandu. To everyone's relief, when Sunday dawned damply, the road had been cleared, but for single-line traffic only – just. Vehicles were forced to creep along so near the edge that no one wanted to look, except, we hoped, our sturdy Tibetan driver who'd probably seen much worse when he'd escaped from the Chinese. Everywhere farmers, police and road workers were shaving each other's heads and rubbing ash on their faces. Lowering clouds and more washouts across the road added to the vaguely apocalyptic feel of it all.

It was mourning dark when we finally lurched into Kathmandu. Number One guide advised us not to go out in case 'some people in town were getting too upset'. He also said that we should be ready an hour earlier than the scheduled departure time tomorrow morning because although the airport had been closed all day, if it were suddenly to open tomorrow, there would be a huge rush and long queues. A copy of *The Kathmandu Post* for Sunday, June 3rd (which I still have) informed us that the late King's brother, Prince Gyanendra, had been appointed

Regent while the Crown Prince was still 'incapacitated'. Number Two guide said he'd heard that the Crown Prince was already dead.

In the hotel lobby was a quite large gilded idol of some smiling Hindu deity with arms surplus to requirements. There were joss sticks burning round him and flower offerings, with a portrait of their late Majesties. The fairly big yellow god still had his two eyes, but there were scratches round them as if, at dead of night, some sacrilegious tourists had tried a removal job in misplaced homage to the poem, but got cold feet.

To the astonishment of all, the airport miraculously opened the next day, the plane was on time, and we got home according to plan, but by then it had closed again, and stayed closed for several days more because the Crown Prince really was dead by now, and his uncle was to be crowned King. I pointed out that Kate Adie jackets were good for something anyway, and still wear it when I'm feeling intrepid if I think no one will laugh. But really, it was the beginning of the end of two thousand years of monarchy in Nepal. In 2007 King Gyanendra was retired and the monarchy abolished and by 2008 the Maoists, always waiting in the wings, had more or less taken over.

Don't Play Footsie with the Putse

The putse fly's Latin name sounds quite elegant – Cordylobia anthropophagia – until you realize the last part meant human-eater, and that human is you.

When travelling in Tropical Africa, always make sure your underwear is thoroughly ironed. Sounds like advice to long-gone colonials with a train of bearers in tow? So who's looking, and what needs ironing anyway, in these days of drip-dry everything? Just rinse out the smalls and hang them on the nearest bush. Put on when dry, and away you go.

Except that a few days after my bush laundry session, I started to itch around my waistband, normally a place where mosquitoes wouldn't venture. But somehow they didn't feel like mosquito bites, and they didn't go away, whatever I put on them. They soon turned into nasty, red pimply bumps, four of them in a neat line, and I was getting curious, not to say tetchy. But what I saw when I got round to having a good look made me almost glad the afflicted area was somewhere I could see for myself - because if someone else had tried to explain what was going on down there, it would have sounded like this:

'Well, there's a sort of black pin-heady thing inside the bumps. Hey! That one's moving!'

Whaat!

It's true. Inside each bump was a maggot. They actually wriggled, and believe me, so did I. I was now an official hatchery for baby putses.

The putse fly, aka the tumbu fly, or common blowfly, is common all over tropical Africa wherever dead things hang around for a bit, which is to say almost everywhere. It's like a blue-bottle, except that it's as green as an African beer bottle. The Latin name sounds quite elegant – *Cordylobia anthropophagia* – until you realize the last part meant human-eater, and that human is you.

The putse's preferred method of reproduction is to lay its eggs in rotting flesh. That way, the maggots can hatch out into a smelly supply of their favourite food. But some curious kind of intelligence has taught this creature that if it can't get a good carcass, a line of damp washing will do.

How does it *know* that the next stage in the lifecycle of a pair of drying knickers is to be pulled on unironed by the owner? Body warmth does the rest. The tiny whitish maggots hatch out and burrow into the skin so neatly that the victim hardly feels a thing. After all, Africa is a pretty itchy place at the best of times.

I couldn't help feeling slightly victimised. We'd only been staying with friends in Lusaka and gone down to Victoria Falls for a few days in the rondavel camp. It was hardly pioneer territory, and here I was, infested with maggots.

The old hands said not to panic. *Ha!* The best thing was to cover the bumps with Vaseline. The maggots would try to come up for air, head first, and could then be pinched out cleanly, or blood-poisoning would set in. Or maybe I'd prefer to have it done at the hospital, followed by a course of antibiotics. But I'd seen that hospital, so they left me on my own, with only a jar of Vaseline and a steady hand to stop me turning into a wormery.

What they didn't say was that it hurt like hell, but it was worth it for the relief of seeing the first little brute pop out in one piece, still wriggling, and only slightly shorter than something you'd find in a pea pod. When it was all over, I passed them round among the more prurient of my friends, and toyed with the idea of pickling the little wrigglers in best South African brandy for posterity. In the end, I couldn't resist the pure glee of squishing them, one by one.

After that, I became something of an expert, because a putse epidemic was now in full swing in Lusaka. Not a washing line was safe. People I hardly knew would turn up with a jar of Vaseline and ask to be de-maggotted. Amazingly, I made some good friends that way. No one died of blood-poisoning, but the news soon got round, and by the end of the week, everyone was ironing everything. Even charcoal-burning irons weren't to be sneezed at, considering the alternative.

Then someone remembered that King Herod was supposed to have died from being eaten alive by worms. Had the slaves been skimping on the ironing? Did Salome lose her bottle when it came to the pinch – or did she quietly lose the Vaseline? So much for historical theory – but don't let it happen to you.

Zim-Zam, Thank You, Ma'am

Getting ripped off up the Zambezi.

Don't you just love border crossings? There's always a tingle in the air. Maybe it's the mug shots of wanted criminals and lists of prohibited goods on the walls, or Uzi-toting guards trying to look bored. Will everything be in order? Will they let you through?

If you want scenery as well, they don't come much more spectacular than the Zimbabwe-Zambia border on the Zambezi at Victoria Falls. But where you get border crossings, you get villains, which could be part of the buzz. You're warned not to change money on the street. But then, the cash point is down – *the* cash point. So naturally, the only two places that might change sterling for Zimbabwe dollars have impatient multi-lingual queues shuffling several times round the block. Homing in like buzzards on a road kill are various shifty characters with bulging pockets, but you're still hankering for those really cheap bush boots from the place that doesn't take credit cards.

Zimbabwe dollars, Zambian kwacha – I have to admit to a double-take when I saw the discrepancy in the exchange rates, and that should have warned me. At that time, the Zim dollar was about 60 to the pound sterling, while the poor old Zambian kwacha was pushing 3,600. (These days, the situation is even crazier than that, with the Zim dollar virtually worthless and the Zambian kwacha holding its own). Yet I was old enough to remember the days when both the Zim dollar and the kwacha had been less than 20 to the pound, and the two kinds of notes had been clearly distinguishable. Border crossings in times of fiscal uncertainty are not good places for those weak at mental arithmetic.

But even common sense should have warned me that, with one currency unit now worth 60 times its neighbour's and looking very similar, here was a scam waiting to happen, and probably to me.

'Mama,' said a soft voice at my shoulder. 'You want taxi, carvings, cheap lodgings, change money?'

'Well, as it happens...' I said. And that was it.

I showed him mine – a £20 note. He showed me his – a grubby wad of Zim dollar hundreds. Apologetically, he flicked through it saying he hadn't quite got the necessary 1200 Zim, but would fetch some more. He didn't even suggest that I handed over my £20, just asked me nicely to wait behind the taxis because there were police about. Which there certainly were.

While he was gone, I chatted to a young lad, who may or may not have been his sidekick, about the dreadful price of mealie meal in Zimbabwe these days. Then my man was back with an even thicker wad. 'See, plenty Zim,' he said, flicking them briskly. Unfortunately, I didn't notice where his thumb was as he began counting through the one hundred notes with an expert corner flick.

We'd got to eleven hundred, when he suddenly pushed my share at me, with several more hundreds, saying, 'Okay, take – police are coming.' He didn't even have to snatch my £20; I handed it over like a lamb, whereupon he vanished in a way that suggested years of practice.

The young lad stayed to watch as I automatically recounted the bills. I loved that bit. ' . . . twelve hundred, *thirteen* hundred? Funny, he's given me one hundred too much...'

Then it hit me. Never in a million years would one of these guys give you too much. Actually it *was* funny. The wad consisted entirely of hundred *kwacha* notes, and he'd had his thumb over the 'K'. He'd given me not 1200 Zim dollars worth £20, but 1300 Zambian kwacha – worth around 36p. In fact it was so funny I started to laugh. After all, it was my own stupid fault, and it could have been a lot more than £19.64p that I'd just donated directly to the Zambezi Sinking Fund for the Unemployed. Cut out the middleman, I say.

Then it got funnier. 'Aaay, mama,' said the lad in what sounded like genuine sympathy. 'These people are all thieves. But since these kwacha things are no good to you, you can give them to me.'

Taking a deep breath, I told him I was going to give them to the first beggar I saw – who turned out to be a blind old lady sitting beside the road, singing *Jesus Wants me for a Sunbeam* or something similar. I put the wad into her hand, apologising that they were only kwacha, and said someone would give her Zim dollars for them.

The lad was right behind me. He spoke to the blind lady, and I caught the word 'fifties'. Unable to believe my ears, I gawked as he took the wad of hundreds and handed her a 10 Zim note (18p) – half their value.

I grabbed his collar and explained carefully that if he didn't give her exactly 20 Zim dollars for the kwacha, I would call that policeman over there. At which he shrugged and handed her the other 10. Then, with a blithe 'Enjoy your stay in Zimbabwe, mama', he too vanished.

'God will bless you, my children,' said the blind old lady, now 36p richer, and carried on singing.

A Sprinkling of Islands

It's fun to imagine what you could do with that kind of money.
I could buy that island I've always wanted to buy all my
life, and live there with my family.

(Johnny Depp)

When they play the flute in Zanzibar,
they dance as far as the Lakes.

(19th-century Swaheli saying)

The Comoros - Islands of the Moon

It's a man's world on the mysterious Indian Ocean island of Grande Comore, where women are considered too weak to go fishing from canoes. But Comorian women have their own ways of doing things and are tougher than they look.

You've set your alarm to catch the first light of a tropical dawn streaming over the volcanic peaks. From your balcony, the Indian Ocean beyond the coral reef is turning from silver to deep sapphire. So it's off across the spotless white sand and into the shallow, swimming-pool-clear waters of the lagoon for a dip before breakfast. Sounds like Paradise? For you maybe, but for Yasmine Amadou, waking up in a still-dark fishing village not half a mile from the hotel, Paradise it isn't.

The dawn light is the only alarm in Bangoi-Kouni, and in all the other fishing villages of Grande Comore, but the women are already stirring. Yasmine is also going for a dip before breakfast. The round trip, down to the lagoon with the other fisherwomen and back again with the catch, will take about three hours if they're lucky. Until then, there will be no breakfast. Sometimes there isn't even enough paraffin to boil water for tea. Or there's no tea.

In the dry season, there is never enough water to wash properly, so a rub down with a piece of damp towel has to do. But for Yasmine it's a normal day. In the Comores, the fisherwomen start working young. She says she was about six years old when she was first allowed to go out fishing with the women. 'That is when you're old enough not to fall over in the water, and to learn that sea urchins hurt and which fish can poison you.'

Now she's twenty-two, and she's been doing this every day except for the few years at primary school. I ask her if it's hard work. 'It's not so bad,' she says with a slow smile. 'The women have their own cooperatives. Nobody calls herself the boss, and we all get a fair share of the catch.'

They speak French here, or Swahili, or the Comorian dialect which has some Arabic thrown in. So cries of *'Bonjour, Mama Cherie,'* greet Yasmine's mother, a big woman of about forty, as the women emerge from their huts and collect their fishing gear. *'Salaam, ma tante.'* (Peace to you, Aunty), *'Hey, Desirée, bouge-toi!'* (Shift yourself, Desirée). All these languages are hardly surprising, considering the position of these islands, in the Mozambique Channel between the southern African coast and the northern tip of Madagascar.

'Is England a part of Africa?' Yasmine asks. And why not? To most Europeans, the Comores, also known as the Federal Islamic Republic of Comoros, might as well be on the dark side of the moon. In fact the islands were first settled by Persian traders who called them the Islands of the Moon. Trading with the East African coast brought the Swahili language, and African slaves. In fact slavery wasn't finally abolished here until 1904. Then the French took over, so the only English speakers most Comorians know are from South Africa and passing cruise ships, or they're hardy international backpacker types. Even the biggest hotel on Grande Comore with the best beaches has now been abandoned by tour operators and is all but derelict.

Language problems apart, it isn't easy to get talking to the women. Grande Comore, the largest of the islands, is almost 100% Muslim, so it's a man's world here. The women wear the *chironi,* a length of bright cotton cloth that covers the arms, shoulders, and often the head. They go fishing fully dressed, wading up to their waists in the shallow waters of the lagoons, and don't like being approached, especially by men and anyone with a camera.

Risking my French, I ask Yasmine if she's married yet, and she giggles and looks at Mama Cherie.

'Here we have two kinds of marriage,' Mama explains. *'Grand mariage,* and *petit mariage.* But a *grand mariage* costs a lot of money. The husband must save for many years and all his relatives have to help him.'

Getting married in the Comores is certainly a complicated business, but some of it is in the woman's favour. As soon as a daughter is born, the father starts to build a house for her, which sounds a pretty good idea. It may be only a simple concrete base with wooden supports and woven palm-leaf walls, but it gives a girl some standing, and is a start to the long business of preparing for the wedding.

The real burden falls on the groom. For a *grand mariage*, he could pay a bride price of up to 250 grammes of gold jewellery, 10 trunks of clothing, 10 cows and the equivalent of up to £10,000 to the bride's relatives. The ceremonies, based on Yemeni/Swahili legends of the wedding of King Solomon to the Queen of Sheba, can go on for over a week and the whole neighbourhood is invited, so a lot of the cash goes on food, transport, and professional singers, drummers and dancers who are expected to keep going all night.

This does seem a bit O.T.T. for an island as poor as this one, and I said so later, as tactfully as I could, to Aboubakar, our guide.

To my relief, he agreed. 'It's a disgrace. The government even tried to ban it once. It holds back development. More than half our people have no paid work, and most don't have electricity or piped water. The money saved for *grand mariage* should be invested in a small business or a well, not blown away in one big party,' he declared. 'Why can't everyone have a *petit mariage*, where the couple make their promises at the mosque or to each other, and the bride price can be a simply token, like a torch or a new ballpoint?'

Back at the beach, Mama Cherie and Yasmine aren't so sure.

'I will make a *petit mariage* soon,' says Yasmine. 'But I would like one day to have a *grand mariage* because it's good for the women. Your husband gets respect from it. He could even be invited onto the village council. He comes to live in your house, which you keep, even after a divorce. Everyone can see what you're worth, and what is yours by right – the jewellery, the clothes. That's good for us.'

'It makes me proud to help give my son a *grand mariage*,' agrees Mama Cherie. 'Then he'll look after me when I'm old and can't fish any more.'

They hitch up their long skirts and *chironis* and wade into the turquoise water. I follow to watch them laying their nets, which are mostly pieces of old mosquito net or faded *chironis* sewn together. The early birds enjoying a leisurely breakfast on the hotel terrace don't give them a second glance.

But Yasmine remembers several days when absolutely everyone looked up. One was when a fisherman in his canoe out by the reef caught a live Coelocanth 'fossil fish'.

'Everyone came running, swimming, diving,' she laughs. 'They said the scientists must see it. So the fisherman asked them for 40 million francs, but it died, and now it's stuffed and in the hotel Dive Shop. Maybe he was thinking of his own *grand mariage*. Then he would really have been a big man.'

They also remember the day when a hijacked Ethiopian Airlines plane came in low over the water, obviously in trouble.

'Suddenly it went like this.' Yasmine waggles her arms to demonstrate the last dramatic moments before it plunged into the sea just beyond the reef. 'They say that was when the hijackers shot the pilot in the head.' She mimes that too. 'It was terrible. There were bodies everywhere. We waded out to help, but we are never allowed in the boats. The men say we women are too weak.'

It was some years later, in June 2009, that a Yemenia Airbus went into the sea near the capital, Moroni. There was only one survivor from the 153 people on board – a girl of Comorian origin who had clung to the wreckage for as many hours as the years of her young life – thirteen. Weak? I don't think so. Looking at them singing, shouting and joking as they beat the water to drive the fish, it doesn't seem possible that the men consider them not strong enough to paddle a *galawa*, the local out-rigger canoe.

I suggest to Yasmine that maybe it's just the men's way of keeping them in their place, and she smiles. 'But we have our own fishing,' she says. 'We like to do it our way, without them interfering, and that's the best.'

There's a shout of triumph from Mama Cherie. She's spotted a small octopus, which will fetch a good price at a restaurant. But otherwise, the catch is meagre. On they go, wading through the shallows to another likely spot, avoiding sea urchins spines and jagged coral with a grace born from years of practice. There will be no welcoming showers and fluffy towels when they get back to the village, but there will be breakfast – *sharoula* – a kind of porridge made from green bananas and cassava mixed with a little coconut milk and fish.

Even if things improve economically for the Comoros, which is the smallest and poorest of the Arab League countries, and tourism revives the international hotel business, the chances are that Yasmine, Mama Cherie and the rest of the Bangoi-Kouni women's co-operative will still be out there pulling in their nets and dreaming of a *grand mariage* in the family, when life, for at least a week, will seem like one long party.

The Black Lemurs of Madagascar

*The water is shallow and there is no pier, so it is always a wet landing.
Then it's off with the boots, into the clear warm water up to your
knees and onto the sandy beach.*

The lemurs certainly saw us before we saw them, and it was debatable
which group was the more excited about it, the graceful ones up in the
trees, or their clumsier distant relatives trundling along the hot, damp
forest path to the rendezvous. For us, it was the promise of a close
encounter with one of the world's most endearing creatures, but for
them it was more likely the prospect of a banana bonanza.

If there is one fact that most people can quote about lemurs, it's
that they come from Madagascar, that vast, still-mysterious island
which detached itself from the coast of East Africa long before humans
appeared on the scene. It was here that the early lemur types survived
and thrived, free of competition from larger primates and carnivores
that stayed home in Africa. Madagascar now has around forty types
of lemur, including not just the well-known ring-tails and the white-
furred, dancing sifakas, but delightful oddities like the moon-eyed potto,
and the weird, wiry-haired aye-aye. That's the shy little Captain Hook of
the family, usually spotted only in David Attenborough documentaries,
with its middle, extra-long, curved claw for tapping on branches and
winkling unsuspecting grubs out of their holes. The only other surviving
lemurs are in the Comoros islands to the north of Madagascar.

What we had come to see were the black lemurs (*Lemur macaco*) or
makis. Their range is mainly along the north-west coast of Madagascar
which is very wet compared with the rest of island, so the forest is quite
dense, making the dark makis difficult to spot. Fortunately, a colony of
these black lemurs has made its home on an offshore island called Nosy
Komba, only a boat ride from Nosy Bé, the main resort island in the
north.

They certainly have a way with words in Madagascar, particularly
the place names. Try jumping into a *taxi-brousse* and asking for the

Reserve Naturelle Intégrale de Tsimanampetsotsa. Or take the capital, Antananarivo. Even the locals now call it simply Tana for short. Then you find that the coastline is peppered with places called Nosy-Something.

Once you realize that 'nosy' means 'island', things become easier. Nosy Bé, which means Big Island, is just what it says – the largest island of a chain that adds dramatic impact to the sweeping panorama of the north-west coast. With its 'capital' Hellville – surely another name for the notebook – it's a favourite destination for package tours and makes a splendid base for touring other 'Nosys' in the area.

Lying like a beautifully rounded pebble between Nosy Bé and the mainland is Nosy Komba (or more correctly, Nosy Ambarivorato). The Komba part is a local name for the lemurs which are the island's most famous inhabitants. It is only here on Nosy Komba that the black lemur has its own place in the sun. Happily, for both lemurs and islanders alike, a local *fady* or taboo forbade hunting them, on the grounds that anything so appealing must be beloved by the ancestors – a notion which, when you see the makis, seems perfectly reasonable. Never having been hunted, they have no fear of humans. Although living wild in what is now a reserve, they are tame enough to take fruit from the hand. It is the prospect of getting up close to these enchanting creatures that brings visitors to the island – thankfully not in sufficient numbers, as yet, to spoil its sleepy charm.

Arrival on Nosy Komba is invariably by small boat, and usually from Hellville (named after a French admiral so not as bad as it sounds) about five kilometers away. Thirty minutes by motor launch is the usual journey time, but by *pirogue* (local canoe), it can take several hours if the wind is against you. The water is shallow and there is no pier, so it is always a wet landing. But that's no real hardship. It's just off with the boots if you don't want wet feet for the rest of the day, into the clear warm water up to your knees, and onto the sandy beach.

The local kiddies rush out with welcome songs and a coy little dance, the girls' faces painted with fetching little swirly patterns in white and yellow. It looks like wash day. Among the fishing nets drying over rickety palm-trunk frames are rope lines festooned with dozens of white cloths. But it's not the village laundry; these are beautifully embroidered tablecloths and bedspreads fit for a bride's trousseau, and in former days, that's what they were.

It seems that the wives of French colonists set the fishermen's womenfolk to work on the soft, dense unbleached local cotton, teaching them the art of cutwork, embroidery and dainty appliqué designs for lacy curtains, tablecloths, pillowcases and spreads of all shapes and sizes. Local flowers, birds, butterflies, sea-life and shells were soon incorporated into the designs, and the result is hand-crafted individual pieces as pretty as any you'll see in expensive shops elsewhere, at prices so reasonable that it seems unkind to haggle. Around US$20 for a lovely tablecloth is, after all, pretty good value for something which must have taken several weeks of work, as anyone who has ever chatted her way through needlework lessons at school will recognize. Local currency (Malagasy francs) can be used, but prices are in US dollars for convenience, even in this remote place, since those who make it to Nosy Komba are a very mixed international bunch indeed.

Fringing the landing beach is the largest village on the island. Called Ampangorina, it's all very laid back, with leaning palms, wandering pepper vines, and Indian almond, pawpaw, mango and cashew nut trees among the fishermen's little wooden houses and hen-pecked backyards.

Children take your hand and show you the spiky, green-yellow flowers on strangely warped ylang-ylang trees. Their tortured shapes come from heavy pruning, with stones tied on to weigh down the branches for easy plucking by the women and children. The scent is so sweet and heady, it's like walking into the perfumery of a large department store – hardly surprising, since ylang-ylang oil is an important ingredient for the French perfume industry. Sitting gossiping on their doorsteps, the women will shyly sell you tiny, sticky bottles of this heavenly stuff, along with vanilla pods, nutmeg and all kinds of things that wouldn't pass EU food regulations, but would be terrific in a fish curry.

There's a kerfuffle as a fishing *pirogue* lands with the morning catch. With no refrigeration available, the women have to act fast. Children make a noisy game of helping their fathers push the dugout with its wobbly out-riggers of mango wood above the high-water line. Up come the nets, and out come the knives. The remains go straight back into the sea, and several of our group quickly lose the urge to paddle. There's another beach not far away that's kept clean, with some simple bungalows for those who want to stay for a few days and enjoy the swimming and snorkelling.

For those who can stay, the extinct volcano at the heart of Nosy Komba is 612 metres high, and they say the view from the top makes the five to six hour trek each way worth every step. Only the truly sound of wind and limb should tackle the walk down the other side to reach the lovely beach of Anjiabe. There are no tracks round the coast, and the only other way of getting to Anjiabe is by a round-island pirogue trip with shared paddling.

But the rest of us had an urgent appointment with some lemurs. In fact, the makis were getting quite impatient. From their vantage points in the high trees of the reserve, they'd already spotted us pottering round the village and were squealing with excitement. It's an odd mewling cry, rather like cats hoping to be let in rather than spoiling for a fight. All lemurs tend to be sociable by nature, and the makis are no exception.

In a clearing by a big shady acacia tree, a rough branch framework has been put up. A couple of the leading males are already there waiting for us, showing off their skills on the parallel bars. And that's when we learn that only the male makis are black. The females are smaller and a light chestnut brown with black velvet faces set off by terrifically smart white face-ruffs and ear tufts. The outfit is completed by black gloves and matching socks... Already our group is besotted, and it's easy to get quite carried away when a female with a tiny baby lands with a soft plop on my shoulder. The urge to kidnap one and take it home is almost overwhelming.

An elegant black suede hand, complete with neat finger nails, reaches politely for the small green banana I'm offering, while I crane my neck to admire the baby clinging round her middle. The mother takes a nibble, looks a little pensive, then tosses it to the ground. 'They actually prefer mangoes,' says our guide, the local school teacher, 'but they're not ripe at the moment.'

Meanwhile, we are all whispering excitedly about whether the makis are more like monkeys, or large cats with hands. One of the men chuckles as two males land on him, one on each shoulder. The fur is a bit foxy, we agree, as we gingerly stroke them. Not wiry, not silky, but bushy and slightly coarse. They haven't got that highly-strung, aggressive curiosity of monkeys, perhaps because, as our guide tells us, they are not quite as bright as their more advanced primate cousins. The makis lack true binocular vision, but their sense of smell is very acute. You almost expect them to purr. They don't seem inclined to bite, their table manners are positively refined, and any squabbling is very low key.

Bored with bananas, the males try some more gymnastics on the pole framework, their long tails acting like a fifth limb, and the cameras click away. Soon it's possible to pick out established pairs, one black, the other chestnut, as they watch us intently to see if we have any surprise mangos up our sleeves. Perhaps it's just as well our offerings are largely rejected, and that feeding lemurs outside the reserve is strictly forbidden. Too many unripe bananas aren't good for nursing mothers, and it's best not to get them too used to 'freebies' which could make them lazy and dependent. Apparently lemur parents are believers in tough love. A mother in a tight spot will sometime throw her offspring to another, who might easily drop it. But now they seem to have decided that their entertainment is over for the day, and the females take their leave, followed reluctantly, we would like to feel, by the males.

Nobody wants to go back to the boat, but it's time to run the gauntlet of the children again, pass round pens (not sweets or money), and perhaps to fall for some carvings of the makis in polished black haematite or wood, made by the people who know them best. After all, what is a souvenir but a reminder of something too rare and wonderful to take home?

Those little carved lemurs also seem like a symbol of one of the better relationships struck up between man and the animal kingdom. The people of Nosy Komba protected the makis as creatures beloved by the ancestors and worthy of admiration and respect, while the lemurs have rewarded their protectors by drawing in fascinated visitors who provide some much-needed extra income for the islanders. That seems like a pretty fair deal, and here at least, it seems to be working – for all those concerned.

The Vallée de Mai

On a lovely island in the Seychelles, there is a magical place that some say is the original Garden of Eden.

No visit to the island of Praslin, the second largest of the Seychelles, would be complete without a walk around the intriguing and unique Vallée de Mai. If you arrive by air at Amitié, as most visitors do after a twenty-minute flight from Mahé, you should get a splendid view of the surrounding reefs, and be able to pick out, towards the south-centre of the island, the dense, dark green of the Praslin National Park, the core of which is the Vallée de Mai.

If arriving by sea, whether on a cruise ship small enough to anchor in the channel between Praslin and La Digue or by a local boat from Mahé, you will almost certainly step ashore on the picturesque little jetty at Baie Ste Anne. From there it is only a ten-minute drive to the Park entrance and Visitors' Centre. Alternatively, the more energetic can take a pleasant couple of kilometres' stroll along the very quiet 'main road', pausing to admire Praslin's only set of traffic lights.

With an area of less than twenty hectares, the Vallée de Mai is one of the smallest UNESCO Nature World Heritage Sites anywhere, so even a full tour takes only three to four hours, with time to linger. For those on half-day trips, the Park has well-marked, graded walks of either one hour or over two hours – just about long enough to absorb the sheer strangeness of the place.

And be in no doubt, the Vallée de Mai is certainly strange. It was declared a Nature World Heritage Site because there is nowhere else on earth quite like it. This isolated, secluded patch of rustling, dark palm forest is a unique remnant of the prehistoric forests of Gondwanaland, the huge southern land mass that rifted and drifted to form what eventually became Africa, Madagascar, India – and of course the tiny granite chunk in the Indian Ocean that is now Praslin. Elsewhere more advanced hardwood species soon crowded out the ancient palm forests, but here, millions of years of isolation from the mainland and comparatively late settlement by man have helped it to survive.

If that isn't impressive enough, the Vallée de Mai has another claim to botanical fame. The dominant palm species is a star in its own right – the extraordinary *coco de mer* (*Lodoicea seychellarum*). This huge palm has both a male and female form, and to see a pair of mature *cocos de mer* is to wonder if Nature has a sense of humour – or perhaps of the absurd. The male *coco* can grow 30 metres tall, and produces a giant, musty-smelling catkin of pollen that had Victorian ladies blushing at its shape and sheer size. The female palm manages only a modest 24 metres, but of course does all the work, by producing the world's largest seeds weighing between 8 and 15 kg when mature. Rarely, nuts heavier than 20 kg have been recorded and that would be your full flight baggage allowance falling on your head, should you doze off underneath one at the wrong moment.

You'd have to be unlucky, though, because the *coco de mer* never does things in a hurry. Even its sex cannot be determined until the plant reaches maturity, which can take between 20 and 40 years. So slow is the growth that some of them in the Vallée de Mai have been estimated to be over 800 years old. The nut itself takes six or seven years to ripen, surely another record – but when it does, it is truly a thing to behold. If the male flower caused maidenly blushes, the fruit certainly gave some Victorian plant-hunting gentlemen severe palpitations. Unhusked, in all its glory, it resembles – well, which part of the human female anatomy is for you to decide.

Perhaps it was seeing too many *coco de mer* nuts that reminded General Charles Gordon, of *Khartoum* fame, of Eve naked in Paradise, because he spent much of his time on Praslin, between wars in China and the Sudan, trying to prove that the Vallée de Mai was the site of the Garden of Eden. Or maybe Gordon spotted, as we did, the scaly tail of a green gecko slinking into one of the male palm catkins, its favourite lurking place, and thought of the serpent in Paradise, up to no good as usual.

Someone probably pointed out that there was a distinct shortage of apple trees on Praslin, and definitely no snakes, only the green gecko, the bronze-eyed gecko and the Seychelles skink by the way of reptiles, but this didn't shake the good General's belief one bit. He even went on to claim that the *coco de mer* was the Tree of Knowledge of Good and Evil, which probably tells us more about him than it does about the *coco*. Even today, botanists aren't sure exactly how pollination takes place, although local folklore has it that on windy nights, the male *cocos* uproot and advance towards the females, sighing and rattling their fronds.

Even the name 'sea coconut' is the result of a misunderstanding. When these nuts were first noticed washed up on various Indian Ocean shores, it was assumed that they must be the fruit of some giant underwater palm tree, until their one and only source on Praslin was discovered as late as 1768.

Meanwhile, among the mysterious rustlings of the Vallée de Mai, our guide is listening for the call of a black parrot, and tells us that bulbuls, an introduced species, do tend to bully these rare native parrots which are difficult to spot in the deep shade. There is some nervousness about the size of the spiders responsible for those webs up there, strung like fishing nets between the palm trunks, and everyone is amazed at the vast quantities of huge, dried out fallen fronds and other dead leaves and branches on the forest floor. It looks as if the whole lot would burn at the drop of a match, but it is this absolutely natural huge thickness of decaying material that keeps the forest floor beneath from ever drying out completely, and so ensures its survival and regeneration. No gardener or forester will ever have seen leaf litter to compare with this. Even a youngish *coco de mer* frond can be fourteen metres long, with a central rib built like a house gutter, so imagine what centuries of higgledy-piggledy fallen layers of them look like with no one tidying up. But then, who said Nature, or even Paradise, was tidy?

The Visitors' Centre has a display of *coco de mer* products, and it's worth trying to pick up one of these world famous nuts to get an idea of the density of the material inside. It is often compared to, and carved like, ivory, and there was quite a trade in the nuts to China and Indonesia, both whole and carved, before it was stopped just in time to save the parent plants from extinction. Now there's a controlled harvest of 3,000 nuts a year, which go mainly to India or are made into tourist items by local craftsmen. Most large botanical gardens round the world have a pair of these highly prized palms, and there is a female *coco* in Sri Lanka whose nuts have whitewashed numbers on them and are secured by padlocked wire netting to the trunk, such is the degree of interest in them.

It is even possible to make a jelly-like dessert from the unripe nuts, but this isn't encouraged these days. For a taste of the exotic, better stick to millionaire's salad, or 'heart of palm', so called because it takes the whole young growing shoot of another kind of palm, the *palmiste*, to make a starter for only ten people, killing the plant in the process. If it's on the menu in Praslin, it won't be from local *palmistes* growing wild alongside the *coco de mer* in the Vallée de Mai, because they are now also protected. It will almost certainly have been imported from Mauritius where it's grown commercially, unless your host is prepared for a hefty fine.

Even today, it doesn't take an overheated imagination to see Praslin as the next best thing to Paradise, with its lush vegetation and rounded granite outcrops that glow pink in the sunset. There's no mention of limpid turquoise lagoons and dazzling white sand in Paradise, but that sort of thing would rather be expected these days, and Praslin has them at every turn of the track. So, after paying your respects to the Vallée de Mai, what better than to head for a pristine beach and chill out, Eden style? Well, almost – sunbathing *au naturel* is forbidden here, and respecting local wishes is as much part of responsible tourism as protecting the unique environment of this truly lovely island.

Lost in Old Zanzibar

They used to say it was the scent of cloves on the warm monsoon wind that told you when your ship was coming into Zanzibar. And still today, the very name of this fascinating island off Africa's east coast spells mystery, intrigue and high adventure.

The stylish way to arrive in Zanzibar is by sea, which usually means a cruise ship or ferry from the Tanzanian mainland, because that's what guarantees a view of the famous Zanzibar skyline from the water. As the boat noses into Stone Town harbour, dodging cheeky fishing *dhows* under its bows, the scene that greets you doesn't seem to have changed for centuries.

What a relief to find it free of high-rise blocks and ugly cargo terminals! Zanzibar still looks like Zanzibar should, with its mosque domes and minarets, the Portuguese Fort, the spires of the two cathedrals, and the wedding-cake white of the Sultan's Palace and merchants' houses on the old waterfront dominating the skyline. You may not catch the scent of cloves just yet, but as the rising sun silhouettes the palm trees there is bound to be the incense whiff of cooking fires, mingled perhaps with the Indian Ocean smell of grilled fresh fish and drying coconut husks, or the mouth-watering sweetness of cinnamon, coffee and baking bread that says 'Breakfast!' in any language.

Even if arriving by plane, as most visitors actually do, it's certainly worth booking a boat trip at some point just to see that magical skyline. The first stop is usually the old *dhow* harbour. Bobbing at anchor are enough of these ancient handcrafted boats with their patched lateen sails to recall the days when this was East Africa's most prosperous port. Ivory, slaves, silks, sandalwood, spices and precious stones were once the cargoes, borne to and fro on the monsoon winds from as far away as India and even China. Today it's more like mangrove poles for scaffolding, coral rock for reconstruction work or fruit and vegetables, and probably one or two other commodities best not inquired about too closely. Until quite recently, you could get the death penalty for smuggling cloves.

The slave trade that so appalled David Livingstone is remembered at the Anglican Cathedral in Stone Town, and those wishing to pay their respects won't be short of company. Friendly cries of *'Jambo, bwana, memsabu*, you want Slave Market?' would wear down anyone's determination to negotiate the maze of narrow lanes and shadowy archways alone and on foot. The Cathedral, a Victorian oasis of calm and coolness, stands on the site of the Slave Market, with a simple cross on the floor to mark the spot where the whipping post stood. In the crypt, some of the holding chambers – little more than caves in the coralline rock – can still be seen. In the churchyard outside there is a very moving sculptured memorial to this dark side of Zanzibar's long and often bloody history.

If you decide to go it alone, this is when you discover that all maps of Stone Town are quite useless. But then, why not get hopelessly (but quite pleasantly) lost in a warren of unmarked alleys with tiny booths selling everything from matches and batteries to local sweets and pastries? Dead-end courtyards offer tantalising glimpses of Hindu shrines, mosque fountains and family laundry. Soft-footed figures in the all-concealing black *bui-bui*, glide past, kohl-eyed toddlers by the hand, bulging vegetable baskets balanced on heads or hips, while craftsmen chip away in shady yards, restoring the stone lintels, brass-studded doors and lattice shutters that were once the pride of every house in Stone Town.

But it's also part of the Stone Town experience to succumb to an 'official guide' to get you back to the waterfront with old-world Swahili charm, by way of a little photo shop with pictures showing, of all people, Freddie Mercury, the late great leader of the rock band 'Queen', as a baby and a school boy. After cloves, Freddie, who was born in Zanzibar, must surely be the island's most famous export. And what a pleasure to see the House of Wonders, where Freddie's father was a civil servant, as well as the Sultan's Palace (now the People's Palace Museum) and the lovely Old Dispensary all so beautifully restored.

One trip into Stone Town doesn't seem enough, especially now that some of the old buildings have been completely restored as very up-market and tasteful hotels, rental apartments, and restaurants offering local and East-meets-West cuisine. But then, there is so much more of the island to see. A lovely drive north through groves of bananas, coconuts, sugarcane and mangos will get you to some wonderful beaches.

Nungwi Beach is reckoned to be one of the finest in Zanzibar, with offshore reefs and tiny islands that make it a snorkelling and scuba paradise. There's a fishing village with traditional *dhow* building in progress nearby, and here, as elsewhere on the island, great care has been taken to conserve both the cultural and marine environment. But for classical Indian Ocean unspoilt beauty, there's stiff competition from the almost deserted beaches on the east and south around Chwaka and Menai Bays where you can swim with dolphins and visit turtle nesting projects. Rock stars with their families and an occasional A-list celebrity can sometimes be spotted enjoying the 'barefoot luxury' ambience and privacy, while doing their bit for conservation projects.

Even with the sea so warm and inviting, you won't want to miss a visit to Jozani Forest Reserve to see the rare red colobus monkeys, if only to watch them delicately nibbling at the charcoal they filch regularly from the villages. Apparently these acrobatic charmers have a form of diabetes and can only eat the tough leaves of the Indian almond tree. But they've worked out that dosing themselves with charcoal helps their delicate digestions, and are natural-born posers when they spot a camera.

The island's roads have improved a lot recently, even if the driving hasn't, and it's tempting to stop and snap away at the shop signs – 'Snow White Laundry with Rinso'; 'Heathy But Chery (sic) Fresh Bar', and other unexpected joys. Or maybe grab a taxi with the air-con broken, windows missing and *Only God can judge me* on the back, to find yourself lulled almost asleep by the warm, humid air. Then it's time to say, 'Take me to a spice farm,' to wake up and smell some real vanilla, citronella, orange blossom, and at last, m'mm, those wonderful Zanzibar cloves.

Africana

There is always something new coming out of Africa.

(Pliny the Elder, Natural History, Bk VIII)

Send us your sons and we will brain them.

(Roadside billboard for a boys' private academy,
near Benin City, Nigeria)

The Magic of a Balloon Safari

Slowly thousands of square metres of brightly chequered cloth rose billowing into the still air like a giant's Bouncy Castle on the edge of the universe.

Watching dawn come up over the African plains, at treetop height from the comfort of a hot air balloon, has to be one of the better experiences that this world has to offer. The only snag is that if you are going to be up there in time to watch the sun rise, you have to get up before it, and getting dressed before dawn, in a tent, in the middle of one of Africa's greatest wildlife parks, can be a pretty scary business.

For one thing, the monkeys are incredibly cheeky, and they get up very early too. In fact, a small raiding party had managed to unzip our tent door the day before, and we'd returned to find the main light knocked over (and out!) and our complimentary fruit basket in ruins. Sticky paw prints on the ground sheet and pieces of papaw rind, complete with tiny teeth marks and scattered on my still-folded nightdress, had given the culprits away.

And then there was the leopard. At dinner that evening, a waiter had whispered that a leopard had been spotted in the tree outside our tent. Whispered, because he didn't want to start a stampede. By the time we got there, the guards said it had gone, but maybe it had just dozed off...

But things were quickly brought into perspective by the voice of Basil Fawlty in my head tackling a disgruntled guest's complaints head on about the view from Fawlty Towers. 'So what did you expect? Herds of wildebeest sweeping across the Serengeti?'

Well, yes. And this morning we were going to get them, from a few hundred feet up in one of the world's largest hot air balloons. Fig Tree Camp in the Masai Mara is one of a handful of places in Kenya which have regular balloon safaris. Since it's on Kenya's southern border with Tanzania, both the Masai and game animals can move freely into the famous Serengeti Plains, thus ensuring that the annual migration of wildebeest remains one of the greatest natural shows on earth, and Kenya's biggest tourist draw.

A quick swallow of hot coffee, a friendly check to see that we were all dressed warmly enough, and we dutifully piled into an open truck. The landing ground was still in near pitch darkness, but the 16-man team needed to get this monster aloft was already at work, and soon the flaring of gas burners spotlighted the ghostly scene. Slowly, under the team's expert manoeuvring, thousands of square metres of brightly chequered cloth rose billowing into the still air like a giant's Bouncy Castle on the edge of the universe.

The pilot, a New Zealander, was the cheerful sort who inspires confidence, which was just as well. One or two people voiced second thoughts about entrusting themselves to what was, after all, just a load of hot air and a wicker basket. The crew yanked and pushed us unceremoniously over the edge into the 'passenger unit', and there we sat, packed firmly as a picnic into the enormous padded basket, practising the safety drill and feeling like astronauts before a moon shot.

With an eyebrow-singeing burst on the burners, we were off, almost without noticing that we'd left the ground. The timing was perfect. The first rays of dawn were beginning to tint the horizon like verses from *The Rubaiyat of Omar Khayyam*. Had there been piped music playing the theme from *Out of Africa*, I might have cried.

But there was just a wonderful, awed silence – most of the time. Every few minutes, a dragon roar from the burners brought a down-blast of searing air onto us, which was why the thin on top had been advised to wear a hat. It seemed natural to whisper, or just gaze at the amazing play of light and colour as the sun's first rays elongated the dark, jagged shadows of the trees into surreal streaks across the golden grass.

As the light strengthened and our eyes adjusted to the scale, we soon caught glimpses of creatures stirring below. Here, it was a line of ostriches in full stride on some important errand; over there, a family of warthogs emerging purposefully from their burrow. And could that be a lion on the move so early? No – only a hyena, confirmed those who'd been sensible enough to bring binoculars.

But from hundreds of feet up, it wasn't the detail that impressed, it was the vast, grand panorama of it all. Giraffes against the dawn glow; the conflict of light and shadow as the sun rose higher and caught the distant Oloololo Escarpment. The pilot pointed out a patch of fresh green glimpsed far to the south – the Ngorongoro Crater, where most of the great wildebeest herds would be at this time, to make full use of the best grazing. Below us, hundreds of their cousins resident to the Masai Mara could be seen strung out in line, playing follow-my-leader the way only wildebeest seem to do. No photos were ever going to do it justice, but we still had to try, and clicked away as we'd never clicked before.

A real surprise was the whiteness of the tree trunks in the full morning sun as the balloon drifted over them, almost as if someone had been along with a bucket of whitewash and coated them all to match. The bleached bones of old kills showed so clearly from that height, like mouse bones forgotten by the cat on a neighbour's threadbare lawn.

Then someone spotted some humans for a change – a group of red-cloaked Masai *moran* leading their cattle out of a thorn-fenced *manyatta*. Inside the muddy compound, the tiny naked figures of children raced around and pointed up at us. The men waved their spears in greeting, their ochre shadows drawing them out into the magical stick men sorcerers of Bushman cave art.

It was a perfect illustration of how the Masai blended so beautifully with their environment, while here we were, hovering in this huge multicoloured, fire-breathing monster whose great, fat shadow served only to darken the plains as we passed.

The herd animals sometimes showed alarm if a roar from the burners reached their sensitive ears, but with a herd of hippos wallowing contentedly in the Mara river, it was probably just idle curiosity that had them bubbling up to watch us. Suddenly the whole stretch of river seemed to heave as more and more of them popped up for a look, leaving ever widening rings of steely water in their wake. Since it was March, the water was low, and the hippos were congregating at the most favoured places. Up here, the air was free of that sulphurous combination of hippo bathwater, rotting vegetation and African mud that had been strong enough yesterday to have us coughing and spluttering at the same spot. Perhaps it was just the hippos' way of getting a little privacy.

The pilot pointed out the stretch of the river which, in July and early August, is the main wildebeest crossing point on the Mara. The tracks worn by millions of hooves could be seen quite clearly, and somewhere down there lurked the crocodiles that would lie in wait for the young, the old and the slow, blundering their way down the slippery banks and trying to swim across, some for the first or last time in their lives. Wildebeest are fairly vocal even at the best of times, but during the stressful crossing, the half-grunts/half-honks made by these ungainly animals swell to a din that can be heard miles away, and certainly from a drifting balloon.

The landing came all too soon, and in three bone-jarring thumps. 'Whoops!' said the pilot. 'Didn't see the anthill. Now, anyone for breakfast?'

Under a lone acacia tree, the cooks from Fig Tree Camp had set us up in style. Tables spread with linen and china, and comfy chairs were ready and waiting, and from the stoves came the delicious aromas of that most famous of institutions, the 'full English breakfast'. These days that seems to include lots of other goodies, such as waffles, muesli, croissants and all kinds of fruit and juices. Feeling hungry as hunters, but glad that we weren't, we tucked in, while passing groups of zebra and eland eyed us curiously. Shoot them? How could anyone possibly do that, except with a camera? It was the only way to end a glorious morning.

In *Out of Africa*, Karen Blixen writes that an old Kikuyu chief asked her if she had ever seen God when she went flying up so high. When she admitted she hadn't, he replied, 'Then I do not know at all why you go on flying.'

That morning, I think we all knew why.

The Incredible Baobab Tree

Few travellers can resist the rugged charms of the baobab tree, and not just because it's been known to save lives.

Of all tropical trees, the once-seen-never-forgotten baobab is perhaps the most easily identifiable and best loved. There are actually eight species, of which only one is native to Africa where its distinctive silhouette stands out against the low grasses and shrubs of the drier savannas. Madagascar has six of its own, and Australia the remaining one, but all of them have the kind of impact that inspires people to make up special names for them, while early explorers drew sketches that were thought to be a joke when they got home.

The first European to fall under the spell of the African baobab was Michel Adanson, a French naval surgeon visiting Senegal in the 1750s. The species was given its botanical name in his honour – *Adansonia digitata,* with *digitata* referring to the way its large glossy leaves are divided into five (sometimes seven) 'fingers'. Some other names, including the Upside-down tree and the Elephant tree, are more interestingly descriptive, giving clues as to why the baobab makes such a vivid impression.

For a start, the overall bulk and shape of the tree is pretty much unmistakable, even for amateur tree-spotters. Mature baobabs regularly have girths of 12 metres or more and a crown 45 metres across, which gives an impression more of width than height. The massive, squat trunk combined with thick, shortish branches creates an oddly stubby shape which makes it look as if the Swahili legend about it might be true – that an evil *jihn,* annoyed by the baobab's pride in surviving even the worst droughts, uprooted it and stuck it back in upside-down. The strange proportions of the Upside-down tree, as it is often called, show up particularly well during a long dry season when it loses all its leaves.

Another striking characteristic is the pale grey colour and apparent shiny smoothness of the trunk – smooth until you touch it, that is. Then it feels as rough as sharkskin. When half concealed in a grassy thicket, the bulk and colour of the tree-trunk can look quite spookily elephantine. In fact, in thick bush or a bad light, hunters have been known to 'stalk' the looming form of a baobab thinking it was an elephant. No harm done there, you may think, apart from making the hunter feel foolish. On the other hand, mistakes the other way round have sometimes proved fatal.

At the very end of a withering dry season when temperatures are near their highest, and most other vegetation is desiccated and brown, the baobab performs its annual miracle of sprouting bunches of hand-shaped leaves at the very ends of its stubby branches. The new leaves are a welcome addition to the local diet in many parts of its range. Being rich in Vitamin C, they are often used to make a nutritious soup or 'relish' when little else is available. In some areas they are used for animal feed, and game animals with a long reach certainly appreciate them.

As soon as the rains begin, the big, whitish-yellow, trumpet-shaped flowers start to appear. These are frequently visited, and so pollinated, by bats which often roost in the branches or inside the hollow trunks of older trees, attracted by the flowers and nectar or the insects which also come for the nectar. Anyone picking the flowers will usually be rewarded by a handful of ants, if nothing worse. Bees love the flowers too and will often make nests on the branches. Some old baobabs in South Africa have pegs driven into them to make it easier to get at the much prized wild honey.

When the fruits eventually appear, they too are spectacular, dangling like enormous woody pears, but with an attractive velvety green bloom. Give one a good crack, and you will find it packed with white pulp that eventually goes quite powdery, as protection for the black, coin-shaped seeds. The average number of seeds per fruit is 30, which in Christian areas earned it another title – the Judas tree, after the thirty pieces of silver Judas was given for betraying his master. Both pulp and seeds can be chewed for their fizzy, thirst-quenching properties and Vitamin C content, and can also be added to soups. Monkeys are known to like the fruit, giving rise to another name for the tree – the Monkey-bread tree. Mixed with water, the dried pulp produces a pleasant drink, thereby earning it yet another name – the lemonade tree – so it was no wonder that baobabs often become natural snacking places for children and travellers. Their welcome shade also made them popular as traditional meeting places, and the tradition continues today. In Zanzibar, coffee houses are sometimes built round them, or sometimes even inside them.

They also make good landmarks and look-out posts. Their presence in clumps or 'groves' along many ancient tracks, often combined with mango trees (native to India), is also thought to indicate that these routes were once used by slave-traders in both West and East Africa. Such groves could surely tell some sad stories.

Baobab wood is spongy and almost as light as balsa. Because of its water-retaining properties, it is much appreciated by thirsty elephants, so it is quite possible to see both elephants and 'Elephant trees' together during a hard dry season. It is also claimed that chewing the wood or sucking it for its moisture content has sometimes saved the lives of travellers. Large trees are said to hold around 40,000 litres of water in their wood – but that would need an awful lot of chewing, even for an elephant. When the fibrous bark is stripped away, either by elephants, or people in need of its tough fibres to make ropes, fishing traps and baskets, it doesn't appear to harm the tree.

Even when older baobabs become completely hollow, their growth seems unaffected. They have been used as bus shelters, grain stores and water tanks (complete with tap) while still producing leaves and fruit. In Western Australia, where they call it the Boab tree, one was used in the 1890s by the town of Derby as a lock-up. Known as the Boab Prison tree, it is quite a tourist attraction, while on the island of Grande Comore, another huge specimen used as a jail in French colonial times now houses an elderly gentleman who chases visitors away with a stick – clearly proof that both he and his home are still going strong.

There are also persistent stories that ancient baobabs don't actually die in the same way as other trees. Some say that they simply crumble very suddenly, leaving only a heap of fine splinters and dust, which could of course be helped by the presence of ants or termites. Wilder claims suggest that they can be victims of spontaneous combustion, although a lightning strike would seem a more plausible reason for a dying baobab being reduced overnight to ashes.

Tropical hotel resorts will go to the extent of altering building plans to accommodate any baobabs growing on site because visitors love being photographed beside them. The various baobab species are also being studied in dry-zone research stations to see whether more commercial use could be made of their amazing drought-survival abilities and by-products – although they've learnt that one thing baobabs really can't stand is frost.

Madagascar is the only place with natural baobab forests, and the weird shapes of the six species here have become almost national icons. The Australian 'boab' version – *Adansonia gregorii* or sometimes *A. gibbosa*, meaning 'with lumps and bumps' – is actually quite bottle-shaped, with a pinkish tinge to its bark.

Probably the most famous baobab in Africa is the Big Tree, on Zambezi Drive near Victoria Falls which is said to be 1500 years old. Here, early travellers and traders would meet before crossing the river at the Old Drift. On the Zambian side is the Look-out Tree, with a ladder and viewing platform. It is thought that these giants could eventually achieve girths of 30 metres and live to be 3000 years old, as has been claimed for some of their relatives elsewhere.

However, even with regard to longevity, baobabs are full of surprises. Because their fibrous, pithy wood doesn't show annual growth rings as most trees do, it can be difficult to estimate their age accurately, so possibly some of the claims for trees being thousands of years old could prove to be exaggerated. Even so, the larger trees seem to create an irresistible urge among travellers to carve their names into the trunks, perhaps in the hope of showing it to their grandchildren some day.

For true baobab fans, this amazing tree has one last surprise – grown from seed and correctly trimmed, it has been found to do very well in bonzai form. Kits are available on websites, so anyone could grow a perfectly formed mini baobab tree on a warm window-sill. With time and patience, it could even become a family heirloom.

Malawi – Land of the Lake

They call Malawi the warm heart of Africa – and the good news is that this beautiful country is now opening up for visitors and investors alike.

It was David Livingstone who affectionately nicknamed Africa's third largest lake the Lake of Stars. Some say he loved the way pinpoints of tropical sunlight danced on the ripples, and photographers still like to capture this charming effect today. Others maintain that it's because the lake waters catch reflections of the stars at night, and certainly its mirror-like surface under the moon on a calm, starry dry-season evening is a lovely thing to see.

But I rather prefer the third theory – that it must have been the lamps from hundreds of fishing canoes dotting the waters that inspired the great man's choice. Better 'Lake of Stars' perhaps than the official name Livingstone gave it – Lake Nyasa – which was based on a misunderstanding typical of early explorers trying their best to work out the local names for various geographical features. As in: 'What do you call this one, then?' 'We call it *nyasa.*' And down it goes in the notebook, when all it means is 'lake' in several local languages. Just over a hundred years later, Nyasaland became Malawi, and in 1967 the lake got renamed to match, although to the neighbours (Mozambique and Tanzania) who share its shores, it's still Nyasa or local variations of it.

In Livingstone's day, the fishermen's lights were probably glowing charcoal or tiny vegetable oil lamps to lure the myriads of fish for which the lake is famous into their nets. Among the canoes would also have been the *dhows* of Swahili slave traders making for the eastern shore with their human cargos and ivory tusks for the long trek to the coast, their triangular lateen sails 'sinister as sharks' fins', as the official brochure so aptly puts it. Today's fishermen use hurricane lamps fuelled by expensive imported paraffin (kerosene), because somehow in all this profusion of wildlife and wonder, one or two essentials were omitted when Nature, in full rifting mode, formed Lake Malawi – like the provision of a decent oil field and access to the coast. But then, nothing's perfect.

'Welcome to the Warm Heart of Africa' is Malawi's new marketing pitch, but there's a rub. It may be warm, but it's a very long, thin heart. One of Africa's smallest countries, around 20% of it is water (Lakes Malawi, Malombe and Chilwa) and it is landlocked. Its outline snakes north-south along the Great African Rift system for about as far as from London to Barcelona, yet in places it's only 80 miles wide. In fact it's sometimes called 'the country you can see across'. The spectacular rift escarpments add to its beauty but subtract from the land suitable for agriculture, thereby cramming its people (around 15 million of them, according to the latest UN estimate), into what's left. As a result, the Land of the Lake is one of the most densely populated countries on earth, and also one of the poorest, with little to sell but its scenery.

Fortunately, Malawi has largely managed to steer clear of the continent's most notorious afflictions – civil war, wars with neighbours, tribal or religious violence and totalitarian regimes that terrorise the populace and encourage scandalous degrees of corruption. Compared with some of its neighbours, it feels more like the way things used to be – friendly, curious and hopeful. Any guns around are likely to be in the hands of the army and police, or game rangers and guards to scare off poachers or the odd over-enthusiastic elephant, hippo or crocodile.

It was the presence of Lake Malawi and its outflow, the Shire River (pron. *Shirri*) with its seasonal swamps that once made this country a wildlife paradise. The days of the great Elephant Marsh herds may have gone forever, yet there are still plenty of big game animals around, especially in the south – thanks to timely anti-poaching and conservation programmes. Better late than never, there are now re-stocking projects for lion and rhino, and the ivory is mostly staying on the elephants.

One of the most popular national parks is Liwonde, on the Shire. But don't think twenty safari buses to a kill surrounded by bored lions. A pleasant boat trip across the Shire is the best way to reach secluded Mvuu Lodge, where crocodiles big enough to take on a fair-sized antelope are the stars. The tented chalets overlook a creek, so you don't have to go and find them, they come to you. By day they lounge among the water lilies. At night, torchlight shows up half a dozen pairs of eyes drifting only yards away. My friend counted a dozen flumping around below her balcony, including a bossy black 12-footer. The next night I went one better by having an elephant brushing alongside my tent, little more than an arm's length from where I lay rigid in my luxurious, mosquito-netted four-poster bed. What's really weird is that they make so little sound – yet you know it's the only thing it could be. I didn't dare sound the mini-klaxon they give you for such 'emergencies' in case I panicked it. In the morning there were tracks outside, and the guard confirmed that *two* elephants had been down my way in the small hours.

For an encore, there's not much to beat a sun-downer of Malawi gin and tonic beside the river looking for Venus and the Southern Cross while hippo-shaped silhouettes emerge to graze against the last of the light. Follow that with a night game drive. That's when the spotter, in the 'hot seat' riveted to the bonnet, uses a red spotlight that's kinder on the eyes of animals bedding down for the night or on the hunt. I hadn't realized that civet cats were quite so big and handsome. But then, Malawi vodka is pretty good, too.

Next morning it was a river safari; elephants splashing in the shallows snacking on young reeds, roots and all; hippos safely back in the water yawning and honking. Thanks to the lack of lions, there are more warthogs in Liwonde than you'd see almost anywhere, trotting around on urgent business like so many civil servants. Equally determined to be on their way were several fish poachers flushed out by our boat drifting silently on the current.

Liwonde alone has around four hundred bird species, including the raucous Hadeda Ibis, said to be the noisiest bird in Africa, which is to say the world... But when the Hadedas quieten down after their dawn conference, it's such an incredibly peaceful place. At Mvuu we never saw another vehicle on any of the drives – in its own way a rare treat.

On Lake Malawi itself, the wildlife is again mostly water-dependent, from its famous endemic population of multicoloured cichlid fish, and hippos of course, to majestic birds of prey, notably Pel's fishing owl (huge, brown and deceptively fluffy) and fish eagles with their haunting cry. Likewise the activities which bring visitors and their much needed foreign currency are also mainly water based and found in clusters – around Nkata Bay to the north, and the Monkey Bay/Cape Maclear/ Malawi National Park peninsula in the south which is nearer to Lilongwe, the capital. In some ways it's a good thing that the high price of fuel ensures a concentration on water sports that can be done without engines.

At discretely luxurious Pumulani Lodge, our sunset sail in a traditional *dhow* with optional snorkelling was yet another perfect way to end a day. Surrounded by Lake Malawi National Park, the best in eco-design has been employed at this spacious complex. It all blends so well into a stunning wooded drop to a tiny beach of golden sand that the individual greenery-draped lodges are barely visible from the *dhow*. This kind of integration into the landscape is what discerning visitors value far more than 'flash, cash and brash', and it seems to be working well.

Most of the accommodation on the lake provides facilities for water sports and sailing, including mini-fleets of kayaks, which come as solos, or doubles with a back-up paddler for first-timers. Adrenalin junkies can push the boundaries here, while beginners suddenly become hooked on feeling adventurous.

Malawi has always welcomed outsiders, and outside assistance. International stars like Madonna with her much-publicised adoption of a Malawian boy have helped to raise the country's profile and draw attention to recent achievements as well as ongoing needs. Lilongwe now has over a million people, and gives a fair impression of a sprawling teenager waking from a long sleep, hungry and in need of new gear. Old friend South Africa is doing the shopping malls, while new best friend China is fixing and building whatever and wherever it can. The railway to the south, a huge Victorian British undertaking on which the country once depended for imports is out of action at the moment, but there are plans to revitalise that, too.

Madonna stays at the relaxing Kumbali Country Lodge when she's in town, and I can see why; fresh milk, cream and yoghurt from its own dairy herd, home-produced eggs and vegetables, lake fish, and top-class cooking. Originally from South Africa, the family who owns it can be really proud of showing what can be done here, not least of which includes the employment and training of hundreds of local staff for the estate. So near to the airport end of Lilongwe and the Capital Hill cluster of ministries and embassies, it's a thrill to hear the whoop of hyenas and chitterings of monkeys in Kumbali's lovely grounds where familiar English garden flowers mingle with exuberant tropical favourites.

In every market, fresh fish such as chambo and tiny silvery kapenta are a constant reminder that the lake is never far away, and there are plans afoot to increase production of fruit and vegetables by using more of its waters for irrigation. Lake Malawi is 2,300 feet deep in places, so there should be enough left for fish, fishermen, fun, crocs and much needed regular transport to link the many lake-side communities. Livingstone's dream was for an integrated railway, river and lake transport system to bring trade and prosperity to the region, and there are hopes that with wise investment, this could become a reality. Meanwhile, the welcome mat is being rolled out for old and new friends alike by the warm-hearted and resilient people of this spectacular country. The great man would surely have approved, as long as there are still hippos honking and fishing lights twinkling on his beloved Lake of Stars.

Into the Wilderness of Sinai

As holy mountains go, they don't come much holier than Mount Sinai,
aka Gebel Musa or the Mountain of Moses.

Nothing could put Egypt's desert wilderness of Sinai into its historical perspective better than that wonderful scene from David Lean's great desert epic, *Lawrence of Arabia*. A rashly brave Lawrence, played by Peter O'Toole, has announced to his victorious Bedouin army that he will cross the Sinai Desert to take news of their surprise capture of the port of Aqaba to the British in Cairo. But the Bedouin are led by the redoubtable chief, Auda of the Howeitat (who else but Anthony Quinn in a beard?) and Auda is scandalised at this tempting of fate.

'You will cross Sinai with only the children?' he roars, glaring scornfully at Laurence's two outcast servant lads.

'Why not?' retorts Lawrence, whipping up his camel. 'Moses did.'

'But Moses was a prophet,' yells Auda after them, raising his hands at the blasphemy. 'And beloved of God!'

So Lawrence sets out to do the impossible. It might have taken the Children of Israel forty years (although surely they must have been going round in circles) but Lawrence knows he must do it in a matter of days. He does, of course, and the Wilderness shows him a biblical pillar of fire by night and smoke by day – the spiralling local dust storms that plague the Sinai at certain times of the year. But not before he has been humbled for his presumption, when the notorious, shifting desert dunes claim one of his companions in a quicksand.

In fact, Egypt's Sinai Desert has never been a place to take lightly. Identified with the biblical Wilderness of Sin, which is perhaps not quite as interesting as it sounds, 'Sin' simply meaning 'moon' in the local language, the Sinai Peninsula is that inverted triangle of land which separates the Gulf of Suez from the Gulf of Aqaba. But a moonscape it certainly remains, with its stunning rock formations, stony plateaux and echoing canyons or *wadis*. Here you can see not just 'pillars of fire', but salt flats and snow-powdered mountain ranges, their flanks etched sharply by wind and the occasional downpour of welcome rain.

At Sinai's southern tip, the two gulfs converge as the Red Sea, where the coral reefs provide scuba diving and snorkelling to rival Australia's Great Barrier Reef. It is from gleaming white, purpose-built resorts like Sharm el Sheikh and Nuweiba, or more informal settlements such as Ras Muhammad and Dahab, that most of today's visitors attempt to do what Moses and, later, Lawrence did – tackle Sinai.

But these days, most of them don't try to cross it. More often, their goal is to reach the Holy Mountain in the southern part of the Peninsula, and as holy mountains go, they don't come much holier than Mount Sinai. For Christians, Jews and Muslims alike, this is the place where God first spoke from the Burning Bush to Moses (considered a prophet by all three religions). It was here that Moses received the Ten Commandments, handed down on tablets of stone, only to have them spurned by his sinful people. In his anger, Moses smashed the precious tablets, and some might say that the world has been picking up the pieces ever since.

At nearly 7,500ft (2,285m) Mount Sinai, or Gebel Musa (the Mountain of Moses) to give it its local name, stands stern and uncompromising among its rocky neighbours, right at the heart of it all. While it is not actually the highest peak in the area, there is a certain something about this particular mountain. It positively imposes its presence, almost overwhelming the world-famous Monastery of St Catherine and the constant stream of visitors toiling up the stony path to its foot. Or perhaps, it's protecting them – for the Sinai Desert is still the kind of place where even the hardy, half-wild camels need all the protection they can get. Flash floods, sandstorms, freezing night temperatures, losing one's bearings and thirst can catch the foolhardy traveller unaware. There are only a few motorable roads across it, mainly in the flatter northern part, and a bus journey from Sharm el Sheikh to Suez or Cairo along the western coast road will take the best part of a bumpy, dusty day.

But if St Catherine's is the goal, it is a mere three-hour drive rather than forty years in the wilderness, and the air-conditioning certainly helps. In fact the nearest thing to discomfort is having to get up early enough to collect your hotel packed breakfast – and that's only because the monastery gates always close at midday.

As long as you are not expecting monastic desert solitude – there's hardly ever a really quiet time to visit – the trip is a must for those in the area. As the bus climbs into the mountains, there are great ridges of barren limestone, starkly fragmented basalt peaks and sand-floored *wadis* as far as the eye can see. For the last half mile up to the monastery, take a camel from the coach park, or foot-slog it with the rest. In spring, the almond blossom in the monastery orchard is frothy and cool against the broken butterscotch of the rocks. But in summer, be prepared to feel like a nut in hot toffee, even if sensibly equipped with a hat and bottled water.

It was water from the Well of Moses, the site of which is still preserved within the monastery complex, that made the original 3rd-century Christian hermits' settlement possible in this barren, awe-inspiring landscape. By AD 530, the often valuable gifts left by pilgrims were attracting the attentions of marauding Bedouin, so the Byzantine Emperor Justinian provided the Greek Orthodox monks guarding the site of the Well and the Burning Bush with massive grey granite fortification walls that remain to this day.

Then one of the monks dreamed that the body of St Catherine of Alexandria, an Egyptian Christian girl martyred by the Romans, had been transported by angels to the even higher peak right opposite Mount Sinai. Next day, after a stiff climb, the monks found some human remains near the top – a skull with flowing, still-blond-ish hair, and a couple of arm bones. Possibly they reasoned that some butter-fingered angel had dropped the rest, but the added attraction of a virgin martyr's relics, however incomplete, ensured a constant stream of pilgrims throughout the centuries. Mount Sinai's twin peak was named St Catherine's Mountain, and the monastery itself was also dedicated to her.

Inside the walls is a warren of ancient chapels and tiny courtyards. In one of these, neatly enclosed by a low wall and still looking green and sprightly, is the Burning Bush. Or possibly it's a cutting from the original rootstock, now covered by an altar in the adjacent chapel. Apparently, attempts to root it elsewhere always fail. A fire extinguisher is kept beside it, perhaps in case some visitor overcome with religious fervour tries to recreate the original miraculous scene. But that would surely be unworthy. You can almost feel the great weight of holiness this ground has carried for so long.

Today, standing in the main Basilica, it is hard to believe that this entire structure, with many of the icons, striking mosaics and the inner doors, dates from the 6th century. Everyone whispers respectfully in here – even the multi-lingual tour guides.

Of more recent construction, yet blending well into the ancient honeycomb, is the Library. It was from here that St Catherine's most famous treasure, the Codex Sinaiticus, was, let's say, removed rather than actually stolen. This amazing book, written in the 4th century on fine parchment, is the earliest known copy of the New Testament in its original Greek. It was lent to a German scholar in 1859 on the promise that it would be copied and returned. It never was. This Elgin Marbles of the book world, this Rosetta Stone of biblical scholarship, then somehow got presented to the last Tsar of Russia. In 1933, the Soviet government sold it to the British Museum for £100,000, a huge sum at that time, and there it remains, much studied and admired, on public view until this day.

The monks are very philosophical about all this, realizing perhaps that it would need another miracle to get the Codex back. Even without it, the monastery is still one of the world's greatest repositories of ancient manuscripts. Two-thirds are in Greek, while the rest are in Coptic, Arabic, Syriac, Ethiopian, Armenian and Slavonic. Accredited scholars from all over the world are welcome here to study the sacred texts and historic documents, many of which have thrown new light on the development of early languages, international relations and religious thought.

But perhaps the most amazing thing about St Catherine's is that its 1,500-year-old walls have never been breached nor its holy places defiled. Given its position at the crossroads of the often turbulent Middle East, that really is a miracle, and perhaps a sign of hope for peace in the area.

Indeed it is this very crossroads position of Sinai, combined with its fascinating historical and geographical features, that has allowed the current boom in tourist development to take place – something that would not have been possible only thirty years ago. Visitors to Israel or Jordan, whether on a package holiday or backpacking, can now safely extend their itinerary to take in Sharm-el Sheikh, St Catherine's, Suez and Cairo with the minimum of border formalities. Anyone staying in Sharm can take a dawn flight to Cairo or even Luxor to see the sights, and be back in time for a late evening meal at one of the resort's many attractive restaurants. Egyptian, Italian, Chinese, Lebanese, Bedu or 'international' cuisine, the choice is wide.

It's a real pleasure to see young people of a dozen nationalities meeting for fun, water sports and scuba diving at Dahab, which still has something of a laid-back, hippie air about it. The sea is warm enough for swimming all year, and in the cooler months, a stiff north-easterly breeze whisking down the Gulf of Aqaba makes for spectacularly speedy wind surfing. Treks into the desert on foot, by camel, or by quad bikes with their four huge bouncy wheels are becoming increasingly popular, even with the not-so-young.

Most hotels organise Bedouin evenings, with a drive out into the desert to pick up the camels. Then it's mounting up time, guaranteed to produce squeals in several languages and earnest exhortations to lean back as the animals rise from their haunches onto their huge padded feet. Wadi Mandar is just one of the majestic backdrops for a dignified procession, nose to tail, in time to catch the sunset, and all those Lawrence fantasies suddenly seem real. Taking snapshots from a moving camel is not quite as impossible as it sounds, once you have mastered the knee-lock and got to grips with that hypnotic 'ship of the desert' swaying motion.

Whether camel trekking, camping free-style, or recovering from quad bike spills, a traditional meal round a Bedouin campfire with drums, stories and singing is something everyone seems to enjoy, wherever they are from. We listened to a Jewish New Yorker describing dawn from the top of Mount Sinai, our Coptic guide's mixed review of the London Underground, and a Swedish couple excitedly looking forward to their first wreck dive. But it was also mentioned that the Pope had been welcomed in Cairo and made a special pilgrimage to St Catherine's, and how Sharm el Sheikh is now a favoured meeting place for Middle East peace talks.

As for the desert night skies, you may not see a pillar of fire, said our guide, but if you don't spot the Milky Way, several planets, some recognizable constellations and a sprinkling of meteorites, then you must drink more mint tea until you do. There were six nationalities and several branches of three major religions round our campfire that night, and surely the stars of Sinai were the brighter for it.

Publication List

Short Stories To Take You Away From it All

SOUTH FOR THE WINTER, 3rd place, Writers Monthly, Short Story comp 1994.

FLIGHT PATH, Woman's Realm Summer Reading Special, 1992.

NOWHERE MAN, 2nd place, Catherine Cookson Cup, 1983, Woman's Realm, 1990.

WISH YOU WERE HERE, Woman's Realm; Margriet (Netherlands), 1988.

THE ROAD TO KACHINGA Woman's Realm, (serialised) 1989

A LONG WAY TO GO, unpublished.

THE HAND THAT ROCKS THE CRADLE, Woman's Realm Summer Special, 2001.

NOT TO BE OPENED UNTIL CHRISTMAS, Annabel, 1983.

IN PERUGIA, unpublished.

OUT OF SEASON, Woman's Weekly Christmas Special, 1999.

GIRL ON A DONKEY, 1st place, Solander, Historical Novel Society Short Story Comp, 2000.

THE TRUMPET VINE, 1st place, Endocrine Research Short Story Comp, 1990; TV Quick, 1991.

LOVE IS LIKE A BUTTERFLY, Family Circle, 1989.

VILLA ROSA, Woman's Realm, 1986.

Travel Writing People & Places

OUT OF AFRICA: IN THE FOOTSTEPS OF KAREN BLIXEN, South Africa Media, 2007; Emirates in-flight, 2007; Asante magazine, Air Uganda in-flight, 2011.

AGATHA CHRISTIE'S OTHER CAREER, Peninsula Publishing, 2008; Oryx in-flight magazine, 2007.

PADDLING HER OWN CANOE - THE AMAZING MARY KINGSLEY, extracted from Kate Nivison's lecture on 'Saga Ruby', West Africa Cruise, 2010.

TRAVELS WITH MY DAUGHTER, The Lady, 1999

HANDS ACROSS THE SEA, Good Humour magazine, 1990.

ONE NIGHT IN LAGOS is the tailpiece for Kate Nivison's novel, 'The Wine is Red', Completely Novel, 2009.

NEPAL – END OF AN ERA, extracts Peninsula Publishing, 2003; Air Arabia in-flight magazine, 2009.

DON'T PLAY FOOTSIE WITH THE PUTSE, 2nd place, LAM Comp, 1988, Adventure Magazine, 1998.

ZIM-ZAM, THANK YOU, MA'AM, Global Travel magazine, 2003.

COMOROS, ON THE ISLANDS OF THE MOON, Eva, 1998; Manx Tails, 1999; Oceania News, 1999; Europa Press (Denmark) 1999; Peninsula Publishing, 2002.

THE BLACK LEMURS OF MADAGASCAR, Peninsula Publishing, 2003; Interair magazine 2001; Take a Break, 2003; Gulf Media, 2006.

THE VALLÉE DE MAI, SEYCHELLES, Take a Break, 2010; Win & Go, 2003; Oryx magazine, 2003.

LOST IN OLD ZANZIBAR, Peninsula Publishing, 2001; Your Life, 2001; Oryx in-flight magazine, 2006.

THE MAGIC OF A BALLOON SAFARI, Manx Tails, 1999; Peninsula Publishing, 2000.

THE INCREDIBLE BAOBAB TREE, Interair magazine, 2000.

MALAWI, LAND OF THE LAKE, Selamta, Ethiopian Airways magazine, 2011; Zambian Traveller, 2011; Manx Life, 2011.

INTO THE WILDERNESS OF SINAI, Manx Tails, 2001; Peninsula Publishing, 2001.